To Dirk Bakker
with Kindest regards
from

Jo. van der Elst

The Last Flowering of the Middle Ages

January 10th 1945.

PORTRAIT OF A LADY by ROGER VAN DER WEYDEN. National Gallery of Art, Washington
(14½ x 10⅜)

PLATE I

The Last Flowering
of the
Middle Ages

By

BARON JOSEPH VAN DER ELST

GARDEN CITY, NEW YORK

Doubleday, Doran & Company, Inc.

MCMXLIV

To the people of my second home,
the United States of America,
in the hope that they may find in this record
of the painters and people of old Flanders
many of the fundamentals of our common Western civilization
which the United Nations are now fighting
to preserve.

Contents

Illustrations

ILLUSTRATIONS

[8]

Introduction

IN THIS turbulent twentieth century it may seem strange to stop and consider, even cursorily, the people and painters of Flanders of five centuries ago. What have they to do with us; or we with them? What possible enlightenment or inspiration does the medieval world offer us of today? And of what value to a nation engaged in fighting the most desperate war in its history are the richly colored, but frequently quaint and childlike, little panel paintings which represent the high flowering of art in the Low Countries during the fifteenth century?

To the majority of Americans the Middle Ages seem very long ago and far away. For many generations education in the Western world has proceeded on the premise that the medieval world came to a much-to-be-desired end with the Renaissance, at which time a brand-new, infinitely richer, and more glorious world began. This is a convenient way of disposing of much historical data which are difficult to explain and awkward to place in relation to current ideas and ideals. As a matter of historical and psychological fact, no period extending roughly over seven centuries and some thirty successive generations of human beings can ever be said to come to a close. History flows continuously, like a great river; it refuses to be dammed up into arbitrary periods and "ages"; it goes on, not only repeating itself, but carrying in its current all the waters, bitter and sweet, that have emptied into it. The spate which flooded western Europe during the sixteenth century with new and inciting ideas, and which swept Europeans to the far corners of the earth, was not an unprecedented accident. It was rather the direct and inevitable consequence of the thought and the way of life of the men and women of the preceding centuries. All that came to the surface during that vigorous and expansive era we call the Renaissance was already in the stream, poured into it by generations of men who lived—as thoughtful men live today—sternly occupied with the business of the present, but with their hopes and their dreams directed toward the future.

The Middle Ages and the spirit which moved the people of the centuries from the time of Charlemagne to the discovery of America did not come to an end with the invention of the printing press and the big news of 1492. Men and women do not change so readily or so swiftly as all that. The spirit of the Middle Ages went on living long after people began to talk of trade with the Americas as once they had talked of commerce with Venice and Constantinople; even though there were shops selling books which formerly had to be copied out by hand in the monastery workshops; even though many of the ideals which the age of chivalry had believed in and followed loyally were turned to ridicule by Cervantes.

The Middle Ages had faults, and many of them, like all the great periods of the past. But a hostile, derisive attitude toward it is an error, if only because we owe it so much. Those centuries during which Christianity spread over Europe brought a vast amount of beauty and tenderness to men. As Jules Romains has said so well: "*Puis le Christianisme est venu baigner de sa douceur, de sa miséricorde, de sa charité, sans orgeuil et sans limite, la tradition greco-latine.* [Then came Christianity and bathed the Greco-Latin heritage with its tenderness, its forgiveness, its limitless charity, and its boundless humility]."

Today, interest in the Middle Ages is inspired by something more urgent than mere historical curiosity. In seeking an ideal after which to fashion a better world, it is inevitable that we should examine our own way of life and the sources from which it derives. That examination reveals what may be startling to many and which must be thought-provoking to all: the twentieth century with its peculiar problems bears an amazing similarity to the fifteenth century, which may be considered the last flowering of the Middle Ages. Then, as today, the world stood in one era watching the first faint light of an approaching dawn. Then, as today, men were appraising the past for its value to the future. Then, as today, workers were finding a voice in government, and a vigorous and articulate middle class was making its demands heard in all the cities of Europe. Above all, then, as today, men were learning to think in terms of a rapidly expanding world.

The sibyls which van Eyck painted in the spandrels of his *Adoration of the Lamb* altarpiece seem to tell us that the fifteenth century knew itself to be fateful. Certainly the forces then at work were soon to fuse and become the great civilizing power of Europe and the Americas. These forces were nowhere so vigorous, and therefore so easy to observe, as in Flanders. During that century this little country, much of it man-made land, therefore doomed to a continuous battle for existence against the tides and winds of the North Sea, played a dominant role in European politics, economics, commerce, industry, fashion, and all the arts. England was impoverished and sorely spent by the brutal Wars of the Roses. London, during the first half of the fifteenth century, had less population than Ypres, and counted for less in the European economy. France was devastated by the Hundred Years' War and was torn by internal strife. But Flanders, the richest and most progressive territory held by the dukes of Burgundy, was strongly industrialized and extremely powerful.

There are many approaches to history. One is by way of the pictures painted by the masters of old Flanders who were moved to fervor by the spirit of their time, which was necessarily the spirit of the Middle Ages. Their horizon was not bounded by narrow limits, because they lived at what was then the crossroads of the world. They were proud and loyal citizens of a little country which was the economic capital of Europe. In the narrow streets of Bruges the citizens rubbed elbows with sailors from all the Mediterranean ports, with merchants from the cities east of the Rhine, with British woolgrowers, and with bearded fur traders from Novgorod. In the market places of Bruges and Ghent one heard the gossip of every court and capital.

The men of Flanders did not see themselves apart from this rapidly expanding world. They were of it, as though already conscious that some of their spirit would spread across the Atlantic, there to take root and flourish in the great democracies of the West.

Great art is imbued with the spirit of its time, and lives forever. The pictures which were painted in the workshops of the Flemish masters during the fifteenth century were inspired by and reflected the way of life of the Flemings of that time. "A school of painting," said Taine in his essay *The Art of Painting in the Low Countries*, "which has lasted almost four hundred years, which includes so many masterpieces and stamps all its works with an original and common character, is a national work; moreover, it is linked with the national life and its root is in the national character. . . .

"I shall show you," he continued, "the seed; that is, the race, with its fundamental and indelible qualities as these have persisted under all circumstances and in all climates; then the plant, which is to say the people themselves . . . and finally, the flower, that is to say the art—and notably the art of painting—toward which all this development tends."

With this justification, let us examine the texture of the life of fifteenth-century Flanders into which Jan van Eyck, Roger van der Weyden, Petrus Christus, and Hugo van der Goes, among many other masters, were born, and which attracted and absorbed the German Memling and the Dutchmen Dirk Bouts and Gerard David. In examining that life we shall find some explanation of what may puzzle us in the pictures painted by these masters. In the paintings, when we come to them, we may uncover the truth about a period which has been less understood and more severely criticized than any other but which still affects the pattern of our civilization.

Only a few of the masters of the Flemish school are taken up in this volume. Besides these great ones are scores of lesser known but good painters whose works are extremely interesting. Nor is it possible in this book to discuss all the pictures attributed to each master; pictures have been selected which are outstanding and which reveal the artist's style.

In the passing of the centuries a web of legends has been spun around these pictures which have been so much prayed to, so deeply loved, and which enchanted the slowly awakening souls of our forefathers. Much of this lore is discounted by the art critics who would strip it away and view the pictures merely as products of the masters' skill, with no relation to the time in which they were painted or to the way of life of the men of that time. My purpose is otherwise. It is to tell something about the nation of artists and craftsmen who made possible this unique flowering of art at the close of the Middle Ages. To do this I must speak of them in the language of the heart, in the spirit of Beethoven when he wrote at the opening of his *Missa Solemnis:* "From the heart it comes; may it find its way to other hearts."

PART I

The Times and the Men Who Made Them

ARNOLFINI AND HIS WIFE by JAN VAN EYCK. National Gallery, London (33¾ x 25)

PLATE 2

I

𝔐𝔢𝔫 𝔬𝔣 𝔉𝔩𝔞𝔫𝔡𝔢𝔯𝔰

THE STRENGTH of medieval Flanders had its roots in the spirit of the peasants and hard-working townsfolk in the counties which comprise modern Belgium. Here, in the low lands lying between the Meuse and the Scheldt, the first democracy in northern Europe was born.

As far back as 1066, practically a century and a half before the signing of Magna Charta, the little town of Huy, close to Liége, demanded and won from its feudal lords a charter in which the rights of the individual citizens of that town were proclaimed. Long before the first Duke of Burgundy cast longing eyes at Flanders, many of the towns in the Low Countries had forced their overlords to acknowledge the freedom and rights of the citizens and to grant the towns privileges which were incorporated in charters. The free towns built town halls, usually with belfries in which the precious charters were kept behind strongly barred iron doors. The belfries, and their clanging bells rung to call the citizens to arms whenever their privileges were threatened, became symbols of free Flanders and of the liberty-loving spirit of the Flemings.

The bells of Bruges, Ghent, Ypres, Louvain, and Courtrai sounded a carillon of freedom through the Middle Ages in which, centuries later, they were to be joined by the pealing of Philadelphia's Liberty Bell.

The counts of Flanders and their successors, the dukes of Burgundy, were compelled to recognize the rights of the citizenry as laid down in those ancient charters of freedom—charters which were to inspire the authors of the American Bill of Rights.

In evaluating the Middle Ages, no one can afford to overlook the fact that the ancient rights of the individual, the basis of modern democracy, were then being established in Flanders. It was not accomplished without blood, sweat, and tears. The people of Belgium still celebrate the anniversary of the Battle of the Golden Spurs each July—that month in which so many national independence days are observed. In 1302, under the leadership of a Flemish weaver, Pieter de Coninck, an improvised army of artisans and peasants, fighting desperately for freedom, defeated the French forces outside Courtrai. When the battle was over, nearly seven hundred golden spurs—one for each French knight who fell in the fray—were gathered on the battlefield. The spurs were hung up in the cathedral at Courtrai as a thank offering and emblem of the Flemings' victory. Whereupon the victors shouldered their arms and went back to their farms and their workshops. The Flemings who stood for their rights at Courtrai were the spiritual progenitors of the embattled farmers who held the rude bridge at Concord.

Among these people and in this setting the great masters of Flemish painting lived and worked. The towns they knew are sadly altered today. Bruges, once the busiest port and the banking center of western Europe, dozes beside its canals like an old man nodding in the chimney corner, dreaming of his vigorous youth and his first love. Ypres, whose streets once throbbed with the rattle of looms, is a city of memories, sorely wounded in the last war. Ghent, whose dark Château des Comtes was the scene of so much Flemish history, is a bustling modern town. The businessmen of Brussels, descendants of those known to van der Weyden and Bruegel, are no different from men of affairs of any other national capital.

But there is one place where the spirit and the way of life of the people of medieval Flanders are still to be found: that is in the paintings made by the masters of that time. In those little panel pictures the amazing fifteenth century still lives and speaks to us.

The pictures of the masters are magic casements through which we look into the world of long ago. Great paintings are born of a spirit to express truths; if not truths, certainly sentiments. They are the ideas, the visual expression of thought, in the midst of which men live and work. They are movements of the minds of men arrested for a moment; ideas in suspension, significant to all who have the ability to see. Like all art, they are the color and poetry of life.

By far the greater number of fifteenth-century paintings of the Flemish masters are religious in subject and treatment. This does not remove them from us or make them impossible for this age to understand and to love. Even if some people have lost faith in the ideas which gave birth to these pictures, the paintings themselves remain a part of the treasure of Western civilization, a portion of the birthright of the Western world which the United Nations are fighting to preserve. These little panels, still glowing with color after the passing of five centuries, speaking great truths on which the entire structure of Western civilization is based, belong to all of us, no matter on which shore we live or what religion we profess. They are as much a part of the civilization of every city and small town in the United States as of the old towns of Belgium where their painters lived.

THE HOUSE OF BURGUNDY

The dukes of Burgundy were descended from a younger son of that king of France whom the Black Prince took captive at Poitiers. With the ambition which was to become a characteristic of their line, the first duke promptly set about making himself as rich and as powerful as his older brother, who had inherited the throne of France. His first step toward this end was to marry the daughter and heiress of the Count of Flanders.

The success of this union established a family precedent to marry prudently, choosing brides with lands in the Low Countries adjacent to Flanders and Artois, the two counties acquired by the first marriage. Fifty-six years later, when Philip the Good succeeded to the dukedom, the House of Burgundy was the richest and strongest dynasty in Europe, with holdings that stretched from the Somme to the Zuider Zee, and from the Atlantic very nearly to the Rhine Valley. Philip the Good, who engaged Jan van Eyck as his court painter and "valet," was known in his times as the Great Duke of the West.

The dukes of Burgundy did not make Flanders great; it was the extraordinary fertility of Flanders' fields (which caused Froissart to marvel) and the humming industry of the little towns on the waterways of Flanders and Brabant which created the unparalleled prestige of the House of Burgundy. Chastelain, the chronicler of the reigns of Philip the Good and his son Charles the Bold, justly remarks that the princes of Burgundy knew well their power "to be born more of Flanders than of France."

The heyday of Burgundian splendor came to an abrupt end toward the close of the fifteenth century with the death of Charles the Bold. That century which saw the greatness of Flanders may be said to have begun with Jan van Eyck and to have ended with Jerome Bosch. The great Flemish masters of painting were all men of their times. It is impossible to study their work without becoming aware of the thought and way of life of the men who painted these pictures and of those for whom the pictures were painted. In the *Madonna* by van Eyck, which is one of the treasures of the National Gallery at Melbourne (COLOR PLATE 107), is found all the proud sumptuousness that distinguished the court of Burgundy under van Eyck's master, Philip the Good. Even the size of this panel (8¾ by 6 inches) is significant. It is like tiny Flanders, tightly bound between its rivers and the sea; yet rich, glowing, vigorous, and self-confident. The Melbourne *Madonna* is fifteenth-century Flanders. No other country and no other period could have produced it.

The same is true, though in a strikingly different way, of Bruegel's *Massacre of the Innocents* which was painted in the sixteenth century when prosperity, power, and peace had fled the Low Countries, and when men remembered the great days of Philip and his son Charles with regret. Bruegel, like van Eyck, was a man of his own times. It is not the slaughter of the Jewish children by Herod's soldiers that he portrays, but the sack of a Flemish village at the hands of Philip II's Spanish men-at-arms. In this picture Bruegel is as mighty a propagandist as Goya was to be. The anguish of all who suffer persecution gives this picture a meaning that is universal and timeless. The woman who sits in the snow with her child's dead body across her knees, his pitiful playthings beside her, is the last of a long line of Flemish "Women of Sorrows." She is Mary. She is Andromache. She is a thousand women who mourn their dead in the war-torn cities of the modern world.

THE PROSPERITY OF FLANDERS

The court of Burgundy was famed throughout Europe for its splendor, for the fine clothes worn by the duke and his household, and for the richness of all the appointments. The sideboards in the ducal

VICTORY OF THE FLEMISH UNDER PHILIP VAN ARTEVELDE BEFORE THE WALLS OF BRUGES IN 1381.
Fifteenth-century illumination from a Chronicle of Froissart

PLATE 3

HANS MEMLING. Tommaso Portinari. Metropolitan Museum, New York.
Courtesy Metropolitan Museum of Art (*17 x 13*)

Plate 4

HANS MEMLING. MARIA PORTINARI. Metropolitan Museum, New York.
Courtesy Metropolitan Museum of Art (*17 x 13*)

PLATE 5

LEGEND OF THESEUS. Fifteenth-century book illumination. National Library, Vienna.

PLATE 6

castles groaned under the weight of gold and silver plate, much of which was encrusted with jewels. This was not vulgar display but a convenient way of storing the state treasure. The ewers and platters could always be melted down and minted to pay the duke's archers or to provide a daughter with a royal dowry. The court of Burgundy put to shame the miserly household of Louis XI of France. Readers of *Quentin Durward* will remember Louis's jealousy of his richer and more powerful cousin.

Olivier de la Marche, who was master of ceremonies at the court of Charles the Bold, wrote a book on the etiquette of the ducal household at the request of the English king, who seems to have been looking around for inspiration and advice. Olivier describes the complicated service of bread masters, carvers, cupbearers, cooks, and also of the ordered course of a banquet that was brought to an end by all noblemen of the court filing past the duke seated at table *"pour lui donner gloire* [in order to give him glory]."

In the kitchen of the old palace at Dijon may still be seen the six gigantic chimneys, all needed to roast the whole oxen, boars, and sheep stuffed with plump capons and pigeons, which were provided for the duke's table. Presiding over the kitchen was the chief cook, who sat on a dais, "and he must hold in his hand a wooden ladle, which serves him for a double purpose: on the one hand to taste soup and broth; on the other to chase the scullions from the kitchen to their work and to beat them if need be."

The Great Duke's household was also the most cultivated court north of the Alps, and it encouraged and commissioned the finest craftsmen in northern Europe. When the duke sent a present to a king it might be a set of costly tapestries, or a Book of Hours, exquisitely illuminated by some monkish artist. In 1389 Duke Philip, being then in Flanders, sent the King of France a New Year's gift of a purse of gold, with a lady in a lily on it, holding in her hand a diamond worth six hundred livres. He sent the Queen a golden picture of the Burial of our Lord, with Our Lady near Him, and the Duke of Berry a St. Catherine of gold.

All these were undoubtedly the work of Flemish artists and craftsmen, working in little shops in the narrow, winding streets of Ghent or Louvain or Bruges, under the strict rules of the medieval guilds and for prices fixed by the wardens of the guild to which the artists belonged.

The prosperity of Flanders throughout the fourteenth and fifteenth centuries, the love of lavish display which was a family characteristic of the members of the House of Burgundy, and the desire of the wealthy Flemish burghers to follow the lead of their sovereigns and surround themselves with rich and beautiful things, drew to the Flemish towns merchants and businessmen from all the countries of Europe. The finest fabrics made on the looms in Florence and Lucca were sent to Bruges to be sold. There is a legend that the reredos of green-and-gold brocade which van Eyck painted as a sumptuous background for the Melbourne *Madonna* was woven by the Arnolfinis in Lucca for Philip the Good. The Arnolfinis played a prominent role in Flanders during the fifteenth century. Giovanni Arnolfini made a huge fortune in silks, velvets, furs, spices, ornaments, jewels, and works of art. It is said he introduced to Flanders the gold brocades which had been first manufactured in Italy in the fourteenth century. The portrait of the merchant and his bride by Jan van Eyck (COLOR PLATE 2) shows them in a bedchamber which is probably typical of the homes of prosperous Flemish merchants of the period. To quote Pirenne, writing of the Flemings during the long, prosperous, peaceful reign of Philip the Good: *"Ils regorgent de bien-être. On y respire la joie de vivre, le sensualisme épais et luxuriant qui, depuis lors, est resté un des traits caractéristiques des mœurs nationales* [They swell with prosperity. One breathes there the joy of living, the rich and luxuriant sensualism which has remained since then one of the characteristic national traits]."

The Medici maintained an office of their banking business in Bruges. The head of that branch during the reign of Charles the Bold was Tommaso Portinari, one of the boldest and shrewdest businessmen of the Middle Ages. Portinari was a Florentine, a descendant of that Portinari whose young daughter Beatrice inflamed the heart of Dante. Tommaso himself was a lover of the arts, who recognized the ability of the Flemish painters. He commissioned Hugo van der Goes to paint an altarpiece for his family chapel in Florence, which, when it arrived in Italy, caused a sensation among the painters there. Portraits of Tommaso and his wife Maria and their children appear in the wings of the triptych (PLATES 72, 74). As though this were not sufficient fame, the agent of the Medici had himself and his wife painted by Hans Memling. These portraits now hang in the Metropolitan Museum of Art in New York (PLATES 4, 5).

From time to time the stubborn and liberty-loving Flemings rebelled against their sovereigns over points of detail. They were jealous of their hard-won rights as citizens and insistent on their dignity. But in their hearts they were loyal to the House of Burgundy, however much they grumbled. For one thing, they knew that the dukes had the prosperity of Flanders at heart, since Flanders was their principal source of income. They knew that the House of Burgundy would defend Flanders against all enemies, and to this end made profitable trade treaties with England—treaties which lined the purses of the men of Ghent and Bruges with gold.

While all this prosperity weighed heavily with the Flemings, who knew a good thing when it came their way, the show that attended the prosperity—the processions, the *joyeuses entrées*, the tournaments, archery meets, courts of love, and tableaux which Philip and his son staged whenever they made a progress through their domains—gratified the Flemings' love of color and rich display. These gala occasions gave exercise to the imagination of Flemish artists and craftsmen and they gave all who worked on the displays, as well as all who witnessed them, the thrilling sense of living in a wonderland. The good people of little Flanders felt their pride swell, knowing that all this grandeur caused Frenchmen and Englishmen to stare in astonishment.

The fifteenth-century artist who made the miniatures to illustrate the story of Theseus (PLATE 6) depicted a scene which he himself may well have witnessed when the Great Duke of the West was making a triumphal progress. According to H. Aubert, this painter, "if he was not a Fleming by birth, he was in all cases very much influenced by Flemish art."

The dress worn by the Athenians in the pictures is that worn by the townsfolk of fifteenth-century Flanders. The garb of the five widows of slain warriors has been made familiar to us by many Sorrowing Madonnas painted by the Flemish masters. Theseus rides in a golden chariot with his wife and his sister Emilia. The citizens who crowd the windows, the maidservant who peeks through the half-opened door, the trumpeters, the procession of burghers, all are as they might have been seen in Bruges on the day of Charles the Bold's marriage to his English bride.

In the second miniature the attitudes of the kneeling men and women are those you would have seen in any church during the fifteenth century. To this day, in Flanders, it is not unusual to see women praying before an altar above which hangs one of the panels painted by a medieval master, with arms extended in the form of a cross, as the pagan Emilia is shown praying to Venus.

This interpretation of the famous Greek story is deliciously naïve. Theseus had brought home as captives two personable youths, Arcitas and Palemon. Both fell in love with the hero's sister Emilia.

She could not make up her mind which one to accept, and it was decided to hold a tourney in which Arcitas and one hundred of his warriors would fight Palemon and an equal number of his followers.

The fifteenth-century painter shows us Arcitas praying before the statue of Mars on the eve of the decisive tourney, while his rival Palemon entreats Diana to give him victory in the lists. Meanwhile Emilia, who had fallen in love with both suitors, cannot decide which she wishes to win and so, with commendable impartiality, prays to Venus for both of them.

The chroniclers of the period—Froissart, Chastelain, and Olivier de la Marche—have left us accounts of many festivities and ceremonies which emblazon the pages of history. There was apparently no limit to the lavishness with which these rulers expressed joy or grief. Birth and death were occasions for extravagant display. When Duke John—called "the Fearless"—was murdered, his heir Philip the Good staged a funeral of grandiose proportions. When he and his retinue rode out to meet the kings of France and England who came to honor the dead duke, Philip wore a mantle of black velvet so long that it covered him and hung down to his charger's hoofs. The company "carried two thousand black vanes, to say nothing of the standards and banners seven yards long, of the same mourning color."[1]

Historians have criticized the "bad taste" of these displays. In refutation of this charge it must be remembered that the men who planned them, who designed the decorations, the scenery for the *tableaux vivants*, the costumes, banners, armor, and harness were artists of a very high degree of skill, whose taste—to judge from those of their works which remain in the great museums and private collections—was vastly superior to that of most modern impresarios. It is hard to believe that decorations and tableaux which Hugo van der Goes, Jacques Daret, and very possibly Hans Memling designed for the celebrations in honor of Charles the Bold's marriage to Princess Margaret of York were in bad taste. It was another taste than that of our day, but whether better or worse must be a matter of opinion.

That wedding, in which the middle-aged and twice-widowed duke allied himself with England's House of York, took place in Bruges in the midsummer of 1468. It marks the climax of the story of Burgundian pageantry and the high tide of Flemish prestige. It is, therefore, a fitting moment at which to open the story of the Flemish masters, many of whom were employed as decorators.

[1] *The Waning of the Middle Ages,* by J. Huizinga.

THE WEDDING DANCE by Peter Bruegel. Institute of Arts, Detroit, Mich. (47⅝ x 62¾)

Plate 7

II

The Flemish Parade

As WAS TRUE of all royal weddings of the Middle Ages, the nuptials of Charles and Margaret were more than a marriage. They were an affair of international importance, the culmination of many long years of mutually profitable trade between Flanders and England. When the first Duke of Burgundy married the heiress of Flanders he acquired with her and her lands the traditional friendship of the British. During the long reign of Philip the Good, in which the British repeatedly enlisted the aid of Flanders in their claims on France, the duke's shrewd Burgundian chancellor, Nicolas Rolin, had seized the opportunity to draw up treaties between Flanders and England which were exceedingly profitable for the duke and for the Flemings. Nicolas Rolin, "sprung from the little people" of the old town of Autun in Burgundy, had a vision of a glorious and powerful Flanders with busy, populous towns and with the commerce of the world riding on the waters of its rivers. Some of the splendor of the chancellor's dream remains for us to see today in the background of the altarpiece he commissioned Jan van Eyck to paint for a chapel in his birthplace of Autun (PLATE 44).

All in all, Charles, whose early years had been influenced by the great chancellor, thought he had done well in making his third marriage an alliance with the House of York which had recently succeeded in quelling its rivals of Lancaster. He was determined to let the world know how important the event was to him and to his country. This meant that the whole ceremony, from the betrothal to the wedding banquets and processions, had to be a work of art.

The great square of Bruges was to be hung with banners, and the streets along its twisting canals were to be filled with pavilions and displays. The ducal palace and the gardens had to be made ready to receive the important guests. A special banquet hall was built and transported by water from Brussels to Bruges. Everything was to be as impressive and gorgeous as possible.

To accomplish all this, wood carvers, tapestry makers, glass blowers, jewelers, goldsmiths, sculptors, architects, and painters were called from every workshop in the Low Countries. At the duke's command they were to turn the old town of Bruges into a fantastic and colorful fairyland.

The artists, whose names make up a veritable Who's Who of Flemish art for the second half of the fifteenth century, included Jacques Daret, Hugo van der Goes, and many others known today for achievements of a very different character. It is recorded that van der Goes worked ten and a half days on the decorations for the wedding. None of the chroniclers mention Memling as among the craftsmen employed on this occasion, but as he was then living in Bruges, it seems likely he was employed in some way. It is probable that there were no special entries in the archives concerning local artists and craftsmen. The lists mention only those from out of town, with special attention to one or two who came on horseback, and so had to be paid higher wages.

It is possible that Dirk Bouts was there, making the journey from Louvain with the delegation sent by that city, and elbowing his way to a good place to see the parade. Dirk had just completed his famous altar of the Holy Sacrament. His contract specified that he should not do any other work until the altarpiece was completed, but an artist of Bouts's intense love for human beings would never have missed a gathering such as this, which drew men from all the provinces of the Low Countries and from beyond the sea.

Van der Goes, Daret, and the others, there in a business capacity, were engaged as glorified interior decorators and caterers. Commissions of this kind were common in the late Middle Ages, when art was in all respects an inherent part of daily life. Everything turned out by a studio in those days was intended for use, either in the home or in the church. Nothing was meant for collectors or museums.

Artists in Flanders (as elsewhere in Europe, for that matter) were called upon to undertake a great many projects that made for more gracious living. These included not only furniture, designs for tapestries and pictures, but also costumes for parties, armor and harness, street decorations for public celebrations, scenery for plays and tableaux which were staged along the route of the processions, and plans for entertainments. One result of this art-for-living point of view was the development of an art which everyone understood without the aid of critics or art directors. Indeed, the artist's outlook, like his employment, was completely practical. In the course of his work he might turn from more impressive and permanent tasks to design table decorations for a ducal banquet or mechanical lions and dragons to figure in the tableaux. Whatever he made, even though not of durable construction, it was his pride and his obligation to make expertly and beautifully. Unlike the decorations made for entertainments in Italy at that time, whatever was designed for the court of Burgundy was made of rare and costly materials.

There was general enthusiasm for the wedding. Charles was popular with the Flemings, and an alliance with England even more so. Above all, the good people of Flanders relished a show such as the House of Burgundy knew how to stage.

There was nothing in the bride's experience to make her anything but wide-eyed at this spectacle of lavish living. No doubt the Flemish burghers chuckled with self-satisfaction at the amazement shown by "the gallant troop of knights and gentlemen and more than fourscore ladies of rank" who accompanied the bride across the Channel. As they said to each other, in the Flemish idiom, this fair-haired English girl was falling with her nose in a butter tub.

John Paxton, "the younger," one of the gentlemen who attended Princess Margaret, gave an account of the wedding festivities in a letter to his mother, expressing his wonder at the luxury of the court and the pageants and tournaments in which knights and citizens vied with each other in the display of gold and silver, precious stones, silks and rare damasks. . . . "By my troth, I never hert of so great plenty as there is. . . . And as for the Duke's court, as of Lords and Ladies and Gentylwomen, Knyts, Lawyers, and Gentylmen, I hert never of non lyck to it, save King Artourys Cort. They are the goodliest fellowship that ever came along, and best can behave themselves, and most like gentlemen." A compliment indeed, from an Englishman of 1463, even in speaking of the Flemings.

It was on a June day that the fleet of sixteen vessels commanded by the Lord Admiral of England came into the harbor of Sluys, the picturesque, now-almost-forgotten village at the entrance to the port of Damme. Margaret, still a little green and peckish from the Channel crossing, was met with great ceremony by her future mother-in-law, the Duchess Isabella.

Charles had not yet seen his bride. It is probable that he had seen, and approved, a portrait of her, as his father had taken the Portuguese Princess Isabella on the strength of the portrait of her by Jan van Eyck. It seems not unlikely that Charles's mother, who had been a "picture bride," would have suggested sending a Flemish painter over to England to paint the English princess for her son's approval.

The only known portrait of Margaret of York is found in an illuminated *Chronicle of Flanders* (PLATE 10) by an unknown miniaturist. It was painted in Bruges about ten years after the marriage. There is also a tradition that Margaret of York and Princess Mary of Burgundy served as models for the two saints in Memling's *Mystic Marriage of St. Catherine* (PLATE 9).

On the following day Charles came for a first glimpse of his bride. "Upon his arrival," wrote Olivier de la Marche to Gilles du Mas, maître d'hôtel to the Duke of Brittany, "when they saw each other the greetings were very ceremonious, and then the two sat down on a bench and chatted comfortably for a time. After some conversation the Bishop of Salisbury questioned Margaret as to what she thought of being betrothed to Charles. She answered that 'it was just for this and nothing else that the King of England had sent her over' and she was quite ready to fulfill the King's command. Whereupon the bishop took their hands and betrothed them. . . . Dame Margaret remained at Sluys until the following Saturday and was visited by monseigneur. On Saturday the boats were richly decorated to conduct my lady to Damme, where the next day 'monseigneur wedded her as was suitable,' and the nuptial benediction was duly pronounced by the Bishop of Salisbury in the church of Damme."

The letter-writing John Paxton says in his quaint old English: ". . . Margaret was maryed on Sunday last past at a town that is called Dame III myle owt of Brugge at V of the clok in the morning. . . ." One wonders whether it was the early hour of the nuptials or Charles's casual frame of mind that caused him, according to the chroniclers, to fall asleep for a time during the ceremony.

Today, Damme is a village of less than one thousand persons. It is hard to realize that five centuries ago this city had a population of 50,000 with hundreds of ships from many nations lying before it at anchor in the Zwyn. The square before the Gothic town hall is now empty and the Church of Our Lady, where the marriage took place, is falling into ruin and appears strangely out of place and proportion with its surroundings. In spite of this it is possible to imagine vividly the bridal party, emerging from the church just at the moment of a glorious sunrise over Flanders. Perhaps Margaret stops a moment, dazzled by the gaily-costumed and cheering crowd. She is surrounded by flocks of children, who join in the enthusiastic welcome for the new fairy-tale Duchess of Burgundy. She then enters a horse litter, draped with cloth of gold. She appears very young and rather touching beside her battle-scarred bridegroom, with his tawny skin and black hair. Charles is a full-blooded man in whose clear blue eyes, even when in repose, can be seen something of the obstinacy and mad courage which were to earn for him the nickname *"le Téméraire."*

From Damme, the ducal parade started for Bruges, the duke riding beside his bride's litter. Behind the bride came thirteen of her English ladies, sufficiently recovered from their seasickness to ride on hackneys. Behind these followed five chariots, in the first of which rode the Duchess of Norfolk, reputed to be the most beautiful woman in England. "In this array Madame proceeded to Bruges and entered at the gate called Sainte Croix." In the words of the chronicler, "she was clad in white silver cloth made like a wedding garment; as was proper she wore on her head a crown girt with diamonds," above which she had placed with her own hands a simple chaplet of roses, presented to her by nuns at her entrance to the town. Her other jewels were appropriate and sumptuous. White doves were let loose at intervals to circle around the litter and settle down to ride upon the poles.

The route of the procession, from the city gate to the palace, gave the designers and craftsmen an opportunity to show what they could do. The streets fluttered with banners of silk and velvet emblazoned with the arms of Burgundy and of England. The house fronts were hung with tapestries from the factories of Arras and with curtains of magnificent Florentine brocade. Dun-colored Bruges must have glowed and sparkled with color that summer day. The fifteenth century is famous for its love for and lavish use of color. The weavers' looms turned out magnificent materials, and the traders shipped these to all the great cities to be sold to nobles and to citizens who were rising in wealth, prestige, and self-importance. Their houses, which had been rather grim, began to take on the appearance of comfort. You have only to study the paintings of van Eyck and Memling to see how richly furnished many of those fifteenth-century houses were. Brocade and velvet wall hangings brought the colors of the southlands to the gray north. When the Flemish masters wished to paint the Madonna, the Mother of God, their piety would not permit them to give her a background less sumptuous than that used for the ladies of the House of Burgundy.

Through the decorated streets and past houses, every window of which was crowded with spectators, moved the wedding procession. It was as gorgeous and as glittering as the setting. Charles had spent more than 40,000 francs merely for the wool and the cloth of gold used for the costumes of his household. The nobles of the Low Countries, who had to buy their own wedding finery, appeared in every style of doublet and mantle obtainable in a period distinguished for the splendor of its dressmaking and tailoring. Their horses' trappings glistened with gold buckles, colored glass jewels, and fringes of silver bells. After the nobles came the duke's trumpeters and other musicians, followed by troops of archers wearing wedding finery in honor of their duke. An able marksman himself, the duke took pride in his archers.

After them marched the Church dignitaries, whose vestments outdid the robes of the courtiers in richness of texture and color. Bishops and archbishops were attended by priests and acolytes bearing treasures from the churches. Following the churchmen came the burgomasters of all the Flemish towns, displaying their gold chains of office, as can be seen in their portraits. They were good, solid, hard-headed Flemings enjoying to the full this occasion of national pride, and no doubt looking forward to the banquet to which they were invited as representatives of the free towns.

The second part of the parade was made up of the "nations," meaning the representatives of the many foreign trading companies which had offices in Flanders. They included agents of the Hanseatic League, merchants of Venice, Lucca, Genoa, Lisbon, and London, and the bankers of the rival Florentine houses of Medici and Pazzi.

It was ever the policy of the House of Burgundy to offer opportunities for profitable enterprise and advancement to clever and able foreigners who, in enriching themselves, would also promote Flemish industry and foreign trade. As the Flemings were little inclined to seafaring, the spread of Flemish-made goods depended on traders from abroad. Many of these foreigners served Flanders well. Nicolas Rolin, the Frenchman, was a good example of this zeal. Though the chancellor aroused jealousy among his contemporaries, it is noteworthy that their animosity was directed toward the dubious quality of his piety, and not toward his work. According to Jacques du Clerq: "The aforesaid chancellor was reputed one of the wise men of the kingdom, to speak temporally; for as to spiritual matters, I shall be silent." In his portrait, van Eyck has not portrayed the face of an easy-going man; yet neither does he seem avaricious. There is ambition and much stubborn will in the forward jut of the nose, but no greed. It is certain that he dreamed of a rich and glorious Flanders, and exercised his considerable talents as jurist, financier, and statesman to make that dream a reality. If he himself prospered in the process, this seems to us of today no more than his due.

Giovanni Arnolfini was another foreigner who served Flanders well. He was knighted by the duke for his services and made a member of the Council. He also acquired the customs lease of the port of Gravelingen through which an enormous import of British wool passed annually; but there is no record that the Italian misused his privileges or caused the Flemish merchants and cloth weavers to lose money.

Arnolfini was succeeded in his post as purchasing agent by Angelo di Jacopo Tani, the Florentine agent of the Medici. Jacopo Tani and his junior partner Tommaso Portinari advanced huge sums not only to the duke but to the English king as well. They were financially interested in this alliance, and as they marched in the parade of "nations" their minds may have been busy computing the interest on their loans. We know Portinari charged the English king 120 per cent, England being considered a bad money risk in those days.

But for all that they had put up the money for the festivities, they did not stint the splendor of their appearance there that summer day. The Florentines in the parade were represented by sixty torchbearers, four pages, ten merchants, ten executives, and twenty-eight squires on horseback. The Spanish "nation" comprised sixty torchbearers, thirty-four merchants, and twenty-eight pages. While the Germans, with less flair for making a splendid appearance, but with an eye to business, sent one hundred and eight merchants and six pages.

Leading the Florentines in the Great Duke's wedding procession was Tommaso Portinari, whose portrait Memling was to paint (PLATE 4). That wily businessman had already managed to oust the elder Jacopo Tani from his post of authority in the Medici branch in Bruges, and was maneuvering to get the reins into his own hands. Doubtless Portinari was pleased with himself and with the occasion. His position with the duke was assured. Through his wife (PLATE 5) he was connected with the Baroncellis, another family of Florentine bankers with strong roots in Flanders. He had two sons and a daughter through whom to extend his profitable relationships. From his countinghouse Portinari spun a web of international finance worthy the admiration of modern bankers. It was said he had a stake in every venture by land and sea during the last half of the fifteenth century. An inveterate gambler, and a persistent believer in the greatness of the House of Burgundy, he continued to lend money to Charles throughout his reign, even after the Medici ordered him not to do so. When the Great Duke was killed at Nancy, he owed Tommaso Portinari £57,000. This debt remained unpaid, and still Portinari continued to advance sums of money to Mary of Burgundy and to her husband Maximilian I. It seems as though he could not believe prosperity could desert Flanders. His loans to Maximilian were secured by some of the crown jewels, among them a lily set with jewels, the *riche fleur-de-lis*, one of the glories of the medieval jewelers' art, which weighed nineteen pounds. This was not redeemed by the Hapsburgs until 1502, after the death of Portinari in Florence.

After the merchants of Venice and Florence in the parade came the Spaniards and the Genoese. The latter contributed to the occasion a large float portraying the legend of St. George and the dragon. "Representations" of this kind appeared in all the state processions of the fifteenth century. They are not to be thought of as resembling the floats used in the Mardi Gras celebrations. They were not grotesque, and the costumes worn by the characters on them were as real as the faith in the legends they represented. Distortions would not have been convincing to these literal-minded people, as is shown in their paintings. The costumes worn on the floats, like those used in the Mystery Plays put on to celebrate the Church feast days, were frequently borrowed from the churches. The saints and angels

CHARLES THE BOLD attributed to ROGER VAN DER WEYDEN.
Kaiser Friedrich Museum, Berlin (*19¼ x 12½*)

PLATE 8

HANS MEMLING. The Mystic Marriage of St. Catherine. According to a tradition, Margaret of York and the Princess Mary of Burgundy served as models for the two Saints, St. John's Hospital, Bruges (*68 x 68*)

Plate 9

CHARLES THE BOLD AND MARGARET OF YORK from a fifteenth-century book illumination of the *Chronicle of Flanders*. Manuscript 435, Morgan Library. Courtesy Morgan Library

PLATE 10

THE JUST JUDGES by Jan van Eyck   THE CHRISTIAN KNIGHTS by Jan van Eyck

Plate 11

appeared in vestments. In earlier centuries, angels were pictured dressed in long white robes like nightgowns; but in van Eyck's altarpiece in Ghent the heavenly host wear glorious brocades in all the canonical colors; van Eyck and the other Flemings had seen angels so represented in the mysteries and on the floats used in the *Ommegangs* (processions). Van Eyck's angels, like those in many other Flemish paintings, have no wings. No thrifty Fleming would cut holes in precious silken copes so that wings could be fastened to the actor's back. The Flemish populace had become accustomed through the Mystery Plays to accept angels without wings.

The chief guilds were represented in the company that followed the foreign "nations." The guilds were the centuries-old backbone of a society that was already beginning to transform itself from medievalism into the modern way of life. They were the economic warp and woof of the democracy which flourished in Flanders though the counties paid homage to the dukes of Burgundy. The guilds had done their part in making this celebration a momentous occasion. The companies of guildmen—with the emblems of their patron saints and attended by their journeymen and apprentices—marched along the cobblestoned streets that day with a conscious pride in their own work and in their civic importance.

While this multicolored parade wound its way through the streets of Bruges, across the market place over which the great belfry towered, and up to the ducal palace, "the great bells tolled among them like the chanting of friars."

Later that day a tourney was held in the market place, in which Antoine, the Great Bastard of Burgundy, pledged himself to take on all who might come against him. Wedding guests and many of the townfolk and sightseers crowded into the Grand Place for the entertainment. When the trumpets announced Antoine victor for the day, the bells pealed again, and the crowds pushed out into the side streets to drink from fountains flowing with Rhenish and Burgundian wines.

The wooden banqueting hall that had been ferried from Brussels to Bruges must have seemed stupendous to the people. It was 140 feet long, 70 feet wide, and more than 60 feet high, and it was set up in the grounds adjoining the palace, where it was made ready for the feast and the entertainments. One might reflect for a moment on how strange this building must have seemed as it was freighted to Bruges between the lush meadows bordered by poplars and willows along the canals. Then it nosed its way to dock in the shipyard, and there it was met by the same busy throng of carpenters, painters, and decorators, who were working on the pageantry for Duke Charles.

The decorations of the hall for the banquet that night, and for the banquets held in it every succeeding night for the ten days the duke appointed for rejoicing over his wedding, gave expression to the fantasy possessed by the Flemish artists and craftsmen of that period. The descriptions given by Olivier de la Marche and Chastelain are most astounding passages in the story of a most astounding time. A forty-foot tower was set up, painted with heraldic devices and adorned with mechanical boars, wolves, and monkeys, to be operated by puppeteers so that they danced and sang. The interior of the hall was hung with tapestries depicting the story of Jason and the Golden Fleece, a tribute to the Order of the Golden Fleece, founded at Bruges by Charles's father and on whose rolls was newly inscribed the name of the King of England.

Inside, the hall was lighted by bronze chandeliers shaped like castles. They were surrounded by artificial forests, where wandered extravagant Gothic monsters. Piled high on a huge cupboard in the center of the hall was much of the duke's collection of plate and golden vessels. It was a striking reminder that Charles, unlike many of his fellow sovereigns of the day, did not have to melt down his platters and goblets in order to pay for spreading the wedding board. A table was set for the bride and groom and for the most important guests under a canopy. Down the center stretched a huge lake framed in silver. In its waters floated thirty ships, each so marked as to represent a territory of the duke's domain. Some of them were seven feet long and rigged like the galleons which dropped anchor in the Zwyn before the ports of Bruges and Damme. This marvelous fleet of carriers brought food to the guests seated around the table. Small boats were loaded with lemons, olives, rare fruits, and spices. After the main course dessert was brought in, borne aloft on the shoulders of the retinue of servants. The sweets were pastries in the shape of castles with very real bastions and battlements. Cooks and chefs had to be as skillful architects as the designers of the chandeliers and the tableaux. From one of the huge pies emerged a whole band of musicians, vigorously playing their instruments.

During the banquet the diners were entertained with a fifteenth-century version of a floor show, where once more the love of the fantastic was exhibited. In addition to songs by minstrels, juggling acts, and dances there were elaborate tableaux. The female dwarf of Charles's daughter and heiress, dressed as a shepherdess, rode in on a mechanical lion larger than a horse and gilded all over. She was lifted to the table to be presented to the new duchess. Another number on the bill was a mechanical camel, nine feet high, carrying baskets of live birds and little pet animals which were given away to the ladies as favors. For a climax, thirty swans, each wearing the Order of the Golden Fleece around its neck, moved in solemn procession about the banquet hall.

It is impossible to write of this entertainment except in the language of a fairy tale. Reading the chronicles, it is easy to see how fairy tales originated in the extraordinary happenings of the Gothic age.

The rejoicing over Charles's marriage lasted until the imagination of the designers and entertainment makers ran out. In the course of the ten days the spectators were delighted by a monstrous whale, more than sixty feet long and "so high that men on horseback, riding on either side, would have been unable to see each other across the back." The whale was dragged into the hall by men dressed to represent giants. While the monster flapped its tail and fins, as if swimming, it opened its mouth and spewed out a troupe of Moorish dancers. After their act the audience was amused to see the giants drive the dancers back into the whale's mouth. These fantastic animals, the progenitors of Walt Disney's menagerie, were favorites of the crowds in the Middle Ages. One remembers the mechanical lion, designed by Leonardo da Vinci, which opened its mouth and let fall a shower of golden fleurs-de-lis in honor of the King of France.

On the ninth evening of the celebration the banqueting hall was laid out as a garden of mosaic in precious and semi-precious stones, surrounded by a hedge of gilded bushes. The eyes of the guests were dazzled by incredible golden trees whose branches were hung with jeweled flowers and fruits. Jets of perfumed water sprayed from gold and silver fountains. With such a display, never seen in western Europe, the festivities ended.

The significance of the event cannot be dismissed as mere display, because it was a mark of high tide in Burgundian splendor. The force of a century of great economic prosperity shaped the desires of the prince and formed a firm basis for the development of a class of skilled artisans and craftsmen. The conclave of artists and the co-operation of all the arts proved the ability of Flanders to create splendidly and at the height of the spirit of the times.

The wedding of Charles the Bold marked the high point in the life of a prince who dazzled Europe. Less than ten years later Charles was to engage in a series of disastrous wars in which he fell at Nancy, in January 1477. Two days after the engagement, on the desolate battlefield and at the edge of a frozen pool, the naked body of the Great Duke of the West was found, stripped by ghouls of his clothes and armor. The corpse, partially devoured by wolves, was gashed with three wounds, each of which was mortal.

For a long time the people of Charles's duchy refused to believe that their lord was dead. There was a persistent legend that he would return someday and bring with him the great days of his reign. There had been similar legends about King Arthur and Charlemagne. Ten years after the Battle of Nancy it was not unusual for the common people of Flanders to lend money to be repaid at the return of the Great Duke.

Charles was buried with medieval pomp in the burial place of the dukes of Lorraine. All the inhabitants of the town of Nancy, each one holding a lighted taper, formed the cortege. It is not likely, as they ushered their little twinkling lights into the night, that they were aware they were serving at the funeral of the medieval world—a world that was not to survive Charles the Bold, the last of Europe's great feudal lords.

Charles was dead, and his world tottered. But Flanders lived on. Bruges quickly lost its prestige to Antwerp. The silting up of the Zwyn turned the once busiest port in western Europe into a place of echoes and memories. But in Antwerp the parade of Flemish industry and trade went on. From Antwerp the merchants of the East India Company set sail for the Spice Islands and to trade with the newly found Americas.

One thinks instinctively of the closing lines of De Coster's famous novel of Tuyl Ulenspiegel, the *Don Quixote* of Belgian literature. Tuyl, the vagabond born in Damme, is the personification of the vitality and the unremitting struggle of the Flemish spirit against tyranny. In the end, when the brutal forces against him seem to have conquered, he rises triumphant and still defiant from the grave, exclaiming to Nele, his beloved: "Can one bury Ulenspiegel, the spirit; and Nele, the heart of our Mother Flanders? She also can sleep; but die, never."

FALL OF ICARUS by Peter Bruegel. Brussels Museum ($29\frac{1}{8}$ x $44\frac{3}{4}$)

PLATE 12

III

The Good Black Earth

SCHOOL of painting which covers one hundred years and possesses such marked common characteristics as we find in the work of all the Flemish masters from van Eyck to Gerard David—so distinct and different from other schools of the same period—and which has held its high standing unchallenged throughout five centuries, did not come into existence by chance or merely through the patronage of rich and powerful princes.

The extraordinary vitality of Flemish art may be traced to the fact that that art had its roots in the good black earth of Flanders.

The countryside surrounding the masters of the late Middle Ages, which influenced them profoundly, has changed very little since the young journeyman painter, Hans Memling, left his native Rhineland and trudged across Brabant and Flanders to Bruges.

On either side of the cobblestoned road, humped in the middle to shed the rain, the same flat, green fields stretch under a low sky to a misty horizon. The same unrelenting wind from the North Sea still bends the rows of tall trees that protect golden seas of wheat sprinkled with blood-red poppies. Along the narrow, winding road between Oostkerke and Westcapelle, near Damme, lumber heavy, blue-painted farm carts drawn by the magnificent long-tailed horses which are the farmers' pride. Memling would surely have noticed them if he walked that way. He always had an eye for a horse, as you can tell when you examine the backgrounds of his pictures. In many of them you will find a rider on a white horse trotting along just such a country lane between tree-bordered meadows.

Here and there along the road are shining white farmhouses with red roofs. Often the farms have charming names, such as "Brombeer Hoek (Blackberry Corner)," or "Nonneken Mole (The Mill of

the Little Nuns)." The little nuns may well have been there in their convent beside the mill in Memling's day. If so, then he may have stopped and sat down to rest in the covered porch built for just such wayfarers as he, and probably accepted gratefully the mug of home-brewed beer the lay sister would have offered him.

From his seat in the porch, if it had been spring, he might have studied the lines of willows which separate the fields—short, stubby trees with old, hollow trunks and branches bristling from their knobby heads. In the ditches between road and fields the yellow iris would have been in bloom. And perhaps—just as you would have seen in any May up to that of 1940—a simple parish procession would come along the road: a band of music-making villagers blowing copper trumpets, followed by young girls dressed in white, carrying on their shoulders a flower-decked platform with a statue of the Virgin or the patron saint of the parish, and attended by many little children wearing paper crowns, strewing flowers along the cobblestoned way. From the swinging censers carried by the young acolytes thin, blue spirals of fragrant smoke would have floated upward through the boughs of the blossoming apple trees.

All this, which is part of the Flemish countryside today, was familiar to the masters of five hundred years ago. You may see it in the backgrounds of their pictures; sometimes just a glimpse through a half-opened window; sometimes, as in a number of Memling's open-air portraits, over the shoulders of a good Flemish burgher; and frequently in the altarpieces as "the sweet and blessed country" in which the saints seem very much at home.

This use of landscape distinguishes the painters of the fifteenth century from those of earlier periods who clung to the Byzantine tradition and represented their Madonnas and saints against gold back-

[23]

grounds. At the time that painting passed from the cloisters into the hands of lay artists, the old conventions inherited from the East were broken. It was no longer considered irreverent to paint Our Lady in a setting of this earth; in fact, the masters expressed their devotion by surrounding her with scenes which they admired and loved—the scenery of Flanders.

One of the earliest bits of landscape painting we have is a tiny vignette by an unknown artist in a manuscript illuminated for Duke William of Bavaria in 1417 or thereabouts. By the time van Eyck painted his *Adoration of the Lamb*, landscape had come into its own. Van Eyck, as court painter to Duke Philip the Good, spent much of his time in castles and in surroundings of regal magnificence; nonetheless, the bits of landscape in his pictures are painted with feeling and with loving attention to detail. With Dirk Bouts the development of landscape may be said to have reached its climax. Bouts felt the tranquil luminosity of the Belgian countryside. His misty landscapes are made with infinite love. His skill in this field of painting was so great that he was famous for it all over Europe. In a letter commending him to the attention of the historian Guicciardini, Lampsonius wrote:

. . . Belgium will forever praise to the skies the skill of your hands. Even Nature herself, mother of all things, she whom you depicted in your pictures, was troubled with fear lest your art make you her equal. . . .

High praise, indeed, but not unmerited by this Flemish master.

When one considers how small many of these old pictures are, it is amazing to find how much feeling and what an amount of storytelling the masters put into them. There are often figures in the foreground—the donor, his wife and offspring engaged in pious prayer, attended by their patron saints. Frequently behind them is a landscape that is barely a few inches across, but is full of charm, and eloquent of the Fleming's love of the land. None of these are merely decorative backdrops against which the main figures are posed effectively. The landscape, no matter how small, is an integral part of the picture. Without it, the painter's message would be incomplete.

In these backgrounds the masters seem to be telling us: See, the great events of the Gospels took place here, on this, our earth. It was this world which Christ came to redeem, and the men who till its fields. And if you will glance through the window at the countryside, you will see that this world —the home of man—is, though quite real, still sufficiently ideal to make His sacrifice understandable and worth while.

No one can look at these little landscapes without feeling that the sea lies just over the rim of the farthest hill. The air which blows across the gray-green fields carries the tang of salt. Under the passing clouds, lights and shadows are forever moving across this land where the earth is so flat and the sky is so overpoweringly close. Even when there is room in the picture for just a little bit of sky, this is painted with a sense of the majesty of the heavens.

No other country has so much sky above it as Flanders. As you walk across the polders you have the feeling not only that the firmament is very spacious, but also that it is very close to you. The sky which arches above you is never bright and dry; it is continually filled with moving mists. The sunlight is filtered through the moist air as you see it in the backgrounds of Memling's open-air portraits. Even on sunny days there are clouds.

A Fleming speaks of his clouds like old friends; they are personalities in his landscape, a part of the home scene. As the Belgian poet Verhaeren has said so perfectly:

"O ciel bleu de la Flandre aux nuages si clairs,
Qu'on les prenait pour des anges traversant l'air.

[O blue sky of Flanders with clouds so clear,
You take them for angels floating through the air . . .]"

In this land of haze and mists and ever-moving clouds the scene changes so completely within the space of an hour that the feverish attempts of many artists to capture some of the luminous beauty bring them to despair. Perhaps this explains in part why the persevering attention and study which the old masters gave to landscape developed in many of them a great sensitiveness to light and color as well as devotion to what Verhaeren has called *"Ce coin de sol triste mais doux que nous confia la terre* [This corner of soil, sad and yet sweet, which earth has entrusted to us]."

A LAND MADE BY MAN

The beauty of this humble landscape has been brought about by the close collaboration of man and nature. One thousand years of backbreaking toil have gone into the making of the fertile fields. Up to the time of Charlemagne, Flanders was a region of marsh and woods where the Celtic tribesmen hid from the invading Teutons. After the dismemberment of Charlemagne's empire the Belgian peoples again had to find refuge in the marshes from the Norsemen.

The county of Flanders lay to the north of the

old Roman road which ran from the Rhine at Cologne to Boulogne and was one of the great trade routes of western Europe through many centuries. At strong points along the road local nobles built their fortresses. Monasteries grew up here and there for the entertainment of travelers. The monks encouraged the peasants living in the forested marshlands north of the road to drain the lands, clear them, and make farms.

It is usual to trace the democratic ideas which moved the Flemings during the early Middle Ages, and which distinguished the Flemish way of life from that lived by other peoples of Europe, to the industry that enriched the towns of Flanders and Brabant and to the influence of the artisans' guilds. As a matter of historical fact the democratic spirit of the medieval Flemings had its roots in the soil of the country and in the agricultural system which was established there as soon as the forests were cleared and the lands drained. The network of drainage canals, "waterings," belonged to all who lived on the drained land. Their maintenance was a serious responsibility in which every farmer shared. The man who neglected to keep his ditches and dykes in good working order imperiled his own and his neighbors' crops. If one little watering was stopped up for only a day it could cause untold damage in a countryside where four feet above sea level is considered high ground.

The ancient code of watering laws established courts of farmers with power to try, fine, and punish offenders. The feudal nobles realized the importance of keeping the farmers on the land, if only to hold the North Sea out, and modified the feudal system of villenage in very early times. The peasants paid taxes in farm produce, and by keeping the dykes and waterings in repair. This took the place of military service. The taxes were low and the land that produced them was exceedingly fertile. This made for a vigorous, self-respecting, and prosperous peasantry. The polders by the sea were good for sheep grazing, and very soon the little towns which grew up around the monasteries and castles became wool markets and centers for spinning, weaving, and dyeing. The goods made in Flanders were freighted by the old Roman road to the Rhine for shipment to eastern and southern Europe, while the nations along the Atlantic sent their ships to trade at the coast towns.

Though Flanders became the first industrialized region in western Europe, as well as a banking and trading center, the Flemings never forgot that their privileges as citizens, their prosperity and national prestige came originally from the land. This feeling is deep in the heart of all Flemings to this day. The Flemish countryman's love for his native soil transcends even the traditional land avarice of peasants the world over. He knows the value of the so-called "fat pastures" in the polders, which can be grazed almost all the year round. It takes twenty years to create one of them, and they rent for high prices. The farmer who would neglect to manure his fields is regarded with disdain by the rest of the countryside, for he has diminished the common patrimony. The same scorn is meted out to the man who fails to squash a potato bug between thumb and forefinger as he passes a potato field. His squeamishness makes him a saboteur of the motherland.

When a Flemish farmer dies, his coffin is sometimes borne to the parish churchyard in his own straw-lined farm wagon, drawn by his own farm team, their brass-trimmed harness beautifully polished. Verhaeren, writing of the Belgian dead in World War I, and of the Fleming's deep love for his own native soil, says:

And the earth, who had loved them, made them welcome
So that without even a coffin or a shroud
They were embraced to their very bones by their Motherland.

When some of the Belgian war dead were taken from temporary graves to final interment in the National War Memorial at Dixmude, the bodies were not placed on gun carriages, but in straw-lined farm carts, drawn by the strapping plow horses of Flanders.

It was inevitable that this side of the national spirit should have expressed itself in the work of the old Flemish masters. They devoted many years of their lives to painting Madonnas and Crucifixions; their eyes were on heaven, but their feet were firmly planted on mother earth.

This love of the earth and of the good things which the earth yields has given the Flemings a reputation for sensuality. You have only to know them through their paintings to realize that they enjoy with an almost childish delight all that comes to them through the senses—the feel and the smell and the taste and the sound of things. Van Eyck makes you feel the deep pile of the green velvet folds of St. John's cloak in the famous altarpiece in Ghent; the soft, rich turf, gemmed with flowers, which is the pasture of his Paradise. Memling, the German, who was wooed and won by the Flemish spirit, makes you feel and smell the soft, sweet breeze which colors the cheeks of the men in his open-air portraits. The unknown Master of Flémalle

[25]

who painted the *Adoration* at Dijon left there in the Côte d'Or a precious bit of the cool, misty Flemish countryside. The *Adoration* of van der Goes (PLATE 76) is full of the Flemish feeling for the earth, akin to the feeling of St. Francis who sang: "Be Thou praised, my Lord, for our sister Mother Earth. . . ." You see in this altarpiece the little squirrel running on the rafters of the stable, going on in his innocent, animal way, unawed by the tremendous event which is happening under his twitching nose.

Cornelius Crul, an Antwerp poet of the early sixteenth century, voices this feeling which is at once essentially Franciscan and essentially Flemish:

"Ghij die appelkens, peerkens en nootkens meact
Sijt ghelooft van uwer goeder chyere,
Van vlees, nan visch dat zoo wel smaect
Van broot, van botere, van wijne, van biere.
Ghij cleet ons, ghij licht ons, ghij wermt ons met viere.
Ghij geeft ons ruste, blijscap en ghesonde.
En leert ons metten woorde van uwen monde.
Tleeft al bij u dat is in swereldts ronde
Tsij zijerken, tsij mierken, tsij vloe, tsij das.
Dies segghen wij u Heere, uut goeden gronde:
Benedicamus Domino. Deo gracias

[You, who make little apples, pears, and nuts,
Be praised for your good cheer,
For meat and fish which taste so good,
For bread, for butter, for wine, for beer.
You clothe us, you light us, you warm us with fire.
You give us rest and joy and health.
You teach us with the words of your mouth.
All in this world live because of you
Be it a gnat, be it an ant, be it a flea, be it a badger.
Therefore we praise you, Lord, for good reasons:
Benedicamus Domino. Deo gracias] . . ."[1]

REALITY, NOT REALISM

You will travel the length and breadth of Belgium without discovering the mountains, crags, and deep rivers the masters show in their landscapes. These are not bits of Flanders at all. They are expressive bits of the Gothic imagination which the masters added to the familiar scene, as a lover hangs a beautiful jewel about the neck of his beloved; not that she needs further adornment, but as an expression of his love.

The people for whom these fifteenth-century pictures were painted were realists in the sense that their own times and their own surroundings possessed them completely. They saw nothing ridiculous in tapestries and engravings which represented Greek heroes in medieval armor and helmets. No

more did their feeling for reality demand that the landscape in their pictures be a factual representation of the Flemish scene. They wanted the "feel" of Flanders; and after that desire was satisfied they employed their imagination taking familiar scenes and embroidering them with a very real kind of fantasy.

It is certain that none of the loyal citizens of Bruges who knelt reverently to pray before the *Madonna of the Rose Garden* (PLATE 15) were wounded in their local pride by the appearance of dramatic mountains added to the prosaic countryside. Some very literal persons might declare that the mountains have no right to be there at all. Certainly there are no bold cliffs, nor so much as a simple hill, anywhere near Bruges. The hills in the picture are deliberate additions to the landscape. It may be they are meant to remind us that "As the hills stand round about Jerusalem, even so the Lord standeth round about His people." The ring of hills guarding Bruges is in a way a symbolic repetition of the message of the foreground of the picture, where there is an enclosed garden—symbol of the purity of Mary and of the Christian's soul.

It would be hard to find a more perfect representation of the peace which passeth all understanding than this picture. It is now in the Museum of Fine Arts, Detroit, Michigan.

It is generally conceded that Memling was the first painter to give his portraits open-air backgrounds. His fields and bits of woodland shown over the shoulders of sturdy Flemish burghers and Italian merchants are as meaningful as the landscapes in his religious pictures. They are a clue to the psychology of the man portrayed. Usually far off across gray-green meadows is a great house in a wooded park which gives the sense of well-being, affluence, and serenity (PLATE 14).

In all the old Flemish paintings the flowers springing from the grass under the light feet of the Virgin and the saints are painted with exquisite care. They are the flowers that bloomed in medieval gardens. Often there is just one plant of each variety, which was the medieval way of symbolizing. However, gardens in Flanders are never large, and in all of them to this day planting is done with exquisite economy, and with the knowledge that one lily, perfectly placed, gives the eye more delight than a dozen crowded together. The walled garden behind the loggia in which the Madonna is seated in van Eyck's *Madonna of Chancellor Rolin* is just such a garden as you would find behind one of the old houses along a canal in Bruges today.

Even the flowers the masters selected were part

[1]From *Du Genie Flamand* by Jan-Albert Goris.

"*O ciel bleu de la Flandre aux nuages si clairs,
Qu'on les prenait pour des anges traversant l'air.*

[O blue sky of Flanders with clouds so clear,
You take them for angels floating through the air . . .]"

Who would have dreamed you would one day become the scene of battle?
EMILE VERHAEREN

PLATE 13

HANS MEMLING. Portrait of a Man. Staedel Institute, Frankfort (*16½ x 12*)

PLATE 14

THE MASTER OF THE ST. LUCIA LEGEND. Madonna of the Rose Garden.
The Detroit Institute of Arts. Courtesy Detroit Institute of Arts (*31⅛ x 23⅝*)

PLATE 15

ROGER VAN DER WEYDEN. St. Mary Magdalene. Louvre, Paris (24⅛ x 10½)

Plate 16

of the storytelling in the pictures; each flower had its meaning, which was known to the people of the medieval world. The men and women who knelt before the *Adoration of the Lamb* altar in Ghent found comforting and inspiring texts in the flowers van Eyck caused to bloom in his Paradise. The columbine—medieval symbol of sorrow and suffering—springs meaningfully from the rocks in many of the religious pictures.

"PEASANT BRUEGEL"

In thinking of Flemish country life and its influences upon the art of the country it is natural to turn to Bruegel, "Peasant Bruegel," as he has frequently been called, not because he came of farming stock, but because he painted Flemish farmers and country scenes with such astounding vitality. Bruegel's art has temperature and season; it is a climatic and organic transformation of life and nature into great works of art. And it is alive today.

The kermess, which provided him with so many scenes, is still a part of Flemish country life. The word comes from *kerke-misse* (Church mass), a celebration in honor of the local patron saint. As no two adjoining parishes are under the care of the same saint, and as the calendar of saints is lengthy, there is usually a kermess being held somewhere during the months of fine weather. The festivity starts with mass at the parish church, which is specially decorated for the occasion, and continues through the day with processions, dancing, feasting, and much beer drinking. Perhaps the kermess is responsible for the fact that the consumption of beer in Belgium is greater per capita than in any other country in the world.

At many of these festivals you look in vain for the white kerchiefs, bright-colored kirtles and aprons of the buxom countrywomen in Bruegel's kermess scenes. But the spirit of the crowd has changed less than their dress.

In Bruegel's day it was customary for bands of Flemish threshers to cross the Channel to work in the English harvest. Those Flemings took with them to England one of their old harvesting songs—originally a hymn, which had been sung in Italian churches, and later in the Low Countries. It had been turned to secular use and was one of the songs sung in the fields of Flanders when the harvesters swung their scythes. Doubtless Bruegel heard it many times in Brabant. In the course of time, the Flemings fitted doggerel verses to the tune, not very meaningful, but good to swing a scythe to. These verses, falling on unaccustomed English ears, were retranslated into deeper doggerel, all about a "Yankee Doodle Dandy" who came to town riding on a pony. This medieval Flemish song became the musical motif of the American Revolution.

The work of Peasant Bruegel will be discussed in a later chapter, but it seems well to look for a moment at his *Fall of Icarus* (COLOR PLATE 12).

Here the plowman guides his wooden plow through the rich brown soil of Flanders. The shepherd stands among his patient sheep and lifts his eyes to the cloud-filled sky. The sheep wander perilously close to the cliff's edge, but he has no fear for them. His dog is on guard—one of those wonderful Belgian dogs which are trained to do so many useful things, to herd cattle and sheep and trot patiently in harness, pulling the carts with the gleaming brass and copper cans filled with fresh milk through the streets of the little Belgian towns. The fisherman casts his line into the sea from which, no doubt, he will soon draw up a fine mackerel such as you can have served to you in almost any village inn or farmhouse along the Belgian coast. In the distance, sufficiently far removed so that its influences do not tamper too much with the countryman's way of life, is a fairy city, dreaming beside the blue sea. And standing out to sea, headed for the Spice Islands or for the Americas, are two stout galleons, with hope in their sails.

Icarus, the dreamer and reformer, falls from the clouds and is lost in the pitiless sea; but the life of the countryside moves on unchanged and unchanging, knowing not centuries nor epochs, but only the stately procession of the seasons and the bounty of the earth.

IV

The Rise of the Towns

HE little landscapes which give so much charm and atmosphere to the panels painted by the old Flemish masters are seldom rustic scenes. Usually above the treetops, in which a restless wind seems always to be moving, rise the towers of a little city, its walls caressed by light.

There is nothing unsubstantial about these little towns. Though you cannot see, you feel that their streets are full of busyness and the comings and goings of all manner of people, and in the tall, high-shouldered houses whose roofs cluster about the church the human affairs connected with birth, death, working, and courting are going on. The carpenter—like St. Joseph in the Mérode altarpiece by the so-called Master of Flémalle (PLATE 53), is making mousetraps for the housewives of the town. The children are running home from school, or pausing to peer in at an open window to see what is going on inside the room, as do the two youths in Bouts's *Last Supper* (PLATE 69). Dogs are dozing in the sun where it warms the cobblestones, as we see them in so many of the old Flemish pictures. In the Street of the Weavers there is the incessant clack and rattle of shuttles and looms. The Street of the Armorers rings with the blows of hammers on metal. From the cathedral comes the sound of chanting. When an old woman, going in to pray for the safety of her son who is away with the Great Duke's army, opens the church door, the scent of incense is blown out to mingle with the smell of the waffles another old woman is frying for sale at a stand in the market place.

No artist could possibly have painted these little towns, which are no more than bits of background and seldom have any direct connection with the figures or the events depicted, unless he loved them and had a deep-seated, fierce pride in them. The towns, like the landscapes in these old panels, have much to tell us about the spirit and customs of medieval Flanders which made possible the extraordinary flowering of Flemish art.

THE GROWTH OF FLEMISH FREEDOM

The pattern of feudalism, which was practically the same in all parts of Europe, rapidly developed its own variations in Flanders. This was in part due to the terrain itself. When Charlemagne made Aix-la-Chapelle the capital of the Holy Roman Empire, travelers came to it from all parts of Europe. Many of these traveled by the old Roman road and along the convenient waterways of Flanders and Brabant. The towns, originally market towns for the farmers and sheepherders of the polders, throve on this traffic. Even the dismemberment of Charlemagne's empire did not bring depression to the little cities of the Low Countries, for at that time they offered the countryfolk a haven from the invasions of the Norsemen.

The depredations of the Norman and Norse pirates along the coast at the time the urban population and urban industry were increasing made Flanders a market for English wool. In fact, the development of Flemish industry very quickly consumed all that the Low Countries produced, and made necessary the importation from England not only of wool and leather, but foodstuffs as well. Apples from Sussex orchards, hops from Kent, rye, barley, and good British roast beef on the hoof were shipped across the Channel to be sold on the quays of Bruges and Ghent.

The Crusades proved a great impetus to trade. The returning Crusaders brought back to Europe many luxuries for which Europeans soon developed an appetite. From Venice, Genoa, and Constantinople, goods were transported over the sea and on the rivers to western Europe. The towns along the

Rhone and the Rhine, along the Meuse and the Scheldt, boomed on this trade which also brought large profits to the seacoast cities of Flanders, from which goods were transshipped to England and to the Hanseatic cities of the north.

The Crusades had also a political and religious significance for the Flemings. The leader of the First Crusade was Godfrey, ruler of the independent little duchy of Bouillon in the south of modern Belgium, close to the French border. He was selected partly because he spoke French, German, and Flemish. The towns of Brabant and Flanders were well represented in Godfrey's army, which delivered Jerusalem from the infidels. Baldwin, Count of Flanders, became ruler of Constantinople. He sent back from the Holy Land a tiny vial containing the blood of Christ, thus, in a way, fulfilling the dream of the Knights of the Holy Grail. The relic was, and still is, treasured in the chapel of the Counts of Flanders in Bruges, known ever after as the Chapel of the Holy Blood. To this day, once each year through the streets of Bruges moves a solemn pageant celebrating a tradition more than seven hundred years old.

The ideal which inspired the Crusaders found a quick response in the hearts of the Flemings. In order to equip themselves for the Crusade, some of the feudal lords of Brabant, Hainault, and Flanders sold more privileges to the citizens of the towns.

These charters, many of them antedating the Crusades, were the basis for the freedom of the people of modern Belgium. By the end of the twelfth century all the principal cities owned charters giving them the right to their own treasury and to the appointment of local judges and other public officers. The old feudal obligations were largely replaced by taxation.

As the towns grew in power they forced a more equitable distribution of taxation among the nobility, clergy, and citizenry. When the Count of Flanders needed funds he had to apply to the city council for a loan, and the council shrewdly made increased privileges for the citizens of the town the price of the loan. In 1312 Jean II of Brabant was forced to grant his people the right to revolt if their prince did not act upon community complaints within fifteen days. The famous Treaty of Fexhe, signed by the Prince-Bishop of Liége in 1316, after fifty years of popular revolts, is undoubtedly one of the first modern constitutions. The treaty stipulated that only the public assembly could make laws for the city; assemblies were to be held regularly, with the prince-bishop acting merely as chief executive. These newly won privileges (*keure* in Flemish,

chartes communals in French) were symbolized by the magnificent town halls and the towers, in which hung the bells—the proud voice of the town. They rang the Angelus, bidding all within hearing stop in their toil and say a prayer for the good of their souls and for the souls of all men everywhere. Soon after dusk the bells rang the *couvre feu* (curfew)—a warning that all fires must be covered and lights extinguished for the night.

In times of emergency, when the coasts were threatened by pirates, or when the citizens of another city decided to make war on one of their neighbors, the bells spoke, calling the citizens to arms. *The droit du beffroi* (the right to a belfry) was the proudest privilege of every town. Rising above the city walls and visible for miles across the flat landscape, it told approaching travelers that here was a free city; within its commune the rights of the individual were established by law and were protected.

You will find the belfries in the backgrounds of many of the old Flemish pictures. Sometimes they are recognizable, but more frequently the masters mixed imagination with reality in painting the little towns, just as they did in painting the landscapes. They combined landmarks of Ghent, Bruges, Brussels, Tournai, and Utrecht into a composite city which became thereby a symbol of all the gallant, free towns of the Low Countries and of the men of those towns who had struggled to be free.

This is the meaning of the towns in the pictures. They proclaim the dignity of the individual. They are therefore not inappropriate in a religious picture which was intended to lead the observer to a fuller and deeper understanding of the gospel and life of Jesus Christ.

THE GROWTH OF FLEMISH TRADE

A little freedom creates an appetite for more; the citizens of the free towns quickly realized that their own importance and the continuance of their prestige were based upon their skill and labor. The goods they made, because they were made honestly and beautifully, were in demand in all the markets of the then known world. Flemish goods were carted by wagon trains to the great fairs in Champagne, where they commanded high prices. In the middle of the twelfth century a new highroad was constructed between Cologne and Bruges. Trade then flowed along it, as well as north and south by the Scheldt and the Meuse. Bruges, which was originally a little town at the bridge (Brugge), grew into the richest trading and banking city, not only of the Low Countries, but of western Europe. Located midway between the North Cape and the Strait of Gibraltar, it was a natural shipping point for goods to the north and to the south. The first commercial treaty made by England with a foreign power was that concluded by Edward I (Longshanks) with the Flemings in 1272.

At the opening of the fourteenth century there was not a city in western Belgium, from Douai to Saint-Trond, which was not in some way connected with the cloth industry. The ships that ferried British wool and British farm produce across the Channel brought back cargoes of Flemish cloth. They brought Flemish weavers, too, who migrated in response to offers made them by the Plantagenet kings and who built up the textile industry in England.

The commercial relations between Flanders and England were dominated by a powerful association of Flemish importers living in London. Even after the textile industry had been well developed in England, these shrewd merchants managed in such a way that cloth woven in England was sent to Flanders to be finished and dyed. After this it came back to London, where it commanded a high price. The Flemings coined a saying that they "knew how to buy the fox from the English for a groat, and sell it back to them for a guilder."

The textiles made in the Flemish towns were unequaled anywhere else in suppleness, delicacy, and beauty of color. In the south of Flanders the art of dyeing reached its highest perfection.

The people who developed the wool-dyer's craft to such perfection had a strong feeling for color that could be satisfied only by paintings by masters of equal sensitivity. The people who developed the art of clothmaking and the art of the high loom had a strong feeling for texture. The Flemish masters had to satisfy the demands of men in all walks of life who knew exactly how a piece of cloth was made, and how that piece of cloth would drape a figure or fall in folds against a wall.

Very early the town of Arras, then in Flanders, became associated with the art of making "*draps worked in the high-loom fashion*," or tapestries. On July 2, 1313, the Countess Mahaut of Artois ordered six tapestries to be made for her there—proof that the industry was then well advanced. It is believed that Baldwin, Count of Flanders and Emperor in Constantinople, encouraged the importation into Flanders of fabrics made in Egypt by tapestry methods, and these imports hastened the development of weaving on the high loom.

Froissart relates that after the disaster at Nicopolis in 1396, the victorious Bajazet butchered most of the Crusaders, but held a son of the Duke of Burgundy for ransom. The ransom paid was a set of tapestries from Arras, depicting the history of Alexander the Great; and, the chronicler concludes, Bajazet was much pleased with his bargain because, though he had cloth of gold and silver and fine silken curtains, hangings with scenes and figures were then unknown in the East.

The favor of the Count of Flanders, though a vassal of the King of France, was courted by all the princes of Europe, whose fingers itched to get into the rich Flemish pie. William of Normandy, the conqueror of England, married a Flemish countess and was insistent on his family connections with the useful Flemings. Edward III of England took to wife Philippa, daughter of the Count of Hainault, and spent much time in Flanders carrying on his perpetual wars against the French. Their son John, who has gone down in history as "John of Gaunt," was born in the Château des Comtes in Ghent, where the rich brewer and "Captain of Ghent," Jacques van Artevelde, entertained the British sovereigns with a magnificence that caused Froissart, Queen Philippa's secretary, to marvel greatly.

In 1500 Charles V was born in the dark castle in the center of this town of hard-working, hard-fighting weavers and leatherworkers. Ghent caused Charles much annoyance, but he was sufficiently Flemish to respect so stout an adversary, and when the Duke of Alva urged him to raze the city which had opposed him so obstinately, Charles—the story goes—took the duke to the top of the belfry and demanded with that ability to play on words that marks history's favorites: "How many Spanish skins would it take to make a glove [*gand*] of this size?"

At the beginning of the fourteenth century the steadily mounting power of the Flemish burghers such as Jacques van Artevelde reduced the authority of the Count of Flanders and permitted the King of France an abuse of his power. When he, with his queen, visited their domains to the north, the burghers' wives and daughters dressed so magnificently, wore such sumptuous furs and such expensive jewels, that the Queen exclaimed indignantly: "I thought I was the only queen, but I see here more than six hundred."

It may have been the finery of the ladies of Bruges that prompted the King to demand that the Flemings should pay the costs of his visit—a demand which infuriated the citizens of the towns. The leaders of some twenty-five guilds met in the market place of Bruges to discuss the matter. A clothmaker, Pieter de Coninck, found the inspired words given to all men who truly thirst after liberty. He or-

THE BELFRY OF BRUGES

PLATE 17

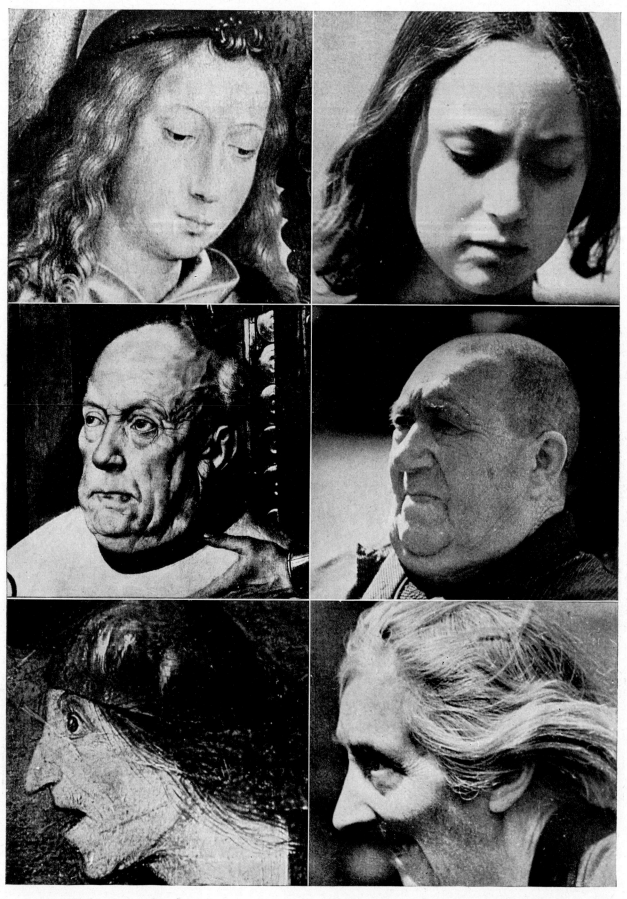

ANGEL by Hans Memling

CANON VAN DER PAELE by van Eyck

MAD MEG by Peter Bruegel

PHOTOGRAPHS OF MODERN
PEOPLE OF FLANDERS

PLATE 18

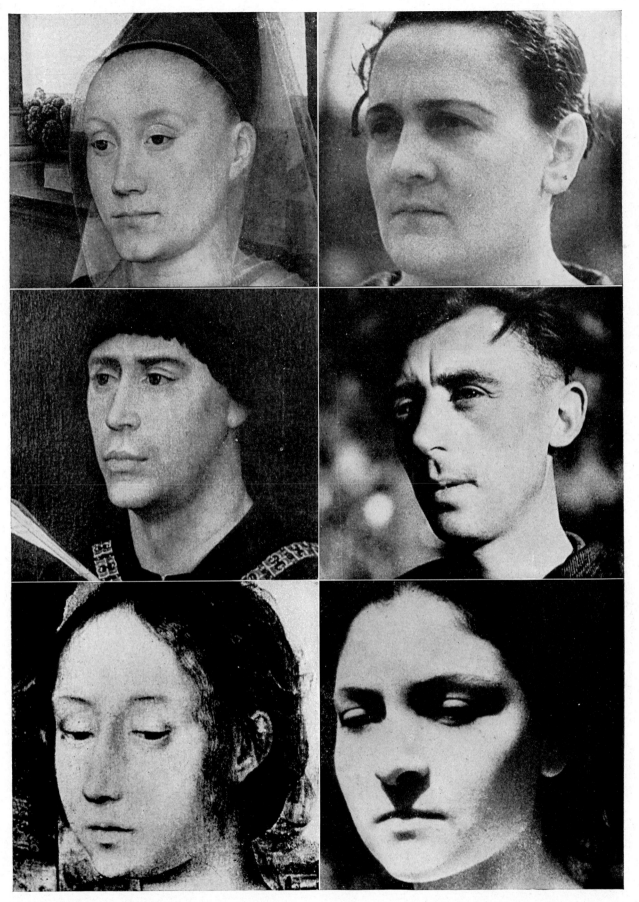

BARBARA MOREEL by MEMLING

PORTRAIT OF A MAN by ROGER VAN DER WEYDEN

ST. MARY MAGDALENE by QUENTIN MASSYS

PHOTOGRAPHS OF MODERN
PEOPLE OF FLANDERS

PLATE 19

MASTER OF BRUGES 1473. Triptych. Virgin and Child with Donors. Guggenheim Collection (*Each panel 28¼ x 14½*)

PLATE 20

ganized the drapers, wool carders, and cloth cutters of the town to defend their rights and resist the French. In the fighting that followed, the French made use of a ruse to garrison two thousand of their men-at-arms within Bruges. This was in defiance of their pledge to leave the armed force outside the town. The Brugeois realized that they had been deceived.

In the night the outraged citizens, armed with butchers' knives and tools of the cloth trade, crept up to the French encampment and massacred the soldiers. That hideous night of flashing knives is known in history as the *Matines de Bruges*. Men fleeing through the streets were pinned against a wall and forced to repeat the Flemish password *"Schild en vriend* [shield and friend]." No Frenchman was capable of pronouncing these words correctly, and those whose tongues betrayed them were immediately stabbed to death.

Some years later the bloodthirsty but none-too-imaginative followers of Wat Tyler, wishing to rid London of the Flemish merchants who had grown overpowerful on banking and trade, resorted to the expedient the Flemings had made use of at the Matins of Bruges. They staged a revolution, and put to death any man who showed a Flemish accent when forced to say "Bread and cheese."

When news of the massacre at Bruges reached the French king, he made preparation to punish the revolutionary Flemings. He raised an army of 40,000 men, led by his brother the Comte d'Artois, and sent them into Flanders. It was this force that the Flemings, led by Coninck and Jan Breydel, chief of the butchers' guild of Bruges, defeated at the Battle of the Golden Spurs.

This victory, which rang through Europe, firmly established the power and prestige of the citizens of the Flemish towns. England, pushing her claims to the throne of France, courted the Flemish burghers and the Flemish communes, each of which could command a substantial army. During the fifteenth century the city of Ghent could raise 80,000 soldiers. After the Battle of the Golden Spurs, Ypres extended its walls to take in a community of weavers who had their houses and workshops outside the ancient city. The federal, military, and political organization divided the country into *châtelleries*, the region around a château; and the Flemish towns extended their powers, though not all their privileges, to the villages which could be seen from the top of their belfries and in which could be heard the sound of the town's bells.

The towns of the fourteenth and fifteenth centuries were small, but they teemed with humanity.

Bruges, from which the vitality ebbed at the close of the fifteenth century when the silting up of the Zwyn closed its harbor to commerce, is very little changed from its aspect of five centuries ago. Its narrow streets are empty of traffic, its canals sleepy waterways for the swans. Its old houses look very much as they looked when young Charles the Bold strutted by to a meeting of the archers' guild. The interiors of many of those houses today are strikingly like the interiors you see in the pictures of the old Flemish masters. And the people you meet on the streets in many of the Flemish towns seem familiar too (PLATES 18, 19). The proprietor of a drugstore looks as though he could have been the donor of a triptych by van der Weyden. A fisherman of Ostend could have sat for the portrait of the Canon van der Paele. A peasant coming into Bruges to sell his farm produce recalls one of the hardy shepherds, who left their flocks on the hill to come to the manger, in van der Goes's altarpiece (PLATE 75). And that pale nun, shepherding unruly orphans across the streetcar track, is amazingly like a Madonna of Dirk Bouts. The same serenity is in her eyes. She is just as gentle with the noisy little boys as Mary with the Christ Child.

THE DEVELOPMENT OF FLEMISH ART

All through the fourteenth century the Flemish communes increased in power and in prosperity. Along the banks of the Zwyn warehouses were built and filled with goods from the Orient, brought in Venetian galleys. The Venetians and the Portuguese, who developed the caravel and built a fleet of them for trade with Bruges and the cities of the Hanse, brought spices and ivory from the newly explored west coasts of Africa. The shippers of the Hanseatic League stocked the docks with timber, wheat, furs, smoked fish, and metals.

All this business drew the bankers. The great moneylenders and promoters such as the Fuggers, the Medici, and their ilk, maintained "factories" in Bruges. The Hanseatic League banked there. And the Popes stored in Bruges the tithes collected north of the Alps.

This prosperity was the background and the rich soil for the greatest flowering of art the world has ever known. Flemish *ymagiers* were kept busy carving statues for the façades of cathedrals, fonts for English churches, and burial monuments which are scattered all over western Europe. High among medieval sculptors stands Claas Sluter, said to be from Holland, whom the first Duke of Burgundy commissioned to build a burial place for himself and his descendants at Champmol, near Dijon.

The meddling of many hands has left us only a poor idea of the original grandeur of the plan and of Sluter's work. Of the ninety mourners around the tomb of the duke, forty have survived. With their cloaked heads and winding robes these mourners are not alone men who weep; they stand as images of grief itself. Had Michelangelo, whose nudes show the struggles of mind and body, seen these figures he could not have failed to praise draperies which speak as loudly as does the flesh. The northern genius portrayed that which is emotionally real while hiding what is corporeal. The northerner always differs from the Italian because he must leave something to mystery and the ineffable.

The cities on the Meuse were centers for coppersmiths, and the products of Dinant, called *dinanderie*, were exported throughout Europe. The merchants of Dinant had a storehouse in London and were members of the Hanseatic League. At Tournai, the goldsmiths made splendid and elaborate reliquaries, chalices, and crosses which have found their way to churches and museums in all parts of the world.

Greatest of Belgian metalworkers was Hugo of Oignies, several of whose works are in the treasury of the Convent of Notre Dame at Namur. Here are a fine cross, reliquaries, a chalice, and a binding for a Book of the Gospels. On one cover is a Christ in majesty, and on the other a Crucifixion with St. John and the Virgin. The figures are framed by two rich bands—one of intertwined foliage done in hammered work, the other with filigree and panels in niello. In his filigree work Hugo was not satisfied, as his predecessors in the art had been, merely to twist metal wires. He added patterns of flowers and leaves, combined with figures of men and animals, in an exoticism that recalls the illuminations in the *Book of Kells*.

In the making of shrines for the relics of the saints, the medieval goldsmith entered into competition with the architect. The reliquary of St. Eloy, patron of goldsmiths and of the guilds of metalworkers, in the cathedral of Tournai, dating from 1247, is one of the most elaborate examples of Gothic imagination and building. The shrine of St. Gertrude at Nivelles, of copper gilt, adorned with statues and precious stones, resembles a cathedral, with a transept, spire, portals, and a rose window.

These two magnificent caskets were doubtless known to Memling when he began work on his shrine of St. Ursula for the Hospital of St. John in Bruges (PLATE 80). The work of the Flemish artists

and craftsmen was not locked away. The rich treasures of the cathedrals and convents were there for use and for the enjoyment of all. The great tapestries, designed by artists of the first rank, commissioned by princes and rich merchants, were hung against the gray walls of the churches on holidays, where the citizens could take pride and delight in the legends they portrayed and in the beauty of the fabrics themselves. The altarpieces painted by Flemish masters on order for rich burghers such as Willem Moreel, head of the grocers' guild of Bruges, were the possession of everyone who came and knelt in prayer before the votive altar.

Moreel is typical of the prosperous merchants of medieval Flanders. He gave a chapel to the Church of St. Jacques in Bruges and commissioned Memling to paint the altarpiece for it (PLATE 36). For the subject he chose St. Christopher, that strong, simple, indomitable, and devoted saint who was so dear to the hearts of the medieval Flemings. Merely to look at a figure of St. Christopher was believed to be sufficient to keep one from disaster throughout the day, so it is to be assumed that the altar ordered by the grocer Moreel was much frequented by the people of Bruges starting out in the morning for their day's work.

The diptych by the same great master made for young Martin Nieuwenhoven of Bruges was probably intended for a private oratory. It gives us an idea of the kind of pictures that hung in the houses of the substantial burghers. Martin Nieuwenhoven was only twenty-three when he ordered the *Madonna*, with his own portrait hanging as a pendant from it. Memling's little portrait shows him very young and dreamy-eyed, yet the records reveal that in later years he was a burgomaster of Bruges.

The burghers such as Willem Moreel, Martin Nieuwenhoven, and Jean des Trompes, and the foreign merchants such as Arnolfini, Tani, and Tommaso Portinari—men of business, with their eyes on the main chance; men who were determined to get on in the world and who knew the value of money; men not far removed from shrewd businessmen of today—were the patrons of the old Flemish masters. Those men who dealt in fine and beautiful articles of trade like scarlet cloth and brocades, furs and leather, paid tribute to the craftsmanship of the Flemish masters of painting. They didn't order portraits and altarpieces as investments for their children and grandchildren, or as gifts to museums. They commissioned the artists to paint these things for their own enjoyment and to hang in the churches, to the glory of God and the edification

ST. BARBARA attributed to the MASTER OF FLÉMALLE.
Prado Museum, Madrid (*39¼ x 18¼*)

PLATE 21

ANNUNCIATION attributed to ROGER VAN DER WEYDEN. Metropolitan Museum, New York. Courtesy Metropolitan Museum of Art (*44 x 32⅜*)

PLATE 22

HANS MEMLING. ANNUNCIATION. Lehman Collection, New York (*44 x 32⅜*)

PLATE 23

MASTER OF THE TIBURTINE SIBYL. St. Anne, the Virgin and Child.
Private collection, New York (*14½ x 9*)

PLATE 24

of the devout. So they, on their part, helped to make possible an era of great artistic achievement.

The pictures were highly valued by the people for whom they were painted, but valued for their content, not as collectors' items. They are mentioned in wills. They were included in dowries. They were made part of the spoils of war. When Charles V abdicated and retired to a monastery to set his soul's affairs in order before his death, he chose to take with him into his cell one picture—van der Weyden's *Descent from the Cross* (PLATE 56). The emperor who could make his choice from the works of the greatest artists Europe had produced selected this one by the great master of Brussels as the inspiration for his last hours.

It is not by accident that monumental painting—and even little panel pictures in the grandeur of their conception can truly be called monumental—made its appearance in Flanders at the time the communes had won their freedom and were in the exercise of their power. The astounding flowering of art in that country during the fifteenth century had its roots in the towns and was developed along with, and in consequence of, the freedom of the Flemish people. It was greatly fostered by the guild system, which was the mark of the medieval faculty for industrial association.

To understand how the masters received their training in painting, and how they conducted their workshops and fulfilled commissions, it is necessary to examine briefly the workings of the painters' guilds.

V

The Medieval Guilds

The origin and growth of the guild system all over Europe during the formative centuries of the Middle Ages is a fascinating story. In Flanders, where trade and industry became important at a date when much of the rest of western Europe was in fief to an agricultural feudalism, the merchant guilds assumed a power and a prestige that set a pattern for all the other guilds organized later.

The guilds of merchants came into being during the eleventh century. During the twelfth century, the period when the great cathedrals were rising and when the arts of building, sculpture, painting, and carving were emerging from the cloister and passing into the hands of lay craftsmen and artists, other guilds of workmen were organized. As the merchants had drawn together to protect their common interests and to fix prices which assured them profit on their enterprises, so the guilds of artisans banded together for the protection and development of their various crafts and trades and—this must not be overlooked—to establish a system of apprenticeship which insured the continuance not only of the trades but of the fine skills which the master craftsmen developed.

As you stroll through any old Flemish city—or, in fact, through the old quarters of practically any city in western Europe—you come upon streets dedicated to glass blowers, goldsmiths, weavers, carpenters, and sword makers. In each of these artisans of that particular trade once lived and did their work. The members of the trades drew together for self-protection and because of similar interests. Thus they kept track of any innovations in their crafts and were able to take joint action when necessary to safeguard their business interests. As the guilds of workers became more powerful, it was usual for each guild to have its own hall for meetings and for the entertainment of guildsmen from foreign cities. These guild houses were usually built around the market square, each with its appropriately sculptured façade on which the arms of the guild appeared. Probably the finest collection of these old guildhalls are those which flank the Grand Place in Brussels. The square is dominated by the noble Hôtel de Ville and by the King's House which opposes it. The Flemish name for the latter, "*Broodhuis,*" tells that this was originally a bread market and the headquarters of the bakers of the city. The bakers of Brussels were so prosperous and their guildhall so magnificent, that the Emperor, Charles V, confiscated it for his own use. Standing proudly beside the Hôtel de Ville is the guildhall of the butchers, marked by a swan; then those of the brewers, the mercers, coopers, grease makers, painters, and tailors.

Distinguished master painters from foreign countries were received at the guildhall with appropriate ceremonies. When Dürer visited Antwerp in 1520, he was received by the painters' guild, which gave a banquet in his honor. He has left us an account of the occasion:

On Sunday, which was St. Oswald's Day, the painters invited me to their guildhall with my wife and maidservant. They had a quantity of silverplate, and costly furniture, and most expensive food. All their wives were with them, and as I was led in to table, everyone stood up in a row on either side, as if they had been bringing in some great lord. Among them were men of very high standing, all of whom behaved with great respect and kindness toward me, saying that in whatever they could be serviceable to me they would do everything for me that lay in their power. And while I sat there in such honor, the syndic of the magistrates of Antwerp came with two servants to me, and gave me four cans of wine in their name, and said to me that they wished thereby to do me honor, and assure me of their good will, and to remember that in whatever I wanted to do they would all be helpful to me. So I thanked them and lay down to sleep.

During the twelfth century, when a cathedral was being built, it was not unusual for all the craftsmen engaged upon it to group themselves together in one association. For instance, at Louvain, those who worked on the church were called Sinte Peeter's Mannen. The cathedral workmen at Ghent were called the men of St. Bavon; at Tournai, the men of St. Mary; and at Nivelles, the men of St. Gertrude. The craftsmen who devoted their skill to the making of crucifixes were called Jhesus Mannen.

From these groups which originally included all who worked on a church building in any capacity the later painters' guilds were formed; and these original groups marked the starting point for the development of art in the hands of laymen. The art of painting did not flourish and flower until it was freed from the cloister which had nourished its early stages. The transition from the Church to the lay craftsmen was made possible by the guild system.

Before the end of the fourteenth century the duties of a painter were most varied; he turned his hand to practically anything that needed coloring. He decorated walls, furniture, armor; painted banners and escutcheons, and worked largely upon things of no religious significance. Only gradually did the monks turn over to the laity the making of objects for use in the churches. The first artists to work independently in Flanders were freed serfs who later became burghers of the city. In the records of old families in the town of Louvain it is not uncommon to find names to which is added the title "pictor."

In many cities, where there were not a sufficient number of workers of one craft to form a strong guild, several crafts joined forces. For example, in Augsburg it was found expedient for the mercers, parchment dealers, shoemakers, importers of spices, and makers of playing cards to unite in one guild. In Lille, the painters and glassmakers formed a union; in Brussels, the goldsmiths, painters, and printers. In Mons, the sword forgers, tapestry weavers, carvers, and painters of images, manuscript illuminators, potters, tailors, and saddlers were all in the same union. Later on, when the guilds had grown in numbers and power, the membership was strictly regulated. For example, at Bruges, during the heyday of the city's prosperity, there were separate guilds for painters and for illuminators. Painters were not allowed to make miniatures, and miniaturists were forbidden to make pictures. The Guild of St. Luke, at Bruges, included painters, saddlers, glassmakers, and mirror makers; the illuminators, calligraphers, and image makers were members of the Guild of St. John. It was decided by a lawsuit that the illuminators might use only water colors, while the making of pictures in oil colors, gold, and silver was the exclusive right of members of the Guild of St. Luke.

Originally, there was little distinction between the man who carved and the man who painted a statue. Almost all the very early painters—those who lived before the fifteenth century—are spoken of in the records under the title of *pictor ymaginum* (painter of images). The men who did the decorative work on the architecture of a cathedral also polychromed the statues. Even in 1440 we read of Roger van der Weyden being paid "forty ridder de 4 gros de Flandre" for coloring a relief belonging to Jean van Evere.

It was in line with the feeling of the men of the Middle Ages that each guild should have its patron saint to whom the members of the guild paid special devotion. The weavers adopted St. Catherine as their patron, probably because she was usually represented with a wheel on which she was martyred, and this seemed an appropriate symbol for workers in the cloth trades. St. Barbara was the patron of the munitions makers. All the guilds of painters, whether in Flanders, Italy, or Bohemia, claim as their patron St. Luke, the evangelist who was believed to have been a painter himself. The winged ox—the apocalyptic beast associated with the author of the third Gospel—appears in the arms of all the painters' guilds. Van der Weyden's *Madonna* in the Boston Museum, in which St. Luke, in a beautiful rosy-red robe with furred sleeves, and a medieval craftsman's hat, sketchbook and pencil in hand, kneels before Our Lady, was probably painted for the chapel of some painters' guild.

THE PAINTERS' GUILDS

Most of the guilds had been in existence for a long time before it became necessary for them to formulate a constitution. The painters' guild of Ghent had reached this stage of progress in 1339. That of Tournai, one of the art centers of old Belgium, drew up its constitution in 1341. The painters' guild of Bruges took the same steps ten years later. We know that there was an active goldsmiths' guild at Louvain during the first half of the fourteenth century because an act of October 16, 1360, made the painters' guild of that city a separate organization. At the same time as the artists of Flanders were banding themselves together for the development and protection of their craft, Guilds of St. Luke were being formed in Florence and in Siena. The Guild of St. Luke in Prague dates its constitution from 1348.

In addition to these chartered guilds, in all the cities of the Low Countries there were religious confraternities which assumed charitable responsibilities. Such, for example, was the Confraternity of Our Lady of the Seven Sorrows at Bruges, which maintained a chapel in the cathedral, made contributions to support masses for the members, and whose members were under vows to aid the sick and destitute, appear at funerals, and take part in Saints' Day processions. Many of the artists belonged to one or another of these confraternities in addition to being members of a painters' guild.

The Guilds of St. Luke also had their religious aspect. The groups usually met in some monastery or in a special chapel before the building of the guildhalls. Each guild had its own chapel and was responsible for the decorations of the altar, gifts of wax for candles, and banners to adorn the cathedral on feast days. In the Church of St. Peter at Louvain one chapel was under the special protection of St. Luke, and the painters and craftsmen of the city went there to invoke his assistance on their projects. Apprentices of the guild were required to furnish a pound of wax apiece for altar candles in the chapel. The painters' guild in Antwerp made it a regulation, in 1434, that each new member should pay a florin to the Church of Our Lady. In the records of the painters' guild at Tournai are preserved the initiation oaths administered to new members by the wardens, and several sermons which were delivered by wardens of the guild to impress the young initiates with the serious and pious purposes of their art.

The dues paid by the members insured each member a Christian burial and a certain number of masses to be said in the guild chapel for the repose of his soul. The same treasury provided a pension for the widow and assured the sons of the deceased free apprenticeship at their father's craft. In this way the medieval guilds—for this benevolent aspect was true of all of them—may be said to represent man's first effort toward social security and group insurance. There was a definite intention to make the arts and trades hereditary in families. For example, of Roger van der Weyden's three sons Jean became a goldsmith; Peter and Goswin became painters. Goswin's son, another Roger, followed in the steps of his famous grandfather. In the sixteenth and seventeenth centuries, when the guild system began to give way, the politicians snapped up these hereditary privileges; so, in Ghent, the illegitimate son of the Emperor, Charles V, and the pretty daughter

of a Ghent butcher claimed the right for himself and his descendants to control the butcher trade in that city.

As organized bodies of men, working for their living and desirous of protecting their craft, the artists' guilds were similar to those of the mercers, butchers, or tanners. Aside from the necessarily different training of apprentices, the organization of the guilds was practically the same. In all of them there was the intent to make the worker recognize his craft or trade, not only as a means of livelihood, but as a way of life, which imposed obligations and conferred privileges. The intent was to make him proud of his guild membership and to give him the feeling that this membership united him with all other workers.

HOW THE GUILDS WERE ORGANIZED

In the painters' guilds there were three groups of members: the apprentices, the paid assistants or companions, and the masters. Each group had a head man who spoke for the group at meetings of the whole guild. The qualifications for membership varied from place to place. For instance, at Ghent the constitution of the Guild of St. Luke stipulated that only residents of the city were eligible for membership. This restriction tended to make the painters' guild at Ghent smaller and less important than the guild of Bruges, or that of Tournai. However, to prove that the guildsmen of Ghent were willing to break their own rule upon occasion, in 1421 they acceded to the request of the Duchess Michelle and admitted to membership the brothers Hubert and Jan van Eyck. This, to their eternal glory.

It was generally required of applicants for admission to a painters' guild that the candidate should have attained the accepted standard of skill in his craft. If he passed certain tests, he was required to pay an entrance fee. In Ghent, this amounted to six livres, with the initiation fee to the warden of eight escalins and a gift to the guild of a silver cup crested with arms and weighing one troy ounce. At Brussels, an applicant was required to pay five pounds and give a specified amount of wine to the warden and the valets of the guild. The painters of Brussels were, apparently, convivial souls, for a banquet was given each new member upon initiation. At Bruges, the entrance fee was two livres for citizens of the city; three livres for foreigners.

All of the painters' guilds in old Belgium seem to have been very strict when it came to admitting bastards to membership. Illegitimate children were accepted as apprentices, but at a much higher fee

ANNUNCIATION by GERARD DAVID. Harkness Collection, New York, N. Y. (*30⅜ x 24¾ each*)

PLATE 25

than was charged for those born in wedlock. At Namur, an outsider who wished to join the guild had to prove that he was of legitimate birth, had to present a recommendation for honesty, and give evidence that he did not leave his home town to escape the clutches of the law. At Saint-Trond the rule of the painters' guild prohibited a bastard from being admitted to membership unless he painted the legend of St. Eloy on the wall of his shop, thus honoring the patron of the goldsmiths. There was a very definite effort on the part of medieval painters and craftsmen to establish themselves and their professions as respectable folk. They would have deplored any suspicion or taint of immorality and the Bohemianism which in later years came to be associated with followers of the arts.

In all the guilds there were strict laws against the admission of women as members, although the painters of Brussels passed an ordinance in 1415 which permitted women to grind colors. This relaxing of the severe early rules against women seems to have gone on, for by the end of the fifteenth century in many cities women could be admitted to the guild of painters under the same conditions and with the same fees as men, provided they could prove that they had a good reputation.

In general, the organization of all the painters' guilds was very much the same, so that a master of Tournai could present himself with his credentials before the wardens of the Guild of St. Luke in Bruges, or Cologne, or Prague, and be sure of proper recognition from his peers. When any of the great Flemish masters traveled to Italy, they were welcomed by the guildsmen of St. Luke in each city they stopped in. So, such a journey was a very enriching one, and the painter came home after having visited the studios of fellow painters all along the route of his travels. He saw hundreds of pictures in process of painting, talked with innumerable painters and craftsmen, and brought back to his own little city in Flanders memories that enriched his work to the end of his days. You can imagine what such a journey meant to Jan van Eyck, when he traveled across France and Spain into Portugal to paint the Princess Isabella, who was to become his master's bride. And to van der Weyden, when he journeyed to Ferrara.

In each city, however, the local guild was organized in accordance with local traditions and requirements. The painters' guild at Louvain was headed by four *meesters* (governors), who kept the accounts and made the annual reports. These officers succeeded each other in groups of two annually. The guild at Brussels had a dean, an assistant dean,

and wardens to manage its affairs. The Guild of St. Luke at Bruges was officered by a dean and two treasurers. In Antwerp, in addition to a president and a dean, there were two commissioners, both officials of the city.

It was the duty of the dean of the guild to maintain the constitution, regulate the quality of work done by the members, and judge and punish any transgressions. It was legally possible for a master craftsman, who had been found guilty by the dean of his guild, to appeal his case to the town magistrate. However, in nearly all the cases of which we have record the town magistrate supported the dean of the guild, and the plaintiff was given an extra fine for insubordination.

REGULATIONS OF THE PAINTERS' GUILDS

There were stipulations in the guild constitutions concerning the pigments to be used. If a master was caught using a substitute for one of these, he was liable to a heavy fine. Such regulations kept the prices for pictures high, and made the cost of production the same in each workshop. There was no chance of one painter underbidding another to get a commission, and being able to do so by using cheap materials. In Antwerp, painters could not accept a statue for polychroming until the guild wardens had approved the quality of its workmanship.

There is no doubt that this strict supervision of works in process of production is the reason why the pictures painted in Flanders during the fifteenth century still remain fresh, rich, clear in color, and undimmed by time. They endure in their pristine beauty because the painters made use of only the best materials available and adhered conscientiously to the guild regulations for preparing the wooden panels for painting.

When you study one of these little panel paintings you find it hard to believe that five centuries have passed since the painter made his last brush stroke on the wood. The surface is surprisingly free from the crow's-feet which disfigure many old pictures. Compare one of these gay and glowing little paintings with a picture by Turner of whom Ruskin, who greatly admired the English master, wrote regretfully: "No picture of Turner's is seen in perfection a month after it is painted."

TECHNIQUE

The regulations governing the use of colors are important because they reveal what the medieval guildsmen considered the best way of making a picture.

The old Flemish masters did not paint on canvas, but on wood. Their first concern, therefore, was to provide themselves with a panel which could be planed perfectly smooth, which would not splinter, warp, or crack, and which would take its priming evenly. The Flemish painter had to know the qualities of woods and more than a little about carpentry. Frequently he had to make his panel of several boards, well selected and joined together so expertly that they would not pull apart.

When it came to painting the panel, it must be remembered that the medieval painter could not buy paints; he had, perforce, to make them himself. He never mixed his colors on a palette. He did not paint quickly, but slowly and precisely, building up one layer of paint smoothly on another, and letting his picture dry level by level. First came the designing of a cartoon; then the making of a panel with its grounding. There followed the underdrawing and underpainting; finally, the lustrous glazes were added to complete the finish.

Our knowledge of how the medieval Flemish painters made their paints comes from the so-called Strasbourg manuscript, a fifteenth-century work on the technique of painting. The manuscript was destroyed by fire in 1870 but fortunately a copy of it had been made some years earlier by an Englishman engaged on a book on the history of oil painting.[1]

The author of the Strasbourg manuscript gives explicit directions as to how to temper all oil colors:

. . . Now I will also teach how all colors are to be tempered with oil . . . and in the first place how the oil is to be prepared for the purpose so that it may be limpid and clear, and that it may dry quickly.

How to prepare oil for the colors. Take the oil of linseed or of hempseed, or old nut oil, as much as you please, and put therein bones that have been long kept, calcined to whiteness, and an equal quantity of pumice stone; let them boil in the oil, removing the scum. Then take the oil from the fire, and let it well cool; and if it is in quantity about a quart, add to it an ounce of white copperas. This will diffuse itself in the oil which will become quite limpid and clear. Afterwards strain the oil through a clean linen cloth into a clean basin, and place it in the sun for four days. Thus it will acquire a thick consistency, and also become as transparent as a fine crystal. And this oil dries very fast and makes all colors beautifully clear and glassy besides. All painters are not acquainted

with it. From its excellence it is called *oleum preciosum*, since half an ounce is well worth a shilling; and with this oil all colors are to be ground and tempered. All colors should be ground stiffly, and then tempered to a half-liquid state, which should be neither too thick nor too thin. . . .

When it came to the pigments for making paints by this or any other method, the Flemish painter had limited resources and very high standards. Most common were the earth colors, ranging through yellows down to a few dull reds, to brown. Their hues could be changed artificially by firing; much as a raw sienna earth is transformed into a burnt sienna.

Blue pigments were hard to acquire and difficult to use. One of the most famed and precious was natural ultramarine, made from grinding down lapis lazuli. Lapis lazuli, from the Badakhshan mines at the headwaters of the Oxus, was an important item of trade in medieval Europe. It was carried by caravan to the port of Acre and thence shipped to Venice. The Venetians re-exported it to the cities of France, Germany, and the Low Countries. The pigment was so rare, it was frequently classified with gold, and its use became a sign of luxury. Jan van Eyck used it in painting his *St. Barbara* (PLATE 29). The great abbot and statesman Suger, who directed the building of the Church of St. Denis in Paris, stipulated in his contracts with craftsmen that lapis lazuli was to be used in the decorations.

The most important blue known to the Flemish and Dutch painters was azurite—a secondary copper ore associated with malachite. In its mineral form azurite is glassy and therefore poor in color saturation. It came chiefly from Hungary.

Because of its vitreous character, azurite had to be ground coarsely to preserve its coloring power. Even in this state it tended to lose itself in the oils that bound it to the painting surface. The result is that many a blue now appears green, dark, and murky.

The saddest chapter in the story of Flemish painting is that of the blues. Ultramarine was too scarce and too costly for common use, and was poor in strength when mixed with oils. Azurite easily lost color in the heavy binders necessitated by its coarse grinding. In a Flemish painting we must always beware of a tone that seems to be green; the artist may have painted it blue.

The red of the Madonna's robes as they swirl about her in so many of the old Flemish panels was almost always made of vermilion. Natural vermilion comes from cinnabar, the ore of mercury. The medieval craftsman could have received this from England, Spain, or other parts of Europe. It was

---

[1] *Materials for a History of Oil Painting*, by Charles Lock Eastlake, published in 1847. An important pioneer work in the history of painting technique.

available, not too costly, and was reliable. Small wonder, then, that the masters used it so generously and so joyously. If only the Flemish blues had stood the passage of time as triumphantly as the reds have.

One of the oldest and most important pigments is white lead. Its preparation from metallic lead and vinegar is described by Pliny. The antique method, which was followed by the medieval painters, was to pack thin strips of lead in clay pots which had separate compartments in the bottom, containing a weak solution of acetic acid. These pots were then buried in the manure heaps for about three months while the heat, acetic vapors, carbon dioxide, oxygen, and water slowly transformed the lead into basic lead carbonate.

Our knowledge of the painting technique of the fifteenth-century masters is drawn chiefly from the poetical treatise on the art by the sixteenth-century Dutch painter, Carel van Mander. The procedure seems to have been as follows: first, small drawings were made with silver point upon grounded papers. Once the panel had been constructed, planed, and primed, the drawing was made on it in a monochrome of neutral tints in freehand, using the preliminary sketches as models. The drawing on the panel was done with egg tempera or water-color medium, and black-and-white pigments were used in it. When the monochrome was completed, a coat of flesh color in an oil medium was laid over it. Over this flesh tint the colors were spread thinly in a shining coat, and the details were drawn in with white. Other films of oil followed the first, and van Mander made it clear that he understood the peculiarities of this material, for he directed that each color should be arranged with certainty and put in its place to avoid later changes.

For more than five centuries there has been a tradition concerning the "secrets" of the brothers van Eyck, which, some historians have believed, were connected with the technique of painting in oils. The origin of this tradition is found in a passage in Vasari's *Lives of the Painters*, which was published in 1550, one hundred and ten years after the death of Jan van Eyck. He says:

A most beautiful invention and a great convenience to the art of painting was the discovery of coloring in oil. The first inventor was John of Bruges, who sent the panel to Naples to King Alphonso; and to the Duke of Urbino, Frederico II, the paintings for his bathroom.

The difficulty with this statement, of course, lies in the two words "invention" and "discovery," which go very badly when used in reference to the arts. In passing, it might be mentioned that the monk Theophilus in the twelfth century and Eraclius a century later give recipes for the use of boiled oils in painting. So much for van Eyck's "invention."

The truth of the matter is that van Eyck did more than invent a process: he evolved a way of using certain available materials in such a manner as to raise old concepts to a new high point of intellectual and spiritual expression. He had the ability to produce singlehanded a whole new way of thinking about pictorial ideas. The method of painting in oils went hand in hand with his new principles of portraying the visual image.

The *St. Barbara* panel of van Eyck, though unfinished, is a fine piece of evidence for the study of the master's method (PLATE 29). One critic has concluded from his study of it that van Eyck began his painting with egg (whether yolk or white of egg he does not state), and over this placed glazes of translucent oil colors, doing the final modeling in egg and applying a surface film of the same medium. Another group of critics hold that a combination of oil with gum or glue could have been a natural and logical procedure whereby the van Eycks arrived at their amazing results. Whatever the painting technique, the *St. Barbara* shows the great amount of painstaking drawing that went into the preparation of every painted panel.

The guilds taught their members the use and significance of symbols, the mystic meaning of colors, and innumerable legends of the saints. All these we find repeated over and over again in medieval sculpture, painting, and tapestries. Originally these secrets were the property of the religious orders, but when art passed into the hands of lay craftsmen, the monks imparted to the laity the knowledge of religious symbols and the legends connected with the most popular saints. The artist might dress a female saint in any way that suited his fancy—frequently in the fashion of the day; but if he intended her to represent the Magdalene he was careful to place in her hands a pot of ointment. Van der Weyden's Mary Magdalene is said to be the most beautiful woman in Flemish art (PLATE 16). Her costume is one that was modish in the fifteenth century. But for all that, she is easily distinguished by the jar of precious ointment which she carries. It was *de rigueur* to paint St. Barbara crowned and holding a miniature tower—in memory of the fortress in which her pagan father imprisoned her for her faith. Nor would any representation of St. Catherine have been approved by the wardens of any painters' guild, or accepted by the medieval public, if the saint had not somewhere near her a broken wheel, the symbol of her martyrdom.

By the scrupulous use of symbols which were generally accepted and understood, the masters packed their little paintings with meaning. The symbols and their meaning were taught to the apprentices in every painter's workshop. So instructed, they found nothing extraordinary in the *Madonna* which Memling painted for young Martin Nieuwenhoven in which the Virgin offers her son a red apple (COLOR PLATE 78). No medieval Fleming would have thought of objecting that mothers did not give little babies raw apples. He saw in the picture what Memling intended he should see—a new and innocent Eve, and a new and infant Adam—the glorious fulfillment of the promise of redemption made to man's first parents.

WHAT ARE PRIMITIVES?

Primitives are fanciful, and they are exciting because they never pretend to be more than they are. Thus, they are intensely sincere. Flemish painting, too, is sincere; but it is not naïve or primitive in the true sense.

That which the modern critic frequently—and quite naïvely—dismisses as photographic naturalism in Flemish painting is actually one of the greatest feats of imagination ever attained in any pictorial art. This is not a quality of true "primitive painting." This fact was already recognized by Professor Huizinga, of the University of Leiden, who wrote:

Yet neither this art nor this faith is primitive. But using the term primitive to designate the masters of the fifteenth century we run the risk of a misunderstanding. They are primitive in a purely chronological sense in so far as, for us, they are the first to come, and no older painting is known to us. But if to this designation we attach the meaning of a primitive spirit we are egregiously mistaken.

The masters who conceived and painted these panels may have believed, as most men of their time did, that the earth was flat, that God made it in six days and rested on the seventh, that the miracles accredited to the saints were as factually true as the miracles of gunpowder and the printing press and other scientific discoveries and inventions of their own time. But when it came to craftsmanship, drawing to scale, and the art of putting paint on an oaken panel so that the colors would live untarnished for centuries, these painters were sophisticated far beyond the standards of today.

Neither their approach to life nor their approach to art can be termed "primitive."

One has only to contrast a few of the pictures painted in Flanders during the fifteenth century with some pictures made in America during the eighteenth and early nineteenth centuries to realize that this nomenclature leads one far astray (PLATE 27). In every land, among all peoples, there have been "primitive artists"; but the Flemish guildsmen who did their work according to the standards of their guilds were too well trained as craftsmen to qualify for the credit due the early American untutored painters who traveled through the states, paying for their board and lodging by painting portraits of their hosts, political posters, and pictures of strong patriotic, if not artistic, significance (PLATE 28).

These American primitives, though painted some three to four centuries after the early Flemish masters painted their little panels, show how very far from primitive the work of the fifteenth-century masters was. When Maurice Barrès said: "There is nothing of real genius which does not hold in its perfection something of the childlike," he might have been speaking of Flemish painting, which, without being primitive, naïve, or childish, is truly childlike in its mixture of mysticism and realism.

APPRENTICESHIP
AND THE MASTER'S SHOP

Tommaso Portinari, banker and promoter; Willem Moreel, the importer of fine spices; Arnolfini, whose wagon trains brought bales of lustrous silks to his shop in Bruges; and William Caxton, governor of the English merchants resident in the Low Countries who had set up his first printing press in his house in Bruges and was experimenting with the new and dangerous art of printing, all carried on their businesses under the same roof that sheltered themselves and their families. This was the medieval way of life.

The same way of life extended to the painters whose homes were their studios.

When a young man desired to become a painter he had first—or rather his parents had to do it for him—to apply to the wardens of the painters' guild in that particular city. If his application was approved, which meant that he showed some promise and that his own and his father's reputation were without blemish, he was accepted and assigned to a master. He then entered the home of the master as a member of the family for the term of his apprenticeship. This lasted usually two to three years. There are instances on record where an apprenticeship was drawn out to last five years; and several times in various cities there were revolts of appren-

PETRUS CHRISTUS. St. Eligius (St. Eloy). Lehman Collection, New York (38½ x 33⅛)

Plate 26

FLEMISH AND AMERICAN PRIMITIVES

THE VIRGIN PAINTED BY ST. LUKE.
Attributed to van der Weyden

A JUST JUDGE by van Eyck

THE YORK FAMILY AT HOME. Museum of
Modern Art

GENERAL GEORGE WASHINGTON Review-
ing the Western Army at Fort Cumberland, Sep-
tember 19, 1794. Bland Gallery, New York

PLATE 27

FLEMISH AND AMERICAN PRIMITIVES

A PRIEST by van der Goes

ARNOLFINI AND HIS BRIDE by van Eyck

REV. SAMUEL BUELL. Long Island Historical
Society

CONVERSATION PIECE. Halladay-Thomas
Collection

PLATE 28

ST. BARBARA by van Eyck. Antwerp Museum ($12\frac{3}{8}$ x $7\frac{1}{4}$)

Plate 29

tices against masters who kept them in apprenticeship, without pay, too long.

In this shop-family life, which was the atmosphere in which the great paintings of fifteenth-century Flanders were created, the apprentice learned infinitely more than how to make white lead by the method described in this chapter, how to season oak for panels and to mortise boards together, how to grind colors, and brew the precious oil. He learned also how to draw, accurately and powerfully. He learned to see how fabrics fell into folds and how the light glowed on their rich texture. He learned the legends of the saints recounted in the *Golden Legend*, which was the treasure house of medieval saint lore. Very early in his apprenticeship, as he held the pot of gold paint for the master and watched the skillful hands paint a wondrous filigree crown of gold and jewels on the brow of a virginal St. Ursula, he learned the necessity for reproducing objects from memory. Above all, he learned the value of doing work well, in accordance with rules worked out by those expert in the craft, and in conformity with standards that were accepted by and religiously followed by the masters of the guild. He learned that there is no quick and easy way to perfection; and he knew that under the guild system he could not make a reputation as a painter unless and until he satisfied all the demands laid down by the guild.

During that long apprenticeship and his experiences as a member of the painter's family he learned a particular approach to his work, and a set of work habits which were the strong warp that made possible the rich texture of Flemish painting.

The young apprentice had plenty of opportunity to watch the master work and to feel close to him. The number of apprentices a master could take at one time was laid down by his guild. These were rarely more than two or three, including members of his own family. At Louvain, the father who had his son working with him could take only one other apprentice. However, these rules were set aside when a shop had a large order which required the services of several assistants.

The master painter was not running a factory nor an art studio. He was engaged in making good paintings, and he took into his workshop only as many helpers as he required to turn out the work he was commissioned to produce. At the same time, his pride in his craft and the rules of his guild constrained him to hand on to younger men what he, himself, had learned of a master and through his own experience. By the regulations of the painters' guild, the master never took into his workshop more apprentices and paid assistants than he could teach and supervise individually. There was no such thing as an art class or an atelier.

Apprentices and paid assistants worked on the paintings or other projects which the master had in hand. Their services were strictly utilitarian, and they were judged by the value of those services to the master. The finished work belonged to the master painter, though all in the shop and even in the family might have had some hand in producing it.

This shop-family life has left its distinct mark on the pictures produced in those medieval Flemish workshops. It is responsible, in large part, for the homeliness of many of the scenes in the religious pictures. We find St. Barbara seated on a bench before the fire in just such a room as the painter's own family living room (PLATE 21). In Memling's *Annunciation* the room probably reproduces one familiar to the painter (PLATE 23). The tiny, walled gardens which you glimpse through an open window or an arcade in many an old Flemish altarpiece are actual gardens of the period. The homely but frequently beautiful ewers and basins which appear in the pictures were the household utensils used in the painters' homes (PLATE 22).

The apprentice received no pay. He was fed, housed, and clothed. He lived as a member of the painter's family. The master was responsible for his well-being and for his moral, social, and religious education. The master was also responsible to the wardens of the guild and to the town for the youth's behavior. Fines for juvenile delinquency on the part of apprentices were collectible from their masters who, no doubt, did not hesitate to discipline unruly lads in their own way.

When the apprentice had completed the term of his apprenticeship satisfactorily he was admitted to the rank of *compagnon*, or paid assistant. This rise in status indicated that he had shown himself capable of learning the fundamentals of the painter's craft. It indicated that in the opinion of the master and of the guild wardens he had in him "the making of a painter."

Many men remained in the rank of paid assistants all their lives; they never produced a masterpiece of their own which won them a higher rating in the guild. They worked in the shops of the masters, doing good work, which helped materially to save the time of the master painter.

A "journeyman"—so called from the fact that he was paid by the day—might travel from town to town across Europe, working here and there, learning and observing. Young men of promise were encouraged to take a *wanderjahr* of this sort, and to bring home sketches of famous buildings in other cities and lands which might become the inspiration of the fantastic little towns for the backgrounds of future altarpieces. Wherever the young journeyman went, he had only to present himself and his credentials to the wardens of the local Guild of St. Luke to be welcomed among his peers, the paid assistants of that city. Upon the payment of certain fees he could take service with a master.

QUALIFICATIONS FOR MASTERSHIP

When a painter made application to his guild for mastership he had to meet certain tests laid down by the local guild. He had first to give assurance that he had completed his apprenticeship successfully and to pay fees which were comparatively heavy. He had also to present to the guild wardens his masterpiece to be judged. At Mons a triptych was required as an examination piece, to be presented before the master constables of the town.

At Tournai, the son of a master could join his father in his own right at the age of twenty-one without any special proof of his ability as a painter. He paid no entrance fees and only half the usual fee to the guild wardens. Amazingly enough, at one time in Brussels no proofs of attainment were required for a mastership. Even apprenticeship was dispensed with by payments for the upkeep of a foundling. In Louvain, only citizens of the town were admitted to mastership in the painters' guild.

It would seem that there were as many kinds of master painters as there were rules and fees for gaining the privilege of the rank.

A master painter could command the prices for his work laid down by his guild. Melchior Broederlain, painter to the first Duke of Burgundy, was paid 200 francs a year, which was exactly twice the pension of the duke's physician. The price of the painting was based upon the time required and the cost of the material used. In the early part of the fourteenth century a higher value was placed on missals and other illuminated books than on carvings. The art of illumination was a part of the large bookmaking industry, and there were set prices for vignettes and initial letters. It was generally figured that a composition which took an experienced artist one day to paint was worth ten sols *tournois*.[2] An artist was expected to turn out an illuminated capital letter with vignette in half a day, at five sols. Painters who applied color to statues or furniture were paid on the same basis as the men who made the original objects. Painters on glass were paid at a rate based on the space they covered: sixteen sols for one foot of

[2]Approximately $3.60.

painting. We have seen how the painters who worked on the decorations and *entremets* for the wedding of Charles the Bold were paid for their day's work.

Dirk Bouts was commissioned to paint four panels of the *Judgment of Otto* for 500 florins. After his death, Hugo van der Goes was asked to estimate the value of the two panels on which Bouts had worked. He set it at 306 florins.[3]

It is impossible for us of today to judge whether the medieval masters were paid adequately for their work. The prices they charged were set by their own guilds. Van Eyck received a salary of 100 livres tournois as court painter to the duke. This has been estimated at about $700. It is interesting to compare the master's modest wages with the values placed on van Eycks in our day, when wealthy collectors and art museums have been known to pay as high as half a million dollars for a small van Eyck panel.

The artists handled their own sales, or their wives kept shop for them. However, in 1460 we find notice of one Nicolas van Holland, *coopman in Schilderien*, an enterprising Dutchman who set up as a dealer in pictures in Louvain where his fellow countryman Dirk Bouts then had his workshop. The archives of Mechlin contain notice of a lottery of a picture from Bruges in 1479.

The first market for pictures was on the Pan in Antwerp, a sort of gallery connected with the Church of Our Lady. It was divided into booths which the church rented to painters and sculptors to be used as shops. In 1480 all sellers of pictures at Antwerp were required to display them at the market for a period of two years, paying two *gros de Flandre* for every square foot of space. This rental provided the painters with storage room and accommodations for themselves when they came to town.

THE SOCIAL POSITION OF PAINTERS

Whatever a master was paid for his work, there seems no doubt that he was a person of importance in the town where he worked. If he enjoyed the favor of the duke, as van Eyck did, he might be rewarded with honors which, though they seem amusing and even childish to us today, were highly coveted at that time.

In 1425, on the nineteenth of May, Philip the

[3]The florin at that time was worth about forty-eight sols: approximately $17.25 in American currency. It is extremely difficult to estimate the values of the medieval coins, as the purchasing power of sums which are small according to modern standards was then very great. It is of some guidance to know that fourteen sols (approximately $5.00) was the value of a fine, fat sheep.

Good made Jan van Eyck his court painter. Van Eyck had been *valet de chambre* to the Bishop of Liége, but was released for service elsewhere upon the bishop's death. The duke had new chains of gold made for his painter, and an order of the year 1426 gave van Eyck two horses and the right to a valet in the livery of the duke. Philip also rented a house belonging to Jean Ravary for his painter; but in 1428 he did as much for the worker in charge of his siege machinery and longbows. It would seem that even in the fifteenth century war matériel was placed on a par with, or given precedence over, art. During his journey to Portugal on behalf of the duke, van Eyck received a sum of 160 livres, the same as Molembaix, governor of Lille, and Mony, the duke's councilor and chamberlain. The order stipulated the painter should march behind these dignitaries in all processions, and immediately in front of the duke's squires, secretaries, and cup-bearers.

The title of valet de chambre was also given to Jean and Nicolas de Voleur, who were simple decorators, and Nicolas received the same salary as van Eyck: 100 livres tournois a year. The title of valet de chambre was also conferred on goldsmiths, master clockmakers, and butchers. It was tantamount to "Purveyor to the Court."

Apparently the duke's treasurers did not have as high a regard for Master van Eyck's services as the duke had, for repeatedly Philip had to order them to pay his artists' salaries. It is not certain that van Eyck ended his career in favor at court. We know that his successor, Daniel Daret, in 1449 was valet de chambre with honors, but without permanent wages. Much of the prestige of the position occupied by van Eyck had disappeared, and no artist again enjoyed such favor in Flanders until the time of Rubens at the court of the Archduke Albert in the seventeenth century.

One would be quite wrong to consider that the successes of the painters allowed them to aspire to aristocratic pretensions. There was always a distinction between the artist and members of the no-bility. Roger van der Weyden, "master worker of painting of Brussels," as he was called by the Abbot of Cambrai, remained all his life a burgher. His rank as "town painter" merely permitted him to wear his mantle on the right shoulder, while workers and valets carried theirs on the left. And he received annually a larger bolt of cloth than that allowed to the town architects.

Dirk Bouts, like the other *meesterwerklieden* and *overste Chapen van der Stadt*, received a robe a year and was allowed ninety *pleken* for a coat lining, as well as a pot of wine to slake his thirst after each procession in which he was obliged to march.

When a painter became an officer of the guild he was required to devote a good share of his time to the guild's business, to the investigation and approval of materials for painters, and to works in progress. The guild system compelled the masters to share in the responsibilities of the civic life; they could not be recluses. Van der Goes served some time as dean of the painters' guild of Ghent before he retired to a monastery. Memling was a highly esteemed burgher of Bruges. In Louvain, artists always enjoyed considerable importance. Several patricians had practiced as painters since early in the fifteenth century and others were related to the families of artists. The families had a custom of dining together, and frequently entertained illustrious visitors.

These obligations and privileges not only made the masters men of their times and of their towns, they tended to make the profession a healthy and normal occupation for well-balanced men. A painter was trained to think of himself first and foremost as a workman, whose products were to be appraised and judged according to established standards. He was compelled by the guild system to assume responsibilities toward his fellow citizens, and toward his fellow artists and craftsmen in particular. These regulations helped to keep the atmosphere in which these men worked and lived sane and wholesome, which also promoted the flowering of a healthy and enduring school of art.

VI

Of Love, The Dream

HE DEVOTION to the Virgin which captured the medieval mind had its influence upon the relations of men and women of the age. It gave women a prestige and power which they had never known before. It is doubtful whether Dante's love for Beatrice could have been possible in a world which had not taken to its heart the Virgin Mother of God's Son.

The stages by which the devotion to the Virgin evolved are clearly traceable in the art of the eleventh to the fifteenth centuries. The earlier artists approached Mary with fear and awe. There is little of womanliness in the stiff and regal figures of their Madonnas. The Byzantine tradition still held the artists' souls and hands within narrow limits of thinking and working. Conforming to that tradition, the Virgin is sometimes represented with a book, symbolizing the wisdom given her by God.

Throughout the twelfth and thirteenth centuries, when the great cathedrals were being built in France, and when devotion to the Virgin was strengthening its hold on the popular mind, it would seem as if a new feeling entered the souls of the artists. Still reverent, they lose their fear of Mary. They begin to paint and carve her image with more and more tenderness. The statues of the Virgin which adorn the doors of the great cathedrals begin to show a womanliness entirely lacking in those carved a century or two earlier. Crowned as Queen of Heaven, she smiles with complete understanding upon the human beings who approach her shrine. She holds the Child as every mother holds her baby —proudly and possessively. The Child's infant fingers reach for her breast, and she smiles.

This tenderness, which was born in the minds of men during the Middle Ages, guided the hands of the artists who illuminated the prayer books. In the miniatures which adorn the pages we seem to enter into a world of innocent gaiety and love. Round-faced angels make music on lutes and zithers to entertain the infant Jesus seated on His mother's knee. In tiny gardens, much like the little flower-filled courtyards behind the high-shouldered old houses of Bruges, the saints gather daisies for a chain to put about the neck of the Christ Child. The Virgin holds her Child carefully, lest He fall, encouraging Him to take His first steps over a flower-strewn lawn, while St. Joseph offers a ripe strawberry as an inducement.

There is an exquisite playfulness in these little paintings which reveals much about the artists who painted them and the people for whom they were made. The history of those centuries is marred by dark and bloody passages. The times were loud with tumults of wars. The Black Death stalked across Europe. And yet if the art of that period is to be trusted as an indication of the mind of the times, there was gaiety, reverence, and freshness of outlook. Even the paintings of the austere Roger van der Weyden are full of intimate and homely details, not only expressive of love of humanity, but also of the realization that humanity in all its phases, even the most humble, is a manifestation of God. In this master's altarpiece of St. John the family life of medieval Flanders is made a background for three dramatic events in the life of St. John the Baptist (PLATE 33). The midwife tends Elizabeth in her great crimson-curtained bed; through an open doorway one can see two neighbor women busy with household duties. These household scenes, which must have been familiar to the people of fifteenth-century Flanders, do not disturb or detract from the dignity of the Virgin, who holds the infant John and shows him to his father. They add to the comfortable domesticity of the scenes portrayed.

Fortunately a fire is not burning beside the bed of Elizabeth. Had there been one, it would have aroused the kind of indignation of such a woman as

THE MASTER OF FRANKFORT. THE PAINTER AND HIS WIFE.
Private collection, New York (15¼ x 10½)

PLATE 30

GERARD DAVID. Wings of the Altarpiece of the Baptism of Christ (*Exterior*).
Madonna with Christ Child. Second Wife of Donor with St. Mary Magdalene. City
Museum, Bruges (*Each 51⅜ x 19*)

Plate 31

GERARD DAVID. Wings of the Altarpiece of the Baptism of Christ (*Interior*).
Donor with Son and St. John. St. Elizabeth with Wife of Donor and Four Daughters.
City Museum, Bruges (*Each 51⅜ x 19*)

Plate 32

ROGER VAN DER WEYDEN. St. John's Altar. THE BIRTH OF ST. JOHN.
Kaiser Friedrich Museum, Berlin (*30 x 18¾*)

PLATE 33

Eleanor of Poitiers, who was once heard to remark with a petulance which strikes not unfamiliarly on our ears: "For a good many years the ladies of Flanders have been putting the bed of a woman newly delivered of a child before the fire; formerly this was never done. What are we coming to? But at present everybody does as he pleases, because of which we may well be afraid that all will go badly."

The intimacy which is found in so many scenes of the religious paintings is no less shown in the portraits of the time. The Flemish woman, in her richly pleated black dress and elaborately folded white wimple, also painted by van der Weyden, withheld no secrets from the painter and withholds none from us (PLATE 55). She is serenely content with her life and her lot. Well-fed and rosy, she is the embodiment of her own self-satisfaction. She is troubled by no frustrations and no anxieties. No doubt she is an excellent housewife who manages her husband's home thriftily and competently. She does not find it hard to be a woman of medieval Flanders. The Italian historian, Guicciardini, remarked of the Flemings: "They have a horror of adultery. Their women are extremely wise and they enjoy great freedom." He goes on to comment, with astonishment, that the women of Flanders make visits by themselves without a chaperon and even go traveling without anyone speaking ill of them. He says: "They are able to take care of themselves." And in addition to this he adds: "They are excellent housekeepers. In spite of the freedom they enjoy, they love their homes and do not neglect them."

The unknown Flemish artist of the fifteenth century who painted the portrait of himself and his wife sharing a plate of June cherries has left us a picture of a happy marriage (PLATE 30). He is called the Master of Frankfort because one of his important pictures hangs in the museum of this town. These two people within their narrow frame are close in spirit as well as in body. The painter clasps his wife with his left arm, and she offers him a flower from the little bouquet on the table. They are both too interested in each other to brush away the fly attracted by the dish of cherries, or the one which has alighted on the woman's headdress. The man who painted this double portrait was a member of the artists' guild of Antwerp. He indicates this in the coat of arms of the Guild of St. Luke, supported by the winged ox, with the motto "*In Jonsten Versaemt* [United in Friendship]," the motto of the Antwerp Guild of Painters since 1480. But more than this is known about him as an individual. He was serious and hard-working, for his face tells us so. He loved his wife and was happy in his marriage; and he and his wife found time to enjoy each other—and to enjoy the good bread of Flanders, with a jug of wine and the luscious black cherries that grew in the orchards around Mechlin.

A note on the back of the panel tells that it was bequeathed to Mrs. Sterling of Kippendare by Mrs. Perry, who resided many years in a cottage on the grounds of Abell Grove, near Epsom, England. The story is told that Mrs. Perry was cook in the household of Sir Richard Ford. One day she saw the children playing with a wooden door, torn from an old cupboard in the attic. They were dragging it about the garden for a cart. The cook rescued the panel, discovered the picture painted on it, and showed it to her employer, who told her if she liked it she could have it.[1]

It must strike anyone who studies the Flemish portraits that the men are invariably dressed in somber colors. The painters of that time reveled in brilliant hues and used them with great expressiveness. They painted the saints in flowing robes of crimson, peacock blue, and moss green. They dressed the angels—beings who might be expected to have no vanity—in shimmering brocades. But the men in the portraits, be they Florentine bankers or Flemish merchants, wear sober black and gray. The historian, Huizinga, relates that during the late Middle Ages the symbolic meanings attached to certain colors, such as blue and green, were so marked as to make them almost unfit for usual wear. "Blue and green were the special colors of love. Blue signified fidelity; green, amorous passion."

> "*Il te fauldra de vert vestir,*
> *C'est la livree aux amoureux*
>
> [You will have to dress in green,
> It is the livery of lovers] . . ."

This medieval color symbolism has come down to us in the superstition which makes it bad luck to wear green at a wedding and lucky for the bride to wear something blue. There is a Flemish saying which goes: "She has thrown a blue cloak around him," which means that a wife has been unfaithful to her husband. Bruegel makes use of this proverb in one of his pictures. In the fifteenth century a man exposed himself to raillery by dressing in blue or green, and, naturally, he would not choose to have his portrait painted in either of these compromising colors.

[1] As shown by Dr. Grete Ring in *Monathefte für Kunstwissenshaft*, Vol. VIII, 1914, p. 263, this picture may be identified with one mentioned in the inventory of 1516 of Margaret of Austria's collection: *Ung autre tableaut d'ung homme et une femme qui est faite d'une bonne main; l'homme tient une tasse et la femme une fleur.*

The romantic spirit of the times was also expressed in the mottoes which the knights wore on their banners, embroidered on their linens, woven into their tapestries, or painted in their books of devotion. Many of these mottoes read like the names of modern perfumes with their suggestion of amorous passion:

Plus que toutes (More than all)
Autre fois mieux (Better next time)
Vostre plaisir (Your pleasure)
Aultre naray (I shall have no other)
Tout pour vous (All for you)
Mon coeur avez (You have my heart)
Pour tourjours (For always)

The medieval sensibilities were exalted, and it is easy to understand how in love, as well as in religion, the people arrived at high peaks of emotion.

François Villon developed such a pessimism mixed with tenderness that at times he produced the atmosphere of decadence, as in the description of the distress of a man who laments that someday the woman he loves will grow old and unlovely:

"*Corps femenin, qui tant es tendre,*
Poly, souef, si precieux,
Te faudra t'il ces maulx attendre?
Oy, ou tout vif aller es cieulx

[Woman's body, which is so soft,
Smooth, suave, and so precious,
Must these evils await you?
Yes, or else you must go to heaven all alive]."

Lest anyone think that the young girls of that faraway time were treated like chattels and had no opportunity to make demands on their parents, here is a translation of a poem by Eustache Deschamps, who died early in the fifteenth century. In it he complains, as innumerable fathers have complained since his time, of the demands made by his daughters:

I do not believe by my own judgment that there is anything so disagreeable, even sickness or torture, to the man who marries his daughter into the estate of chivalry, of a clerk, of the bourgeois or of the laity. I learned this from my daughter who has devoured me to the bones. And I want to say to those who have daughters that the man who has a daughter is without repose.

First you must give her some ground, not for life only, but for always. You must give her dresses, jewelry, gold and silver, velvet, cloth of gold, and precious stones, mantles, rings, furs, a small coat of hair, a rosary of gold, a crown and a bandeau. My God, what a joy! You must give her also vessels, platters, kettles, and pots. Never should I marry a daughter. He who has a daughter is without repose.

She must have many garments, long and short. You must give her a big and expensive wedding. You must have minstrels with many instruments in order to amuse the company. And you must also give her rooms and beds and fine linen.

I don't know how fathers can be such idiots. I have been pressed to the point of screaming. He who has a daughter is without repose.

The love motif crept into decorations of prayer books. In a charming Flemish *Livre d'heures* kept in Dresden, which dates from the fifteenth century, are painted as an illustration for the month of March a young man and a young girl walking very wisely together amid budding nature. The shy attitude of the youth and the awkwardness of the maiden tell that he is declaring his love to her. As a decoration for May there is a happy Flemish landscape, and across the rich green fields rides the same young man, mounted on a white horse, with a falcon on his wrist. Seated behind him in elegant headdress and costume rides the young woman, whose love he entreated in March. It is easy to read this little novel without words. You know that the girl has accepted the young man's love and now, in this wonderful shining morning, which the unknown artist has made eternal, they are riding toward the promise of the distant blue hills.

This spirit of joy, which permeates so much of the paintings of the Middle Ages, is shared by the little saints found in attendance upon the Virgin and her son. Indeed, the great popularity of these pretty little saints stands as evidence of the high regard for woman which characterized Flemish thought during the late Middle Ages.

Though the virgin saints were the beloved patronesses of many of the guilds, as well as of the girls and women of medieval Flanders, it is not a slight to the medieval Flemings to say that the saint most entreated was Mary Magdalene. She, who had been a sinner, and who had experienced the wonderful joy of forgiveness, is admitted to the most intimate and tragic scenes of the Passion by most of the masters. Those people of the fifteenth century loved virtue and honored chastity; but they were also realists in the art of living, and they did not deceive themselves about life. No doubt many of them felt that they could confess their sins to Mary Magdalene, believing she would understand as one who had been a sinner herself and would not be too shocked by their confessions. She, they felt, could be trusted to intercede for them with the Virgin, who, in turn, would present their cause to God. It was customary to dress the Magdalene in a sumptuous, fashionable gown. In van der Weyden's picture of her (Plate 16) she is beautiful, and becomingly attired.

In line with this kind of reasoning is the charming Flemish legend about the nun who ran away from her convent with a lover. Years passed, and she came back disillusioned and destitute, wanting to beg forgiveness and yet scarcely daring to approach the house she had dishonored. What was her amazement to find that no one had ever noticed her absence. Her escapade was undiscovered because the Holy Virgin, to hide her sin, had taken her place in the convent. This miracle had been done for one who, though she had failed in her vows, had never lost faith or her love for the Mother of God.

It is during this period, when devotion to the Virgin had lifted the status of all women, that Mother Eve is found more often in the altarpieces. Van Eyck's Eve, whose white and fruitful body is a vase which holds the human race, occupies an outermost wing of the great *Adoration of the Lamb*. She is not in the same panel with the saints and martyrs, but she is allowed to come closer to them than she would have been permitted to approach in early centuries. There is no suggestion of infamy about her; or about the Eve of Hugo van der Goes, who seems to be listening thoughtfully to the insinuations of the Gothic serpent with his lizard body, claws, and tail, and his wistful human head. This Eve seems not a willful sinner so much as a calculating woman who is doing what she can to better her husband's future (Plate 38).

The devotion to St. Anne, the mother of the Virgin, which spread through France and Flanders during the Middle Ages, helped in its way to make older women revered. St. Anne became the patroness of the mothers of families; and one of the favorite subjects of medieval artists was the education of the Virgin. St. Anne is usually shown seated —a type of the matriarch—teaching the youthful and dutiful Mary to read. She is frequently introduced into paintings of the Virgin and infant Christ. Always she is given the place of honor above the little virgin saints.

I think it is possible, after looking at the miniatures and panel pictures which have come down to us from the late Middle Ages, to realize that women then knew the tenderness of love and the stability of affection. To see this you have only to look at the religious pictures, in which the donors are represented and where you see the husband on the left side of the painting with his sons behind him and his wife on the right side with her daughters behind her, praying to the Madonna and supervised by their patron saints, who seem to encourage them in their devotions and to stand sponsor for them. Such is the painting of the Reyns family by Memling. There is the wife of Jacob Reyns with her twelve daughters kneeling on one side of the altarpiece, while Jacob Reyns with his seven little sons kneels as devoutly on the other side. Here is a happy family of nineteen children, praying with their parents. The altarpiece of the Moreels in Bruges shows a more restrained family—they have but sixteen children. They seem none the less devout than the Reyns, and appear to enjoy the same domestic happiness (Plate 37).

A touching sensibility is shown in the altarpiece commissioned from Gerard David by Jean des Trompes (Plate 32). He was faced by a very delicate situation, because his first wife was dead, after giving birth to several children. He did not want to forget her, or leave her out of the memorial altar. But, at the same time, he did not want to arouse jealousy in his second wife. One feels that he thought this over a long time, and no doubt prayed about it. In the end, he found a charming solution to his problem. On the interior wings he had the painter place himself with his son on one side, and upon the other wing his first wife with her four daughters, both praying in front of a representation of the Baptism of Christ. And on the cover of the right wing Jean des Trompes had the artist paint a portrait of his second wife with her little daughter praying beside her. The new wife gazes sadly, yet devoutly, toward the Madonna with the Christ Child holding in His left hand a bunch of grapes. She seems a trifle scared, as if she was afraid to be alone on the outside wing of the altar. The idea is full of charm. The dead wife is not forgotten by her husband, and the new little wife prays for protection to the Mother of the Christ Child (Plate 31).

Many of the children of the donors of these medieval altarpieces are painted with great sympathy and tenderness. The three youngest sons of Willem Moreel, painted by Memling, are true character studies (Plate 37). The little daughter of Tommaso Portinari, painted by van der Goes (Plate 74), is watched with grave approval by St. Margaret. From the look the saint bends on her you know she is a very good little maid.

These children who remain ever young, innocent, and untouched by the world are the link between us and the Middle Ages. They are of the generation which received the electrifying news of Columbus' discovery of the new world beyond the sea. Their children and grandchildren were to cross the sea and lay the foundations of democracy in the Americas.

VII

The Upward Glance

Two ELEMENTS, realism and mysticism, have always been essential to the Flemish soul and to the particular form of Christianity it developed. Since most paintings of the Flemish school were devoted to religious purposes, an understanding of them depends upon an insight into the spiritual structure of the civilization they represent.

One of the elements, realism, made the people comply with the traditional tenets of the Church, defined by the clergy and the theologians. The other element, mysticism, moved the people to add to the lasting doctrines of the Church the inner light of their own exaltation and their own dreams. Flemish painting of the fifteenth century was a result of the intimate interpenetration of the mysticism of the Flemish people and the fixed dogma of the Church.

The religious thought of the period was greatly influenced by the writings of the Flemish mystic Jan van Ruysbroeck the Admirable, who said of his own work: "My words are strange, but those who love will understand." Ruysbroeck, who "joins the innocence of a child to the knowledge of one who has returned from the dead,"[1] spent all his life in his native province of Brabant. He was canon at the Cathedral of St. Gudule in Brussels. A man who knew him in those days has left us the picture of him as a simple, quiet, shabbily dressed cleric who "went about the streets of Brussels with his mind lifted up to God." Later he and two other priests retired to the old hermitage of Groenendael near Waterloo, and there Ruysbroeck lived out the last thirty-eight years of his life. It is said that he spent hours in the forest each day, sitting under a giant beech tree, writing as the Holy Spirit dictated. He was "unknowing of most of the artifices of speech"; he was "able only to speak of the ineffable."[1] Even in the

fourteenth century, long before the era of the printing press, his writings and his teachings spread throughout old Belgium, Germany, and France, and exerted a profound influence on popular thought. The following quotation is characteristic:

> Those who follow the way of love
> Are the richest of all men living.
> They are bold, frank, and fearless.
> They have neither travail nor care
> For the Holy Ghost bears all their burdens.

There is a story of two priests who made a pilgrimage from Paris to ask his opinion on the state of their souls. They returned shaking their heads, discussing with amazement Ruysbroeck's quiet and profound statement: "You are as holy as you wish to be." By his writings and by his life he made clear his doctrines that the ideal of the Christian soul is a perfect balance between the active life and the contemplative life. This philosophy, which is neither old nor new, has always been considered sound. A mysticism which was so wholesome was bound to survive and have far-reaching effects on art. The masters who painted a century and more after Ruysbroeck's death continued his teaching, and through their pictures passed on his message: love redeems, and true holiness is healthiness of soul.

The block book of the Song of Solomon, reproduced here, is a manifestation of the spiritual *élan* that carried men beyond the garden of this life into the paradise of the world beyond. Ruysbroeck gives us the key to the greatness of these little woodcuts: "When man makes what he is able and when his own weakness prevents him going further, it is up to the infinite goodness of God to perfect the work."

The fifteenth century, like the mid-twentieth century, found word imagery difficult; as a result both periods are characterized by a tremendous popularity of pictures. But fifteenth-century wood-

---

[1] *L'ornement des Noces Spirituelles de Ruysbroeck l'Admirable* by Maurice Maeterlinck.

MATER DOLOROSA by Joos van Cleve. Mr. and Mrs. Charles Hickox, New York, N. Y. (*19¼ x 13⅝*)

PLATE 34

cuts, unlike modern photographs, never dealt with transitory events. They were images of ideas. And as Ruysbroeck intimated, if they did not complete the whole idea for the observer, it did not matter, because faith perfected them.

From the earliest days of Christianity the *Song of Songs* has been the touchstone of mysticism. St. Bernard, the great Cistercian reformer of the twelfth century, preached burning sermons on the basis of its text. But with St. Bernard the flesh faded before the whiter glow of the spirit. Late in the twelfth and in the early thirteenth century, Mary of Ognies and Luitgarde of Tongres, both of old Belgium, envisioned the fire of divine love inspired by the great canticle.

The fifteenth-century woodcutter who made these pictures has interpreted the poem as a song of love between Christ and His mother. The bridegroom of the *Song* is Christ, represented as a dreaming youth, and the bride is Mary, willowy and immaterial as a flame.

THE *SONG OF SONGS*

A bundle of myrrh is my well-beloved unto me; he shall lie all night betwixt my breasts. The picture portrays the Virgin clasping her crucified Son.

I charge you, O ye Daughters of Jerusalem, by the hinds of the field, that ye stir not up, nor awaken my love, till he please. Here, the Virgin has fallen asleep, her head on Christ's knees. Through the open window the Daughters of Jerusalem are watching, with hands folded, this mute scene of tenderness,

while the hinds glide through a dreamland, softly, not to disturb this hour of ecstasy.

My beloved is mine, and I am his; he feedeth among the lilies. Christ turns to the Virgin, a lily in His hand. Over the Virgin, and the Daughters of Jerusalem who attend her, the artist inscribed the well-known line from the *Song of Songs* which was identified in the medieval mind with the Virgin: *I am the rose of Sharon and the lily of the valleys.*

Mary languishes, swooning on her rose-bedecked couch. She gasps to the maidens: *Stay me with raisins, comfort me with apples, for I am sick with love.* To the Daughters of Jerusalem she murmurs: *I adjure you, O Daughters of Jerusalem, if ye find my Beloved, tell Him that I am sick with love.* Hopefully, but with somewhat futile gestures, two of the little girls lift their lamps, attentive and infinitely tender. The third adjusts the coverlet over the feet of Our Lady. In the upper right-hand corner of the woodcut Christ is borne heavenward by four angels. From above He answers: *Thou hast ravished my heart, my sister, my bride, Thou hast ravished my heart with one of thine eyes.* Here the Virgin has arisen and caresses the battlement of a little tower. There is no uniform scale, the figure of Mary being quite out of proportion with the size of the tower. However, this in no way interferes with the interpretation. She says: *What shall we do for our sister in the day when she shall be spoken for? If she be a wall, we shall build upon her a turret of silver; and if she be a door, we will enclose her with boards of cedar.* Our Lady's gentle companions have now changed their guise to militant protectresses, armed with bow and arrow and sword and buckler. They stand guard over the battlements of the silver tower above the door of cedarwood.

In this interpretation, the artist reaches the height of fifteenth-century mysticism. It must be remembered that these pictures were originally meant to be contemplated and meditated over devoutly and at length. They do not yield their full meaning at first glance, but deliberately withhold this until the observer is led gently to a realization of their content.

Thou art all fair, my love, and there is no spot in thee: Christ so speaks to His Mother. She replies: *I held Him and would not let Him go until I had brought Him into my mother's house and into the chamber of her who conceived me.* The earthly lover's bed has been transformed into an altar of heavenly love, decked with flaming red roses. The little picture naïvely asks those who see it to bring Christ into their hearts and not let Him go.

The Virgin is in the closed garden, the gate of which is guarded by an angel. She looks at the Beloved and recites to Him that strange verse from the *Song: Awake, O North Wind, and come, thou South; blow upon my garden, that the spices thereof may flow out.* Four angels with swords and shields are perched on the wall like huge birds. They sing: *A fountain of gardens, a well of living waters, and streams from Lebanon.* Christ whispers with fervor to the Virgin: *A garden enclosed is my sister, my spouse; a spring shut up, a fountain sealed.*

Christ hands to the Virgin a great seal that shows Him nailed on a cross held by God the Father. He says: *Set me a seal upon thine heart.* The Virgin, kneeling, receives the mystic gift and repeats the well-known phrase: *Here is my beloved. Love is strong as Death.*

I sleep, but my heart waketh . . . Christ has fallen asleep in His Mother's arms, on a bed littered with roses. She bends over Him. Her right hand lifts Christ's head with infinite gentleness, a care that only a mother's hand can bestow; but her left arm, in a vain attempt to protect the loved one, seems to clutch at the limp body that has ceased to suffer and has come down from the Cross. But in order that this strange scene should in no way appear ulteriorly suggestive, the old engraver conceived the idea of simultaneously illustrating a passage from another part of the text, *Behold threescore of valiant ones of the most valiant of Israel, surround the bed of Solomon, all of them bearing swords.*

Before the tiny figures of two devout burghers—a kneeling man and his wife—in a charming room stands the willowy figure of the Virgin. *If a man would give all the substance of his house for love, it would utterly be contemned.* This is the inscription of the banderole above their heads, implying that not the burghers' gold and silver plate, their goblets and pitchers as they stand in the heavy cupboard, will buy the way to heavenly love. The people must see it with her when she says: *The flashes thereof are flashes of fire, a very flame of the Lord.* The Virgin emphasizes this description of love with an upraised hand and a gesture of pointing. On the right a third banderole with the inscription: *Many waters cannot quench love, neither can the floods drown it,* floats above the heads of two Daughters of Jerusalem. One of them bears the lighted lamp of the wise Virgin, while the other stands next to a glowing fire. Dreamily, she spills water from a pitcher onto her companion's gown. She also is a wise little Virgin. She does not pour the water on the burning logs because she knows that the invisible flames of love are all around her, that the atmosphere itself is like a consuming fire, and that the contents of her little pitcher will never be able to quench this blaze.

The way in which the simple but forceful wood-cutter has hewn out his images from the bare block and cut the type for the inscriptions in the floating banderoles enhances the beauty of these symbolic interpretations. They are pictorial poetry, lifting the heart and soul to contemplation. Like music, these little pictures detach the beholder from himself and help him to reach the state of prayer.

From the mystic heart of the Middle Ages arose many prayers and rituals of the Church, such as the litanies of Mary. They were adopted by the Church in 1576, but for centuries before that they had grown in the devout hearts of nuns and friars, of young girls and mothers, of all those who asked for the peaceful assurance of Mary's intercession before God. The need constantly grew for new and beautiful words to exalt the Mother of God. The apocryphal gospel of the Nativity described her in these words:

She is so beautiful that one can scarcely sustain the radiant brilliance of her visage. She is so grave that her young companions do not dare to laugh before her nor speak in a loud voice. She is so pure that the angels descend from Heaven in order to speak with her and bring her food.

Later the mystics went far and wide to find the imagery for their metaphors of beauty and for their similes of expression. In the old books of revelations, in the Sermons of St. Bernard, in the Bible, and in some of the old poems, medieval men found phrases and words of praise fitting the glory that they saw in Mary. From all these sources a ritual was composed; and the names were like gems which the devout put into a gorgeous crown to adorn Mary: "Enclosed Garden," "Tower of David," "Sealed Fountain," "Lily of the Valley," "Rose of Sharon," "Mirror without Blemish," "Rose without Thorns," and "Star of the Sea." Also she was the "Field of Grain" and the "Bread of Eternity." The good people saw the Mother of God everywhere; the work of God became her handiwork too. In a way she must have seemed to many of them as something of an earthly mother—yet with infinitely more tenderness and humanity.

The great Dominican poet and philosopher, Heinrich Suso, who lived near Lake Constance in the fourteenth century, found unending inspiration in the Mother of God as she influenced nature. In an old story of his life is revealed the gentle flavor of Suso's tender mysticism:

In his youth, when he saw spring approaching and the flowers commencing to open, he restrained himself from cutting them; but, when it seemed to him that the time had come, he gathered some and took them to his cell. There he wove a crown of them, and he took it to the chapel, where he placed it on the statue of the Virgin. He thought that, as she was the most beautiful flower and in a way the springtime of his heart, she would not refuse the first flowers that he offered to her . . . One morning he was still asleep because he had returned very tired from the countryside after looking for flowers for the Virgin; when the hour for him to get up was drawing near it seemed to him that he was in the midst of a celestial concert that chanted the Magnificat; when it was finished the Virgin approached him and commanded him to sing: O Vernalis rosula (O young rose of spring). He obeyed with joy, and, moreover, three or four beautiful angels that were a part of the concert joined him. . . .

The rose crown of Suso transformed itself slowly into the rosary; the garland offered by men to the Queen of Heaven was reverently bestowed by monks upon their Celestial Beloved. In our days the rosary is called in French chaplet—meaning "little hat," from the medieval rose crown.

In the year 1470 the Dominican monk Alain de la Roche popularized the poetical symbol after Mary had appeared to him in a vision. Alain's rosary was composed of flowers of different colors: red roses for the sorrowful mysteries of Mary's life; white roses for the joyous mysteries; roses of gold for the glorious ones. In the same way many painters, as, for instance, Gerard David, represented this poetical symbol in little scenes arranged in the form of a wreath around Mary.

The devotion to the symbolic chain of the rosary appealed to the mystic spirit of the times and immediately became immensely popular. By the time of the death of Alain de la Roche in 1475, in the region of Cologne and along the Rhine, there had grown up some six thousand "Brotherhoods," pledged to the daily recitation of the rosary. These confraternities expanded tremendously by the end of the century. The movement was completely spontaneous, and it well illustrates the way in which the society of those days was permeated by the fervor of religious mysticism.

THE MYSTERY PLAYS

The constant desire on the part of the people to have more and more detailed accounts of the holy personages who figured so much in their lives, and hence in their art, proved their growing desire for greater realism. They did not exercise what would be called today "a critical faculty," but turned for their information to almost all sources. This popular research for stories and minutiae became most noticeable in the Mystery Plays; this form of medieval dramatic art provided the essential bridge between the popular demands for greater realism of fact and the content of the paintings of those days. Both the plays and the paintings were based upon orthodox belief from the teachings of the Church, but at the same time they carried with them their full measure of mysticism and legend.

At first the performances were in Latin, but as the obvious purpose of the play was to instruct, and even to entertain, they soon came to be given in the vernacular. The sources for the dramas could not be limited to the Bible alone, because obviously it was lacking in the color and wealth of interesting detail necessary to make a reconstruction of the event as vivid, appealing, and believable as possible. It is worth noticing in passing that these were also prime requisites of the paintings. The lives and legends of the saints—particularly the *Golden Legend* and the *Meditations on the Life of Jesus* attributed to St. Bonaventure, as well as the apocryphal Gospels—were searched for embellishments of the established points of belief. One can well imagine how excited the townsfolk were when St. George was to slay the dragon in the public square. Men were eager to play the part of the good shepherd adoring the Christ Child in the manger. Nobody knew exactly how many "wise men" were present to adore the newborn King because St. Matthew did not number them specifically; but the *Golden Legend* was more definite, calling them kings and naming them Caspar, Balthasar, and Melchior. The legend spoke of Balthasar as "dark," and from this to considering him a Moor was only a step. In fact the three kings from the East became associated with the sons of Noah, the founders of the white race, the yellow race, and the black race. So, through the Mystery Plays, into the paintings came the tradition of the carol:

> We three kings of Orient are,
> Bearing gifts we travel afar. . . .

The stories in the *Golden Legend* gave the painters of the Nativity the reason for placing Mary near a column in telling that she braced herself against it at the time when she gave birth to her son. The Nativities usually included this column, just as they included the ox and the ass, who also come down from the same literary sources. Having a sense of drama, the writers of the Mysteries arranged the original stories for stage effect. When they staged their scenes, they gave the actors "props" which made the plays realistic. St. Joseph was shown carrying a bucket of water, warming the swaddling clothes of the infant Christ before the fire, and stirring the pot of Flemish soup which steamed on the hearth. No one who saw the good

saint so employed could fail to know and love him as a kindly and tender protector of the Virgin and of all women. The shepherds, who came to adore, were dressed in rude coats of skins, and brought as offerings their pipes, or a young lamb, or a basket of cheese made of ewes' milk. All those homely details, which linked the stories with the life of the people, became a part of the story itself, so that the masters, when they painted an altarpiece, represented details they were accustomed to see on the stage.

The humanizing influence of the Mysteries which augmented the realism of the painting is most strikingly illustrated by a passage from the *Mystère d'Adam*, where the author does not hesitate to indulge a kind of subtle wit that is wholly delightful. At a moment when Adam is off guard and not noticing what his wife is up to, Satan approaches Eve to give her some confidential advice. She promises discretion, and for this the Devil compliments her. He begins to tempt her by saying that she is much cleverer than her spouse. She is only willing to admit that he is "a little hard." The Devil says to her: "Though he be harder than hell [*plus dure que n'est enfers*], he shall be made soft." He thinks that Adam should take better care of Eve, for as he says to her: "You are fresher than the rose and whiter than crystal, or snow that falls on ice in the vale. The Creator did not mate you well; you are too tender and he is too rough. Nevertheless, you are wiser than he. That's why I have done well to speak with you." So with a time-honored and time-proven kind of flattery, the Devil introduces his temptation, like the man in a drawing room who seeks to ensnare the virtue of a woman who has taken his fancy. A more perfect fusion of realism and mysticism can scarcely be imagined.

RELIGIOUS THEMES

The Mystery Plays formed links between man and idea and had their influence on the paintings. What were the main themes of these elements of faith and belief—painted by the artists and loved by the devout people of those days? In the fifteenth-century paintings of Flanders these themes grouped themselves largely around: (1) the teaching of belief, as in the Sacrament and Last Judgment, (2) the life of Christ and Mary, inspiring sentiments of love and thankfulness in men, and (3) the intercession and example of Mary and the saints. One of the finest examples of this kind of picture, representing a fundamental point of religion, is the Ghent altarpiece by van Eyck; its central theme is the famous apocalyptical vision of the *Adoration of the Lamb*

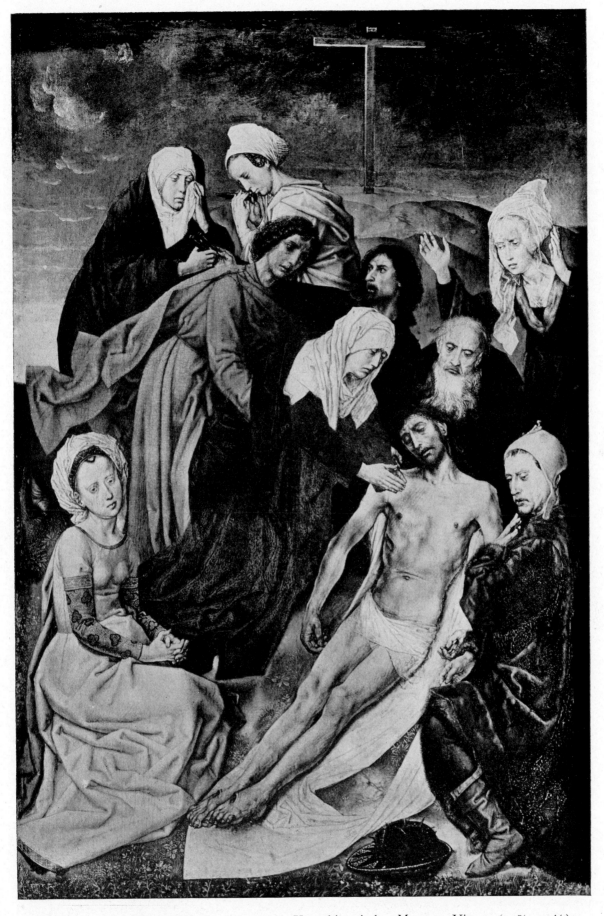

HUGO VAN DER GOES. LAMENTATION. Kunsthistorisches Museum, Vienna (*13⅞ x 9⅛*)

PLATE 35

HANS MEMLING. Moreel Altar. St. Benedict, St. Christopher, St. Giles. City Museum, Bruges (47¼ x 59½)

PLATE 36

HANS MEMLING. Moreel Altar. Willem Moreel with His Five Sons. Barbara Moreel with Eleven Daughters (*Each 47¼ x 30*)

PLATE 37

HUGO VAN DER GOES. Adam and Eve. Kunsthistorisches Museum, Vienna ($13\frac{7}{8}$ x $9\frac{1}{8}$)

PLATE 38

(PLATE 41). Another example is Roger van der Weyden's *Altar of the Seven Sacraments* (PLATES 57, 58). As a single great theme of belief, there is the *Last Supper* as painted by Dirk Bouts (PLATE 69).

Closely related to the idea of teaching, rather than to the idea of touching or inspiring, were the lessons of hope and fear as shown in visions of Heaven and Hell such as Jerome Bosch painted. The depiction of a Last Judgment such as Memling's (PLATE 79) gave a wonderful opportunity to demonstrate the fate that awaited the good and the bad. What this meant to the people is poignantly expressed by the words François Villon put into the mouth of his mother:

> *"Femme je suis povrette et ancienne,*
> *Qui riens ne scai; oncques lettre ne leuz;*
> *Au moustier Voy dont suis paroissienne*
> *Paradise paint, ou sont harpes et luz,*
> *Et ung enfer ou dampnez sont boulluz.*
> *L'ung me fait paour, l'autre joye et liesse*

> [I am a poor little old woman,
> Who knows nothing; I never could read;
> In my parish church I see Paradise painted,
> Where are harps and lutes; and a hell
> Where the damned are boiled.
> The one frightens me, the other brings
> Joy and gladness]."

The religious appeal—less to the mind and more to the heart—was made a pictorial reality in paintings based upon the life of Christ and that of the Virgin, and especially upon the main themes centering around the early and late events of Christ's life.

The most important part of this iconography dealt with the events of the Passion. Some of the scenes were singled out for most elaborate and sensitive treatment. As is true today, the Christmas scene of the Nativity occupied a first ranking position; for it was not only a symbol of the coming of God among men but it was also a touching and dramatic story. There was something wonderful in the three great wise men who came and knelt before the King of Kings. Then, too, there was something exciting about the flight of Joseph and Mary with the Christ Child as they escaped the slaughter by Herod's soldiers. It is interesting to note, however, that there is not a single picture known of the Massacre of the Innocents from the hand of a great Flemish master before Bruegel. This is explained by the fact that the themes of true interest to these people had to be representations before which they could pray, and which carried a spiritual message.

The link between the writings of the mystics and the paintings of our old masters is often striking.

The *Lamentation* of van der Weyden, now in Granada, Spain (PLATE 68), would probably never have been painted in such a way without the vision of St. Bridget, revealed as follows in her Meditations. She saw "the dead body of Christ full of wounds lying in the lap of Mary, who tried to unbend the poor contorted body. She wanted to cross His hands upon His breast, in order to give them the familiar attitude of the dead; but the joints refused to move. Then she threw herself upon the face of her son and covered it with kisses. When she raised up her head, her face was covered with blood. For a long time she held him embraced without wishing to be separated from him. She poured out so many tears that her soul and her flesh seemed to dissolve in tears."

The other large group of images that helped to satisfy the yearnings in the hearts of the people of Flanders was that of Mary and the saints. The holy men and women of the dim past who had given their lives to God were a deep source of pious inspiration. Theirs were ideals of life toward which a man might aspire, and upon which he might model his own way of living. The saints who were persons of merit had the ear of God and could act as advocates for those who prayed to them. They were very near to Mary, and a description of a fine stained-glass window in the Cathedral of Beauvais shows clearly the course of ascension of prayers toward the throne of Heaven. In the window a canon kneels at the feet of his patron, St. Lawrence, and says to him: "St. Lawrence, patron saint of this place, pray to St. Mary for me, a sinner." And the good saint, with his eyes turned toward the Virgin, says: "For this man, Queen of Heaven, would you pray to your Son Jesus?" And she, in turn, addresses Christ on the Cross: "My Son, whom I took care of, for this poor sinner I call unto you." And Jesus, suffering on the Cross, looks at God, saying: "My Father, have mercy on this sinner for the sake of my passion." And the Lord replies: "Moved by so many reasons, I am pleased to take pity on him." There was an order and a simple beauty in the positive protection of the saints. The people called on them in every walk of daily life. They felt safe in their hands; and, moreover, the saints reminded all of them of their duties toward the Church and toward God.

Among the most popular saints in old Belgium were St. Roch, the patron saint of prisoners and the sick, especially those who suffered from the plague; St. Sebastian, sometimes linked with St. Roch, prevented sudden death and warded off pestilence; St. Medard, who had been Bishop of Tournai, was particularly efficient in controlling the weather and was prayed to for rain for the crops; St. Ursula was very popular among young maidens. St. Catherine was the patroness chosen by the weavers, and St. Barbara protected artillerymen and even the great clumsy cannons. Patron saints were frequently chosen by individuals because they had the same name as the man or woman who sought the saint's intercession. Some of the legends of the saints are delightful and have a fairy-tale quality that has endeared them to all times.

St. Hubert was a handsome young French gallant and sportsman. Once, while hunting in the south Belgian forest of Ardennes, on Good Friday, he saw a stag with a crucifix between its antlers. He was so overcome with the awe and the mystery of this event that he realized his own sinful ways. He renounced the world to become a monk; ultimately he was appointed Bishop of Liége.

St. Eloy (St. Eligius) was the patron of blacksmiths and all metalworkers. One day, while at his forge, the Devil came to torment him. He was a man of quick thought and sudden action; he seized a red-hot pincers and tweaked the Devil's nose. This act so discouraged Satan that he did not return to torment St. Eloy again. However, he lodged himself inside a stallion that was brought to the smithy for shoeing. He so upset the creature that it kicked at everyone who came near him. Undismayed, the resourceful St. Eloy detached the horse's leg; and after the hoof was shod, he fixed the leg neatly in place again.

The discomfiture of the Devil was a constant source of amusement to medieval folk—especially in the Mystery Plays, where it provided the only legitimate source of humor—and no doubt the story of St. Eloy was particularly popular.

The teachings of the Church were often indirectly influenced by the mystics. Their demands did not change the basic flow, but they did re-emphasize old principles or bring new ones into light. Such was the case of Alain de la Roche and the rosary. And if it is true that the mystics often affected the established order, it is also true that the established order frequently turned back against the mystics.

The fervent imagination of the fifteenth century came especially under question at the time of the Reformation and Counter Reformation. The leaders in good faith undertook what they considered to be a kind of purification. However, their acts were frequently marred by an arid literal-mindedness. In 1563 the Council of Trent, in its twenty-fifth session, which was its last, discussed the problem of statues and pictures that decorated the churches. The Holy Council forbade any image that recalled an incorrect belief or which might confuse a pure

dogma; images were not to be allowed any "provocative attributes." But they went even further, and the theologian, Molanus, professor at the University of Louvain, stated that there was no reason why St. Peter should be placed before St. Paul nor why the Virgin or St. John should enjoy especially either the right or the left side of a Crucifixion. He contended further that Mary must not be shown as fainting in anguishing grief at the foot of the Cross because it was insulting to her dignity. The doctrines of Molanus and the Council of Trent robbed the old images of the Middle Ages of the soul that had moved them. They lost both their mortal and immortal charm.

The spirit which was to animate the Council of Trent caused the death of medieval art. Under the influence of the reformation movements all the good saints of the *Golden Legend*, who had never been so popular as at the end of the fifteenth century, saw a great part of Christianity move away from them. But they left forever the reflection of their kind faces and tender eyes upon this earth where they had been so much loved. Today there still remain hundreds of churches and streets dedicated to them. Countless processions and kermesses celebrate their feast days. Simple shrines in the shadows of huge trees amid the cornfields constantly remind the countryfolk that the legend of the saints is still alive. Even crossroads and valleys in the country, wells in the villages, and springs in the forests still bear their names. Their marvelous fairy tales continue to enchant the dreams of little children as they fall asleep. Always they are a moving and living part of the ageless poetry of the Old World.

What was this holy spirit which was the real creator of the great art of medieval Flanders; which moved in the souls of masters, quickened their brushes, flamed in their colors like points of fire, and so blessed them with the pentecostal gift of tongues that they spoke, and still speak, to every man in his own language?

The life of a person who is half realist and half mystic is like that of a child, for it is filled with joys and surprises.

There was in the people of medieval Flanders a wealth of that expansive kind of wonder that fills the eyes of children with delight as they seize upon something new or are dazzled by a spectacle filled with exciting and fascinating things.

The medieval man had a way of hearing voices. He said to himself, as did the author of the *Imitation of Christ:* "I would rather *feel* contrition than *know* the definition of it." How unsure and unhappy this same man would be today if he looked around him and then repeated to himself his own words as he said:

"If I knew the whole Bible by heart, and all the philosophical doctrines, what would that profit me without the love of God and His grace?"

Whatever our actual creed may be we must be thankful to this medieval faith for the consolation and peace it brought in these hard days of our forefathers. To the poor, shivering in their cottages, it showed the glistening cupolas of Heaven. To those possessing nothing on earth it promised the flowery meadows of Paradise. To the lonely and bereft, it offered the friendship of all the saints of the *Golden Legend*, who were sweet, smiling, and pure. To the people of the fifteenth century, religion was not only faith, it was a state of mind. The people expected the Holy Virgin, the angels, and the saints to come down on earth at any moment. There was an easy going back and forth between the church triumphant and the church militant. The cross at the pinnacle of the cathedral sphere indicated the undivided boundary between heaven and earth.

These paintings were born out of artists' dreams, of prayers said by the faithful, and of the suffering of the poor. Many of them were inspired by legends that had blossomed throughout centuries in monks' cells or in the narrow streets where lowly people led their humble lives. Modern people will perhaps object that these stories were not true, but who cares, if they created beauty and brought happiness to this earth? With their aid the old Flemish school retained until the end all its freshness of soul, all its childishness of heart. The Flemish masters stayed young because a man is old only when he ceases to love or ceases to be amazed.

For five hundred years these old Flemish pictures have been speaking to human hearts. If some of the pictures seem to modern eyes naïve and hard to understand, that is because the modern world has lost the key which unlocks their meaning. They were painted as acts of faith, and they are intended to be so received. It may be that these pictures painted so many years ago will lead us back to walk again in the garden from which we were evicted.

If you wish to understand fully the warm religious message of these simple Flemish paintings after having looked at one of them, close your eyes, forget your surroundings, and travel in thought back into the fifteenth century.

A *Crucifixion* of van der Weyden is in the Church of St. Gudule in Brussels. The sun shines on it through the stained-glass window; an old woman is praying before it with outstretched arms.

A *Madonna* of Memling is in the house of Willem Moreel in Bruges. All the family are kneeling before it for their evening prayer—the father on one side followed by all his sons, and the mother on the other side with all her daughters, just as in their family altarpiece in the Museum of Bruges (PLATE 37). The little girls are praying very diligently. The boys are more restless—one of them watches a night moth flying around the candles burning before the picture; another one slyly pinches his little brother. The deep, unperturbed voice of Father Moreel repeats the eternal Flemish prayers that have come down through the centuries. Out of doors all is silent in the dark town. The swans do not move on the black waters of the canals. Sometimes the heavy footfalls of the night watchman are heard on the cobblestones of the street. He intones with a loud and deep voice:

> "Christians, ye who sleep,
> Pray God for the dead."

The step of the watchman fades away. All is silent again. Then suddenly the clock in the belfry peacefully strikes the hour while on the turrets of all the patrician homes, guild houses, chapels, and convents of Bruges hundreds of bronze angels stand silently by, their gilded wings outspread over the gabled roofs of the sleeping town.

If you can have such a vision in your mind you will understand at once that Pascal stated for all times the way of the Flemish fifteenth-century glance upward when he said:

"*Le coeur a ses raisons que la raison ne connait pas.* [The heart has its reasons which reason does not know]."

PART II

The Flemish Masters

ST. FRANCIS RECEIVING THE STIGMATA by Jan van Eyck. Johnson Collection,
Philadelphia, Pa. (5 x 5¾)

PLATE 39

Jan van Eyck

THE FAME of Jan van Eyck has come down the centuries uneclipsed and undiminished. Like the great Giotto, the Flemish master who signed many of his pictures with a device meaning "as well as I can," stands unchallenged as the leader of a particular way of thinking and painting.

It can be said justly that Giotto was the father of Renaissance and, indeed, of modern painting. He forecasts the titanic struggles of Michelangelo. But van Eyck, though living a full century later than the first of the great Florentines, is the consummation and the resplendent reflection of the Gothic spirit. His inventions, which had a profound effect on the artists of his time, are not the result of reform and change; they have their roots in the past. They are the full flowering of the spirit of the late Middle Ages. One ventures to say that more can be learned about the Middle Ages and the thought and way of life of the men of that period through the study of van Eyck's pictures than may be gleaned from many books.

There has always been a tendency in writing on Flemish painting to speak of "the brothers van Eyck" as the founders of the school. All that is known of the elder brother, Hubert van Eyck, is that he lived, served as master of the hounds to the Duke of Bavaria, was admitted to the painters' guild of Ghent in 1421, is said to have worked on the *Adoration of the Lamb,* and died in 1426. The sole basis for the theory that Hubert was a greater master of painting than his younger brother Jan is a Latin inscription on the famous altarpiece which may be translated "The painter Hubert van Eyck, to whom no one yet has been found superior, commenced this work. Jan, his brother and follower in art, completed it at the request of Jodocus Vydt.

The sixth of May (1432). You are facing the work."

It is a well-known fact that there was a bitter rivalry between Bruges and Ghent, each town trying to outdo the other. Jan van Eyck was claimed by Bruges, where he lived in attendance on the Duke of Burgundy. It would not have been beyond the citizens of Ghent, during the sixteenth or even the seventeenth century, to have added this inscription to the altarpiece in an effort to build up the prestige of the elder brother who may have made his home in their city.

Friedländer makes the following statement concerning the mystery of the brothers van Eyck:

Since the most recent and careful research has brought to light nothing positive which will identify Hubert, we must hold to the opinion that everything which is preserved of the van Eyck art can be fitted into the development of *one* painter of genius, namely, Jan.

Jan van Eyck, who founded the style of the fifteenth-century Flemish school, was born in the province of Gueldre, probably at Maaseyck, between the years 1385 and 1390. On the basis of some miniatures in a Book of Hours, known to have been commissioned by Wilhelm of Bavaria, Count of Holland, it is believed that Jan van Eyck was in the service of that nobleman as an artist. Later, from 1422 to 1424, he worked for the count's brother, John, at The Hague. By special decree made at Bruges on May 19, 1425, Jan van Eyck was appointed court painter to Philip the Good, Duke of Burgundy.

The duke employed him on a number of missions —proof that the painter was a man of discretion, with a gift for diplomacy. In 1429 the duke sent him to Portugal with orders to paint two portraits of the Infanta Isabella, whose hand the duke sought.

There is pleasure in speculating upon the effect on van Eyck of his journey through the Côte d'Or across the Pyrenees and northern Castile into Portugal. To his eyes, accustomed to the cool, misty, northern landscape, the dry highlands of Castile, brown under the cloudless blue sky, must have seemed strangely exciting. In the towns where the duke's embassy put up, van Eyck saw an architecture in which Moorish artisans had labored and which was very different from the buildings in the cold north. He was to remember the colonnades and patios all his life and to reproduce them in many of his pictures.

In Portugal the painter came in contact with the exotic tropics. The fleets of Portugal were then exploring the coast of Guinea and bringing back from there, and from newly occupied Madeira, cargoes of fruits, spices, ivory, and rare woods. All these were heaped on the black-and-white mosaic pavements of Lisbon and were bargained for by traders whose ships crowded the Tagus. Portugal was entering upon its heroic age under a king who had married an English bride. She was Philippa, a daughter of John of Gaunt. It is not unreasonable to suppose that the queen, whose grandmother, for whom she was named, had been a daughter of Flanders and whose father was proud of his birth in Ghent, would have welcomed the Flemish painter whose art was to aid in bringing about the marriage of her daughter to the Great Duke of the West. Of the two portraits of the young infanta which van Eyck painted in Lisbon, one was sent by the sea route, the other overland to Bruges. One would like to know whether both pictures reached their destination safely, and, if not, which route proved the safer. All that we know is that the duke's embassy waited in Portugal to receive their master's decision about the marriage, and during that time van Eyck visited other parts of Portugal and Spain.

The portrait of the Portuguese princess must have pleased Philip the Good, and the dowry offered by King John must have satisfied the duke's counselors. The marriage was solemnized by proxy in Portugal, after which the new duchess and her train, among whom was van Eyck, set off by ship to Flanders. They had a stormy voyage, almost meeting disaster by shipwreck off Land's End. They reached Flanders in December 1429, and in honor of the event the duke founded the famous Order of the Golden Fleece.

Jan van Eyck was rewarded for his services. He set up a house in Bruges where the duke continued to keep him busy. He married a lady of the town,

named Margaret, whose justly famous portrait is now one of the treasures in the museum at Bruges. It is signed and dated as completed on June 17, 1439. The portrait shows a woman of great strength of character, though it is true the lips are thin and the nose a little long (PLATE 42).

Jan and Margaret van Eyck had one son, who was born in 1434 and at whose christening the duke stood sponsor, represented by the Seigneur de Charny. There is record that when the painter's daughter Lievine became a nun the duke allowed her a dowry of twenty-four francs.

It was during the seven years after his return from Portugal, and while he was living in Bruges, that van Eyck painted his largest and most important works, including the famous altarpiece in Ghent, which Hubert may have begun but which Jan, undoubtedly, completed and made his own. The master who created this vision of Paradise was the man whose eyes had been filled with the luxuriant vegetation of Portugal. He was a Fleming who had seen date palms and orange trees in flower and who carried the memory of the exuberant south back to his workshop in the north.

After eleven years as the great master of Bruges, revered by all the other artists of his time, and sixteen as *valet de chambre* to the Duke of Burgundy, van Eyck died in 1441. He was given a modest funeral, costing only the low price of twelve pounds. According to van Mander, the following inscription was cut on a stone near his burial place in the Church of St. Donatian:

> "*Hic jacet eximia clarus virtute Joannes,*
> *In quo picturae gratia mira fuit;*
> *Spirantes formas, et humum florentibus herbis*
> *Pinxit, et ad vivum quodlibet egit opus.*
> *Quippe illi Phidias et cedere debet Apelles;*
> *Arte illi inferior ac Polycletus erat.*
> *Crudeles igitur, crudeles dicite Parcas,*
> *Quae talem nobis eripuere virum.*
> *Actum sit lachrymis incommutabile factum;*
> *Vivat ut in coelis jam deprecare Deum*

[Here lies John, illustrious for exceptional genius, in whom was a wonderful gift of painting. Breathing forms, and the earth with flowering shrubs, and whatever the work needed, he painted to the life. Indeed Phidias and Apelles should give place to him; and Polycletus was inferior to him in skill. Cruel, therefore, cruel the Fates who robbed us of such a man. Let us commemorate with tears the unalterable fact: and now pray God that he may live in heaven]."

It is interesting that this epitaph, which breathes the spirit of the Renaissance, should have been composed to mark the resting place of the artist whose work eloquently expressed the thought and feeling of the medieval mind.

THE *ADORATION OF THE LAMB*

The altarpiece which the devout Jodocus Vydt of Ghent and his wife Isabella Borluut commissioned for their burial chapel has long been in one of the chapels of the Cathedral of St. Bavon of Ghent (PLATE 41). The altarpiece is a great theological machine. Just as those extraordinary *entremets* celebrated famous legends and kept those legends alive in the minds of the populace, van Eyck's *Adoration of the Lamb* gives, through a medium understandable to all, the vision which dazzled St. John and the promise of salvation. It is an epic poem full of symbols for the devout to meditate upon. In this sense, it is comparable only to Michelangelo's decorations on the ceiling of the Sistine Chapel.

In plan, the altarpiece is much more elaborate than are most of those designed by the Flemish masters. It is arranged with an upper and a lower section, each of which can be opened or closed independently of the other. When the altarpiece is completely closed, the upper section shows a painting of the Annunciation. The room in which the Angel Gabriel appears with his lily and makes his announcement to the young and obedient Mary is typically Flemish, with the homely household furniture such as stood in any solid burgher's house in Ghent. The two figures are painted in neutral tones, which harmonize with the gray-painted statues of St. John the Evangelist and St. John the Baptist which decorate two of the four panels of the lower section of the altarpiece. Panel portraits of Jodocus Vydt and his wife flank the statues of the two saints (PLATE 40).

The reproduction of statues in painting was common in the fifteenth century. These *grisailles*, as they were called, made possible the introduction of many symbols which were familiar to the people of the time. The two Johns are the keynotes of the altarpiece: one as the forerunner of the Lamb of God, the other as the apostle whom Jesus loved and the mystic to whom was given the revelation on the Island of Patmos. The grisailles stand like statues guarding the portals of a church, and the donors kneel in the outer niches in reverent humility. The portraits are painted realistically, and the rich rosy red of Jodocus Vydt's furred robe, which is repeated in his wife's gown, provides the warmest color on the outside of the altarpiece.

When the doors of the altar are open, the full splendor of van Eyck's vision of Paradise bursts upon one with scarcely less bewildering splendor than the Apostle John experienced when the angel revealed to him the things that should be hereafter. The moment which the painter has selected to portray is that described in the verses:

After this I beheld, and, lo, a great multitude, which no man could number, of all nations, and kindreds, and people, and tongues, stood before the throne, and before the Lamb, clothed with white robes, and palms in their hands;

And cried with a loud voice, saying, Salvation to our God which sitteth upon the throne, and unto the Lamb.[1]

The Paradise van Eyck has imagined is a joyous and beautiful one wherein grow many trees bearing all manner of fruits and blossoms, and from which one looks away to the belfries and spires which seem to give assurance that Heaven is situated pleasantly close to Flanders. The mystic vision is brought to earth in the full light of an open Flanders sky (PLATE 41).

The angels who guard the altar on which stands the mystic Lamb bear the symbols of the Passion of our Lord, and on the altar itself appear two inscriptions: "Behold the Lamb of God which taketh away the sins of the world," and "Jesus, the Way, the Truth, and the Life." Before the altar is the "fountain of living water, proceeding from the Throne of God and from the Lamb." At a little distance are groups of saints. St. Agnes, carrying her lamb, St. Barbara with her tower, St. Catherine, and St. Ursula lead the company of virgins. The evangelists kneel on one side of the fountain, reading from their books. On the other side kneel the apostles in dun-colored cloaks. Behind these, pressing close, come popes and bishops in rich red robes, and from the opposite side of the panel a company of crowned kings, prophets, and doctors of the Church.

The wings which flank the large central panel are filled with more figures: knights, judges, pilgrims, and hermits. The hermits are led by the great saints who found inspiration in the desert: St. Paul, St. Anthony, St. Mary Magdalene, and St. Mary of the Egyptians—she who is said to have clothed herself in her own hair and to have remained in the desert, repeating to herself the words of the Gospels which she had never read but which had been magically revealed to her. St. Christopher, gigantic in a red mantle, with a pine tree for a staff, marshals seventeen pilgrims. The groups which fill these four wings symbolize the four cardinal virtues enumerated by St. Thomas Aquinas: Prudence (the pil-

[1]Revelation 7:9–10.

[61]

grims), Temperance (the hermits), Justice (the judges), and Fortitude (the knights).

The upper section of the altarpiece is formed of seven panels curved at the top. In the central one appears the King of Kings. This is not the Ancient of Days, bearded and hoary, portrayed by the artists of the Renaissance. He is the One whom John saw above Patmos, "like a stone of jasper and sardonyx." He is timeless. Below the intricate votive crown at His feet appear the words: "On His head, life without death. On His brow, youth without age. On His right hand, joy without sadness. On His left hand, security without fear." He wears the papal tiara and a red mantle embroidered with flashing jewels. His left hand holds a scepter of rock crystal carved most intricately. His right hand is lifted, blessing all who obey the injunction to "Look unto Me." A Latin inscription on the gold lunette behind the head of the Most High proclaims: "This is God, all-powerful in His divine majesty; of all the best, by the gentleness of His goodness; the most liberal giver, because of His infinite generosity."

And lest this vision of the King of Kings seem too austere and far removed from man, van Eyck has placed behind the throned figure a piece of brocade in which appears the pelican—symbol of self-sacrificing love.

In these panels the master has translated into simple terms for all men of all times, not only the transcendent glory of the apocalyptic vision, but the theology of the great medieval scholastics, such as St. Thomas Aquinas, and the mystics such as St. Bernard of Clairveaux and Ruysbroeck.

Upon the right hand of the Most High sits Mary, the Queen of Heaven, the Mother of the Word. She is radiant, yet her beauty is that of fairness and purity rather than the beauty of wisdom. Her robe is a deep, glowing blue, of that prized ultramarine which was brought by the trade caravans out of the East. She reads from a missal which she supports on a green cloth. The seven stars, the lilies and roses of her filigree crown, almost obliterate the Latin inscription on the lunette behind her head. Translated, this reads: "This one is more brilliant than the sun and all the orders of the stars. Compared to light, she surpasses it; she is the radiance of the eternal light; the mirror without blemish, of Divine Majesty." The white brocade behind her quiet figure has the design in gold of a unicorn—the symbol of chastity.

The figure which fills the panel on the left of the Most High is that of John the Baptist. He wears a green mantle over his hair shirt of penitence. He holds a book of the Gospels, but he does not read.

His hand is raised to call attention and his eyes seem to look far into the distance, beholding the One greater than he, whose shoe's latchet he was unworthy to unloose. The gold lunette behind his head carries the inscription proclaiming his greatness as the forerunner of Christ. There is a reredos of rose-colored brocade behind him and this has a design of a lamb among flowers.

These three glowing panels occupy the space above the large central panel of the lower section of the altarpiece. The panel next to that which is filled with the figure of John the Baptist shows a group of eight singing angels. They wear copes of richly colored brocades. Unlike the Angel Gabriel in the Annunciation scene on the outside of the altarpiece and the fourteen kneeling angels who surround the altar of the Lamb in the central panel, these choiring angels have no wings. Van Mander, in praising van Eyck's great work, claimed to be able to distinguish the note in the scale which each angel is singing from the form of the lips.

The corresponding panel on the other side of the altarpiece shows more angelic musicians. One is seated, playing at an organ; one plays a harp with twenty-four strings, another the fifteenth-century *vielle à archat*, the early form of the viol. It is clear from the position of the musicians and the way in which they handle their instruments that van Eyck knew more about music than did many other painters of the period. The fifteenth and sixteenth centuries were the period of impressive church music, and during that time Flanders was the musical center of Europe. This art, like all others, was fostered by the dukes of Burgundy. Jacob Obrecht, one of the earliest Flemish composers, and the teacher of Erasmus, wrote masses which were played and sung in the cathedrals throughout old Belgium, and Josquin des Pres attained an everlasting fame. It was during this period and in Flanders that organs and instrumental music came into use in churches. The organs of van Eyck's time had no pedals. The organ pedal was invented by the German, Bernhard, later in the fifteenth century.

These five upper panels are brought into harmony by means of an exceedingly elementary device—the lines of perspective of the tiled floor. Without these lines, each figure or group of figures would be a separate icon. As it is, van Eyck has indicated that they are all part of a single idea, though the tiles beneath the feet of the angels are different from the simple red and black squares in the three central panels.

Beyond the celestial choirs are a pair of half panels which complete the wings of the altarpiece.

JAN VAN EYCK. The Ghent Altarpiece (*exterior*). Church of St. Bavon, Ghent

PLATE 40

JAN VAN EYCK. The Ghent Altarpiece (i

of St. Bavon, Ghent

JAN VAN EYCK. The Wife of the Master. City Museum, Bruges (*12½ x 10⅛*)

Plate 42

Here the painter has daringly introduced the nude figures of Adam and Eve. He has placed them in niches, outside the glorious company of Heaven, as when they were expelled from the Garden of Eden for disobedience. What strikes the eye at once is that they are painted from a different level than the other figures in the upper panels, who are viewed from the normal line of vision. Adam and Eve are seen from below; one can actually look at the sole of Adam's right foot. This difference has given rise to a swarm of theories which drive the theorists back to the mystery surrounding Hubert van Eyck and where he, possibly, laid down his brush and Jan took it up.

For all these theories, one does not feel that Adam and Eve are interlopers. They are a vital part of the great story which the altarpiece unfolds before our eyes; for did not their sin make necessary the sacrifice of the Lamb of God for the redemption of the world? There they stand, two simple, rather uncouth Flemish peasants, whose hands are roughened and sunburned from work in the fields. Eve is with child—the mother of all living. There is nothing sensual or alluring in the painting of these nude bodies. Adam and Eve are as realistic as Jodocus and Isabella Vydt. They are sinful and suffering humanity, slow to learn, frequently hard of heart, repeatedly indifferent to the heavenly vision; and yet possessed of an inherent dignity because they are the greatest creation of the Most High, made in His image, whom God so loved that He gave His only begotten Son to redeem.

In its complexity, its wealth of significances and symbols, its dogma and its superb storytelling, the *Adoration of the Lamb* is the *summmum bonum* of the Middle Ages. There is little tenderness in it; it appeals to the intellect rather than to the heart. But for all that, it is essentially medieval in its concept and handling. It *is* the Middle Ages, presented graphically. It has the intellectuality and the logic of the writings of St. Thomas Aquinas.

The altarpiece cannot be seen and understood in a single hour or, indeed, in many hours. It demands to be lived with. The master planned it to disclose its tremendous truths slowly, gradually, grandly to the devout who came daily to kneel in the chapel, to be present at the dramatic moment when the wings of the altar were thrown wide for the sacrifice of the mass and the full glory of the apocalyptic vision was revealed.

In the five centuries since Jan van Eyck completed his great work it has suffered many vicissitudes. Late in the eighteenth century the Emperor Joseph II, the brother of Marie Antoinette of France, paid a visit to Ghent and saw the altarpiece which had caused painters and art lovers to acclaim the genius of the brothers van Eyck. His imperial modesty was horrified by the nakedness of Adam and Eve, and he ordered that the offenders be provided with decent coats of leaves. Fortunately, this was not done. The two panels were merely removed and hidden from view in the crypt of the cathedral. Some time later they were rescued from this dusty seclusion and hung in the Brussels Art Museum.

Meanwhile, the altarpiece was completely dismembered. The central portion was carried off to Paris during the French Revolution and placed in the Louvre. After the defeat of Napoleon on Belgian soil at Waterloo, among the demands made on France by the victors was the return of the panels and the central portion of van Eyck's *Adoration of the Lamb* to Ghent. After the panels were sent back to Belgium, six of them were sold to an English collector, Solly, from whom the King of Prussia bought them in 1821. A full hundred years later a paragraph in the Treaty of Versailles stipulated that the defeated Germans should return the panels to make the altar complete after many years.

For some fifteen years the altarpiece stood intact, the pride of the city of Ghent and one of the art wonders of the world. Then, one morning, when the cathedral was unlocked, it was discovered that the lower panel showing the procession of the Just Judges, with the grisaille of St. John the Evangelist on its outer side, had been stolen. There was a tremendous hue and cry. In the midst of it the authorities received a mysterious message to the effect that the grisaille of St. John could be found, checked, in the luggage room of the Gare du Nord in Brussels, and from whence it was recovered. The inner side of the panel, showing the Just Judges, the message continued, was held for ransom. The thief warned that he had concealed this so cleverly that there was no hope of finding it (PLATE 11).

While negotiations for the ransom of this panel were in progress, the identity of the thief was discovered. He was a former beadle of the cathedral who had speculated heavily, grown rich, then suffered heavy financial reverses. He had thought to recoup his losses through this theft. He suffered a stroke and died without revealing where he had hidden the panel. Van Eyck's *Just Judges* remains lost to this day.

THE ARNOLFINI PORTRAIT

Giovanni Arnolfini had an extraordinarily successful and colorful career even for careerists of the fifteenth century, but his most lasting monument has nothing to do with his wealth or his prestige. It is his portrait by Jan van Eyck (COLOR PLATE 2).

Our knowledge that this picture is a portrait of the silk merchant and his Flemish wife comes from an entry in the inventory of the collection of Margaret of Austria, governor of the Low Countries in the sixteenth century, which reads:

A large picture called Hernoul le Fin (Arnolfini), with his wife in a room, which was given to Madame by Don Diego. His arms appear on the back of the picture. Made by the painter Jan.

The picture was taken to Spain, where it hung in the royal palace until the disturbances of the Napoleonic Wars. In some devious manner it made its way with the French armies to the very battle-field of Waterloo. After the battle a British general appropriated it and took it to England. In 1842 it was acquired by the National Gallery in London for the sum of £730. Van Mander, in his biography of van Eyck, says: "Johannes once painted in oil two portraits in a single scene—a man and a woman as if they had been united in wedlock by Fides." This statement gave rise to the belief, which persisted through several centuries, that the picture represented a wedding scene. It seems far more probable that the double portrait was made some time after the marriage of the silk merchant and his bride.

Like many great pictures painted by the Flemish masters, this nuptial portrait is full of story. The feeling for narrative fills all Flemish painting, and this picture, if we read its symbols, tells us a great deal not only about the husband and wife who stand hand in hand in their nuptial chamber, but about the medieval conception of marriage.

One of the first things one notices in the picture is the single candle burning in the chandelier. Surely Giovanni Arnolfini was not so miserly as this would seem to suggest. Nor is there need for candlelight, for through the open window pours the daylight of the out of doors. The lighted candle is a symbol of the presence of God. One was usually carried into the church in the wedding procession, and after the ceremony it was placed in the room of the newly wedded pair to remind them that they had made their vows to each other in the presence of God. Following the same symbolism, a lighted candle was usually required for the ceremony of taking an oath.

Arnolfini's wife is portrayed as if with child. This may be merely a matter of fifteenth-century fashion—St. Catherine in van Eyck's little triptych in Dresden has exactly the same posture and style of dress. Though the idea may seem amusing to modern minds, there is a kind of sublimity in an aesthetic ideal which makes fecundity an attribute of beauty. There is some reason to believe that this portrait is realistic, for on the carved post of the chair beside the great, crimson-curtained bed appears the figure of St. Margaret triumphing over the dragon. St. Margaret was revered as the protectress of women in childbirth.

The Flemish wife is demure and young, though she looks older than her years in her long-skirted green gown and white linen headdress. She has a faraway look in her eyes. She seems to place her right hand in her husband's left more obediently than fondly. This attitude is understandable when one studies the long-nosed, sallow, shrewd face of the silk merchant. No matter how clever he proved himself in business, he is unable to dominate his great beaver hat. It is not at all unlikely that this portrait of Giovanni Arnolfini inspired Sir John Tenniel's picture of the Mad Hatter in *Alice's Adventures in Wonderland.*

Arnolfini raises his right hand in a gesture of reverence, as though taking an oath. A rosary of amber beads hangs on the back wall of the room, and the convex mirror is adorned with ten medallions, each representing one of the Stations of the Cross. In the mirror, tiny but perfectly recognizable, appear the reflections of two persons, who may be Jan van Eyck and the servant the duke allowed him. That we may have no doubt who painted the portrait the painter has added above the mirror the flamboyant signature in Latin: "Jan van Eyck was here, 1434."

The Arnolfini portrait is one of the world's great pictures which is loved by the general public as much as it is admired by art critics. This portrait study reveals van Eyck's devotion to those things which he could touch and sense from experience with a known world. There can be no doubt that Jan van Eyck saw solid things as living naturally and easily in space. They take their places in his mind with the same simplicity they have in nature. In describing these two people and their surroundings he has chosen specific qualities of things and made them vivid. He delights in the shine of textiles, the hairiness of fur, and the very warp and woof of cloth. He senses that forms in nature diminish and diffuse as they stand away from his place of observation, and he senses the descriptive power of light in making these gradations possible. The art with which the atmosphere and illumination is made to pervade the whole room and the subtle analysis of the personalities of the man and woman are representative of the highest abilities of the Flemish masters.

The composition of the picture in three dimensions is enclosed by the far wall and by the converging side walls of the room. But the most astonishing optical directional force in the picture is the convex mirror which takes the eye of the observer back to the very point where van Eyck was standing when he observed the scene. This subtle device, almost amounting to a trick, gives a clear accent to the whole focus of the composition in space. No less a master than Velásquez was to make use of the same device in his *Maids of Honor*, painted two centuries after van Eyck's time. But in Velásquez' picture it is the man and woman—the Spanish King and Queen—who are reflected in the mirror, not the artist and his surroundings.

PORTRAIT OF MARGARET VAN EYCK

This justly famous portrait of the painter's wife was discovered in a Belgian fish market by Pieter van Lede, who gave it to the museum in Bruges in 1808. It will never be known how many fine flounders were prepared for the oven on the back of this picture of a strong-featured, middle-aged woman (PLATE 42).

Max Friedländer, the celebrated German art critic, considers this an impersonal portrait, which resembles all the other women in van Eyck's pictures. Perhaps it would be truer to say that van Eyck—like many other painters—found in the lady of his heart the ideal type which influenced his conceptions of all women.

We know very little about Margaret van Eyck except that she survived her husband, was granted a small pension for life by the city of Bruges, and in February 1446 bought a chance in a lottery. Van Eyck has signed this portrait with his usual device of Greek letters which spell phonetically the Flemish words *als ich kan* (as well as I can).

THREE MADONNAS BY VAN EYCK

Now that van Eyck has been studied as theologian and portraitist, it will be interesting to see how he combines the earthly and the heavenly vision in three of his most resplendent works, the *Madonna of the Chancellor Rolin* (PLATE 43), the *Madonna of the Canon van der Paele* (PLATE 45), and the tiny Melbourne *Madonna* (COLOR PLATE 107).

Before turning to them, however, it will be an advantage to see exactly how he understands the most venerated of Christian themes, that of the Madonna and Child.

There was no room for this tender subject upon the apocalyptic and hieratic Ghent altarpiece. The Madonna lends herself better to more intimate works to be hung in a house or a devotional chapel. This, undoubtedly, was the function of the tiny but exquisite panel, known as the *Ince Hall Madonna*, which is the great treasure of the National Gallery in Melbourne. It is marvelous how easily the master has solved the problem of expressing an all-pervasive light and atmosphere. The two figures have real dimension and life. This motherly, thoroughly Flemish Madonna with her pert, healthy Child, turning the pages of a great book, is truly amazing and painted with character.

The color organization is unified, diverse, and rich. The blue of the bodice is set off against a powerful red, and this is further enriched by the green-and-gold hanging behind the figures. A harmony of color composition is brought about by the red along the fringe of the canopy, while the blue is echoed in one little spot in the Virgin's gown which peeps out below the great tumbling folds of her mantle. This skillful device was to be repeated many times by the Flemish painters who followed van Eyck.

When it is admitted that the tiny Melbourne *Madonna*, with its almost un-Eyckian loving sentiment, is also grand and monumental, then by comparison the *Madonna of the Canon van der Paele* becomes tremendous in its scale and dignity (PLATE 45). The type of the *Madonna and Child*, though very much larger, is yet the same as that in the Melbourne gallery. But here the figures have an epic grandeur. The Child is erect. He turns His curly head, and for a moment forgets His divine mission as He reaches to play with the brightly colored parakeet and to receive a bunch of flowers from His mother's hand. Above the Virgin's head appears the same inscription the painter placed over the Queen of Heaven in the Ghent altarpiece.

The eyes of the two central figures are directed upon the old canon kneeling at the mailed feet of his patron St. George. The saint has an air of chivalrous sincerity as he presents his namesake to the Madonna. He is stiff and awkward in his complete suit of armor, but he doffs his helmet gallantly to do homage to the Queen of Heaven and to her Son. One recalls that the custom of tipping one's hat as a greeting has come down to us from the Middle Ages when a knight raised the visor of his helmet, so as not to conceal his face in the presence of a lady.

The portrait of the Canon van der Paele is a masterpiece of masterpieces, so exquisite and fine that it has been reproduced here in detail (PLATE 46). His sensitive old hands clasp to his breast a cloth-

JAN VAN EYCK. The Madonna of the Chancellor Rolin. Louvre, Paris (*23½ x 24¼*)

PLATE 43

JAN VAN EYCK. Detail of the Madonna of the Chancellor Rolin

Plate 44

JAN VAN EYCK. THE MADONNA OF THE CANON VAN DER PAELE. City Museum, Bruges (47⅝ x 58½)

JAN VAN EYCK. Detail from the Madonna of the Canon van der Paele. City Museum, Bruges

Plate 46

wrapped missal and a pair of heavy-rimmed spectacles. The light falls through their lenses, magnifying the writing on the page. Above his white surplice is a wrinkled but kindly face. His lips are tightly pursed, but his eyes are raised, awe-struck but confident, to the Madonna. Van Eyck's *Canon van der Paele* is an ideal achievement in the art of portraiture. The canon was elected to his office in the Cathedral of Bruges in 1410 and continued to serve there until his death in 1444. The memorial altarpiece took van Eyck two years to paint, and for eight years before his death the good canon was able to see it and pray before it, just as he is doing in the picture itself.

The other saint in the picture is St. Donatian, patron of the Cathedral of Bruges. Van Eyck has identified him for all time by placing beside him a wheel bearing five lighted candles. This is to commemorate the legend which tells that the saint was once thrown into a river by a group of unfaithful servants. Fortunately Pope Dionysius saw his plight and had the happy inspiration to throw him a life preserver in the form of a candlelit wheel. With the aid of this extraordinary craft, the drowning saint made shore.

The wonder of the *Madonna of the Canon van der Paele* is its timelessness and its truths about nature and about faith. In itself it is as finely wrought as a goldsmith's chalice. It is filled with the promise and hope that make the humble veneration of the donor live to this day.

Like this great picture, the *Madonna of the Chancellor Rolin* (PLATES 43, 44) ranks with the greatest votive pictures. Here again appear a noble Madonna and Child; human yet grand. The Child holds a masterpiece of the medieval goldsmith's work—a crystal orb surmounted by a dazzling cross. He makes the sign of benediction. He is a healthy, earthly Child, yet He is clearly His Father's son. From aloft an angel with peacock wings descends bearing an elaborate crown of gold filigree and flashing jewels, to remind us that the Madonna is also the Queen of Heaven. Clearly it is power and majesty which move Nicolas Rolin, the great chancellor, who labored to create and extend the power of the House of Burgundy, and which he wished to have commemorated by the painter. It is to the glorious Queen of Heaven and to the infant King of Kings that he kneels, not to a humble Mother and Child who face suffering.

The splendor of the foreground is repeated antiphonally in the wonderful background of the picture, with its suggestions of wealth and prosperity. The myriad details of the landscape beyond the loggia are a counterpoint of many notes which embellish the plain song of the divine grace in the movement of the Child's right hand to bless the world.

ST. FRANCIS RECEIVING THE STIGMATA

To St. Francis of Assisi all created things proclaimed the wonder and the glory of God. It is fitting that the painter who sang the praise of the countless wonders of this earth should have made a picture of the saint who could pay a sympathetic tribute to "brother worm."

As a matter of fact, van Eyck seems to have made two such pictures. One is now in the gallery of Turin, the other in the Johnson Collection in the Philadelphia Museum. The latter is reproduced here (COLOR PLATE 39).

The two pictures belonged to one family at one time. By the last testament of Anselmo Adornes, a Genoese living in Bruges since his birth in 1424, the panels depicting St. Francis receiving the stigmata were left to his two daughters who were nuns. This was in 1470. It is possible that van Eyck painted the two pictures for some member of the Adornes family older than Anselmo, who was only seventeen at the time of the master's death. It has been suggested that the first owner might have been named Francesco, and that the face of the saint is his portrait. If so—and it is, of course, no more than a supposition—it would account for the lifelike nature of the figure.[2]

Van Eyck's St. Francis is by no means seized by an ecstatic vision; but then, as has been pointed out, van Eyck was not a painter of drama. The second figure represents Brother Bruno, who was the saint's companion at the time he "saw above him a man having six wings like a seraph, arms extended and feet joined together, attached to a cross. Two of his wings were raised above his head, two others were stretched out in flight, the last two were wrapped about him. . . . His (St. Francis's) heart was completely occupied by this apparition when on his hands and feet began to appear the marks of the nails which he had just seen on the man crucified above him. . . ."

It is interesting to note that van Eyck dressed his Franciscans in the brown habit which he had seen worn by members of the order in Spain and Portugal, rather than the gray worn by the Franciscans in Flanders.

These paintings of St. Francis remain something

[2]Some critics think that the panel in Turin is a copy, ordered by Anselmo, from the original by van Eyck. One notices that the kneeling monk in the Turin picture has two right feet, which could have been a copyist's mistake.

of an enigma. The concern of the critics has always been with the problem of which was painted first, and whether these panels were originally parts of two diptychs. These disputes have obscured the meaning and merit of the pictures themselves. They do not stand among the greatest works of van Eyck, but the excellence of the draftsmanship is undeniable, and the forms have the clarity of the master's incomparable style.

THE GENIUS OF VAN EYCK

In the *Book of Illustrious Men* by Bartolomeo Fazio, which is a Who's Who of the fifteenth century, it is stated that Jan van Eyck studied geometry, the books of Pliny, and other ancient writers, and was learned in the art of distillation and what was then known of the science of chemistry. This statement and the fact that he disguised his modest device *als ich kan* in Greek letters have led some critics to acclaim his genius as arising from books and theory. This is not the case. The development of Jan van Eyck's style proves that he learned by observation; and that observation with him was a matter of penetrating things from the outside toward the inside. What he chose to portray was how things lived, for him, in three-dimensional space. To van Eyck that space was static, in the sense that he stood in one place and looked at it. Van Eyck did not choose to have his observers walk down the streets he painted; he wanted them to look down them. His art is one of the timeless solidity of permanent things, even of the changelessness of open air and light.

To him, all things have definite relationship in space; shapes overlap; floor tiles diminish by perspective; objects in the distance are small and those near by are large; the horizon is bathed in mist. Van Eyck saw these things and felt them to be true. In fact, he had a kind of mystic devotion of faith in what might be called the relativity of things as seen from one static viewpoint. If van Eyck made a great discovery, it was not simply a new way of putting paint on a panel; it was the discovery of a way of thinking objectively about what he saw.

One proof of this is that he treated problems of color tone in exactly the same way he treated problems of volume and perspective. He always retained the same color hue on any surface that was continuously the same. He modeled the surface, not by changing the hue, but by reaching its tonal value.

The third point about the art of van Eyck is that in the treatment of the human form he followed identically the same method of procedure that he followed in handling problems of light and space. He penetrated anatomy from the outside in. This is an explanation for the awkwardness of his figures whenever they make expressive gestures. One recalls the stiffness of St. George presenting George van der Paele to the Madonna and the grimaces of the singing angels in the Ghent altarpiece. This order of thinking applied to van Eyck's approach to psychology and the souls of men. He knew men well; the circumstances of his life at court gave him a shrewd understanding of human motives and human behavior. But van Eyck always analyzed a man from what he read in the man's outer appearance. This is the reason why his portraits have such an intense outward expression. Canon van der Paele, Nicolas Rolin, Margaret van Eyck, and Giovanni Arnolfini are all masterpieces of psychological interpretation in which the master tells you more about these real people by a wrinkle or a curl of hair than other artists who approach man from the inside are able to convey.

The greatness of van Eyck's style is that he started with the epidermis of man and nature and proceeded to analyze this and to translate what he found into hues, intensities, and values of paint. He treated the surfaces of his panels as fields upon which to demonstrate the interrelationship and relativity of all things. In this he expresses his theology —the relative merit of all things in the eyes of God.

To van Eyck, beauty lay in the perfection of a craft, whether this was his own or that of God, or nature's. To him, as to the mystics, there was as much beauty and meaning in a gnat as in the crown of Heaven.

Petrus Christus

ROM the point of view of technique, it is fortunate that Flemish painting began its evolution under the guiding light of the great van Eyck. In many ways, however, van Eyck was an exception. It must be remembered that he was not a popular painter. He was patronized by princes and by wealthy merchants such as Giovanni Arnolfini. He was not representative of the typical guildsman whose craft grew out of and fitted into the homely setting of old Flanders. Van Eyck set the standards of technical perfection for the Flemish school; he freely revealed to all the nature of his "secret." But he did not set the standards of sentiment for the Flemish style.

There is a more human strain in Flemish painting than we find in van Eyck's pictures, and this asserted itself strongly in his pupil, Petrus Christus. The work of this master—the only one who it is certain studied and worked under Jan van Eyck—marks the development of a more popular and more tender heart. It is difficult to give a name to this change in feeling, but it has to do with the way in which the painter approached his subject. Where van Eyck gives the cold splendor of jewels and rich brocades, his follower, Petrus Christus, shows a delight in simple domestic scenes, peasant types, and homely landscapes. It is the same tendency that marked van Eyck's contemporary, the Master of Flémalle, who painted St. Joseph making a mousetrap (PLATE 53).

Like van Eyck, Petrus Christus was not born in West Flanders. It would seem that he was born at Baerle, near Tilburg, in North Brabant, early in the fifteenth century. It is recorded that he bought a house in Bruges in 1443 and settled there with his wife to exercise his craft as a free painter. He had a natural son, named Sebastian, who became an illuminator; and his grandson, a second Petrus, was admitted to the Guild of St. Luke as a master painter in 1501. In this connection see PLATE 26.

In 1453 Petrus Christus was called to Cambrai to make three copies of a picture of the Virgin for the Count of Étampes. Some critics associate him with the "Piero di Burges," who was recorded to have been at the court of the Duke of Milan in 1456, and it is thought that Petrus Christus formed a link in the chain that brought Italian and Flemish painting closer together in the last half of the century.

He is mentioned several times in the archives of the city of Bruges during the fourteen-sixties, and he died there in 1472 or 1473, having outlived his great master by some thirty years.

The sixteenth-century Italian critic and historian, Guicciardini, mentions him under the name of Pietro Christa and places him among the Flemish masters, fourth in merit after van Eyck. Exactly how he came in contact with van Eyck is not known, but of the contact there can be no doubt. Petrus Christus was not a strong personality; he reflected many of the virtues of the styles of other masters, and as van Eyck clearly influenced his earlier work, we can trace the influences of van der Weyden and of Dirk Bouts in the pictures painted in his later years. Like van Eyck, and unlike most other Flemish painters, he frequently signed and dated his pictures. As van Eyck used Greek letters to spell his famous "As well as I can," Petrus Christus used the Greek XPI (Christi) for his signature.

ST. ELOY

One of the most fascinating and enigmatic pictures of the Flemish school is the painting of St. Eloy which is signed "Petr χρι me fecit—a—1449," now in the Philip Lehman family collection in New York City (PLATE 26).

The saint who was the patron of the goldsmiths'

DORMITION OF THE VIRGIN by Petrus Christus. Knoedler Gallery, New York, N. Y. (54½ x 67⅝)

PLATE 47

PETRUS CHRISTUS

guild is shown as a goldsmith in his shop waiting on two customers, a young man and a young woman. He is in the act of weighing gold and in his right hand he holds a ring. Around him are all the tools of his craft. The two young people toward whom he glances over his right shoulder are obviously very much in love.

One critic suggests that this is a double portrait in which Petrus Christus followed the fashion van Eyck used so magnificently in his Arnolfini portrait, and that the picture was made to commemorate the day the young lovers ordered their wedding rings. Friedländer, however, gives as his opinion that the picture was painted for the goldsmiths' guild, possibly to hang in the guildhall. He points out the marked difference between the intimacy with which all the little details of the shop are painted and the more aloof and stylized rendering of the figures.

Another, and quite different, explanation of the picture springs to mind when one recalls that the painter's son, Sebastian, was illegitimate, and that all the guilds had strict regulations regarding the admission to their ranks of persons born out of wedlock. Sebastian was an illuminator, which meant that he would belong to the guild of goldsmiths in Bruges, as illuminators were not classed with painters of the Guild of St. Luke. There was a ruling that any member of the goldsmiths' guild, who was of illegitimate birth, had to place in his shop a picture of St. Eloy. It is quite within the range of possibility that Petrus Christus painted this charming panel for his son to hang in his shop as a kind of license plate. We know that Sebastian had a son, Petrus, who, from the records, appears to have been born in wedlock. Perhaps Sebastian's father made the painting as a wedding gift to his son and his bride. If so, the idea of the picture is subtle and skillful; it meets the requirements of the guild and, at the same time, it proclaims the moral goodness of Sebastian. For him and his bride to be shown in the act of buying a wedding ring from St. Eloy takes the sting out of Sebastian's having to hang the likeness of the saint in his shop for all to know the shame of his own birth.

The painting is done with great care, and all the appointments of the little shop are most charming. On the shelves is a wealth of curios—rings, corals, beads, and precious stones. It seems that the painter had studied attentively van Eyck's portrait of Giovanni Arnolfini and his wife, for he, too, paints a little convex mirror on the table in which are reflected two more customers approaching the good saint's shop.

MADONNA WITH THE CARTHUSIAN MONK

One of the earliest works by Petrus Christus, long thought to have been made by van Eyck himself, is the *Madonna with the Carthusian Monk* which has long hung in the museum in Berlin (PLATE 49). It is obviously inspired by the Maelbecke *Madonna* of van Eyck, and by the *Madonna with a Carthusian Monk* which is generally attributed to van Eyck, now in the Rothschild collection in Paris. Petrus Christus has naïvely moved St. Barbara's tower into the portico from the place van Eyck gave it out of doors beyond the arcade, and he has removed van Eyck's rich brocades. The stiffness of the figures and the lack of inspiration about them show what invariably happens to a painter who follows slavishly the forms of another master and fails to absorb the meaning of those forms.

Perhaps when Petrus Christus painted this picture he was so deeply awed by the power of van Eyck that he was hampered in his own creation.

TWO PORTRAITS

Lest the discussion of this worthy old craftsman of Bruges appear too damaging to his good character, let us turn to two of his really fine portraits in which his weaknesses actually seem to become merits. One of the most charming and even coy portraits ever made of a young girl is the one by Petrus Christus which hangs in the Berlin Gallery (PLATE 50). It speaks fully for itself. Petrus Christus outdid himself in penetrating psychology, and even though he is not ranked among the greatest of the great, he certainly knew what he was doing when he painted this exquisite little picture of a pert young woman. This girl, with the slightly oriental eyes, knew her own mind. One feels sure she arranged her white fur collar very carefully and set her headdress at what she considered the most provocative angle before she allowed the painter to make his preliminary sketches. A calculating young woman, who, perhaps, thought she was revealing little of herself. One wonders whether, after the picture was finished, she realized how completely the artist had understood her and how much of her he makes us understand.

In the Jules Bache Collection, recently bequeathed to the Metropolitan Museum of Art in New York City, is the portrait of a Carthusian monk, signed by Petrus Christus and dated 1446. The coloring is fiery and the portrait has real warmth, which, unfortunately, is lost in a black-

[69]

and-white reproduction (PLATE 48). Why the halo has been given to this follower of St. Bernard is not known. It is possibly an addition by a later artist who wished to turn the monk into a saint for some pious purpose. Perhaps the intent was to make the portrait appear to represent Denis, the great mystic of the Carthusian Order in the Low Countries.

There is a fly painted on the ledge of the lower margin. It has been suggested by some critics that the fly is there to tell us that the person portrayed has died. However, this is more or less surmise. The masters of the fifteenth century who had so recently discovered the power of vivid realism delighted in occasional effects of startling naturalism. Vasari wrote that he had seen cherries which were painted with such vividness that the birds flew in through the open windows to peck at them. This fly by Petrus Christus would certainly tempt a spider. There are two flies in the portrait of the artist and his wife by the unknown master of Frankfort (PLATE 30). In the famous *Madonna* by Carlo Crivelli, also in the Bache Collection, a fly has lighted on the balustrade beside the Child. Seemingly, then, the representation of the fly is no more than a touch of vivid naturalism designed to give the picture scale and depth by its unobtrusive position in the foreground.

There is no question but that these two portraits of the unknown young girl and the unknown monk, with their closeness, penetration, and directness, are exceptionally fine.

THE *DORMITION OF THE VIRGIN*

The *Dormition of the Virgin* (COLOR PLATE 47) was painted between 1440 and 1445, according to M. Friedländer. It is the earliest known rendering of the subject made by a Flemish painter, preceding that by van der Goes (PLATE 77) by some forty years.

The story which the picture tells is taken from the *Golden Legend* in which it is related that Mary survived the ascension of her Son by twenty-four years. When she reached the age of seventy-two, it was announced to her by an angel that she would shortly fall asleep and her soul would be transported to Heaven where her Son awaited her. Furthermore, the angel promised, the twelve apostles would be miraculously transported to her bedside to attend to her last rites.

The first apostle to arrive was St. John, who came enveloped in a white cloud and accompanied by a clap of thunder. He was shortly followed by eleven more clouds and thunderclaps and then the whole company of the apostles was assembled.

This story, with all its dramatic incidents, was entirely in keeping with the pattern of the medieval mysteries, and it is just such a Mystery Play which Petrus Christus has painted. The actors, including the dying Mary, make studied gestures. Here in this large panel the devout could find all the scenes of the drama—one disciple swings his censer, and another exhorts his companions not to mourn, repeating the words of St. John: "My brothers, when she will be dead, none shall weep for fear that the people may say: 'Look how they fear death, these men who preach the resurrection.'" At some distance along the pathway approaches the last of the disciples, St. Thomas, who was reputedly a skeptic and doubted not only Christ's wounds but also the Incarnation. It is to him, the doubter, that the angel appears, bearing the girdle of the Virgin, the emblem of virginal purity.

The final act of the Mystery takes place beneath the great red canopy of the deathbed, the curtains of which have been gathered up in the same way in which the bed curtains are gathered in van Eyck's Arnolfini portrait. Here Christ, surrounded by angels, comes from Heaven to receive the spirit of the Virgin, which is borne upward by angels. Petrus Christus, with his naïve realism, seems to consider spirits as having actual weight. This clumsy representation is also in keeping with the mechanisms used in the Mysteries, by means of which angels were lowered from above and saints were lifted from the platform of the stage to Heaven.

To modern minds, the art of Petrus Christus seems whimsically childlike. To him reality lies only in what he can see and touch. Even this reality is circumscribed by formulas he learned from other masters. He took what he painted not so much from life as from figures representing it. Some of these he found in the art of other masters, some in the Mystery Plays, others come from his uninspired outlook upon the world in which he lived.

But for all this, this old master, who may indeed have been an important link between the painters of the north and those of the south, must not be discounted, for in his childish wonder and simple faith he is always sincere. He was a portraitist of slow but real ability. His religious concepts were understandable by even the most untutored men. He was a laborious craftsman, and produced the enamels and technical perfections of the finest paintings of the Flemish school, though his colors ran perhaps overmuch to brown and wine-red. The last he loved almost to a fault.

Unlike van Eyck, Petrus Christus was in every sense the painter for the little people of Flanders.

PETRUS CHRISTUS. Portrait of a Monk. Bache Collection,
Metropolitan Museum, New York (11½ x 8)

Plate 48

PETRUS CHRISTUS. Madonna with the Carthusian Monk.
Kaiser Friedrich Museum, Berlin (7½ x 5½)

Plate 49

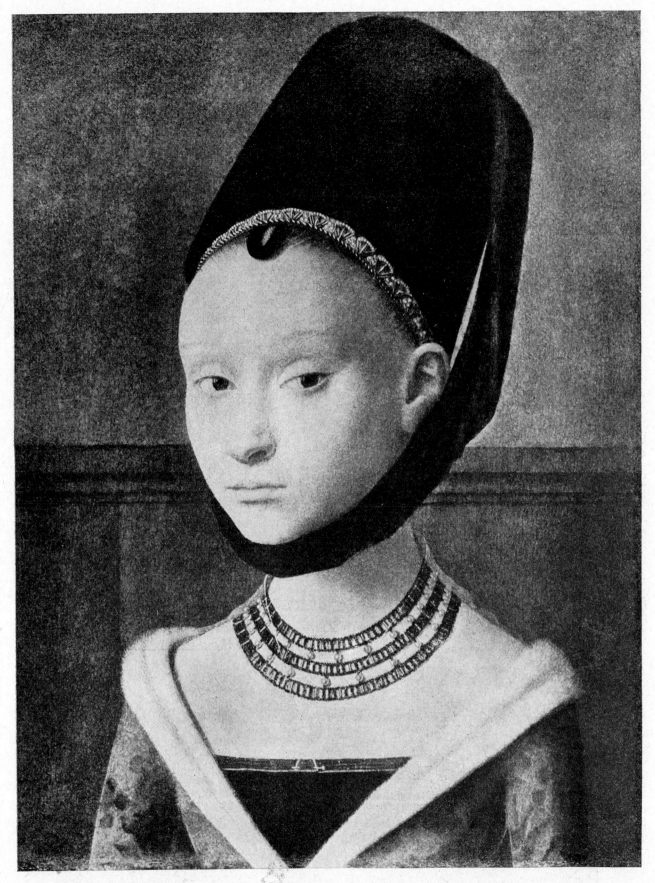

PETRUS CHRISTUS. Portrait of a Woman. Kaiser Friedrich Museum, Berlin (*11 x 8¼*)

Plate 50

PETRUS CHRISTUS. St. Jerome in His Study. Courtesy Detroit Institute of Arts (8¼ x 5¼)

PLATE 51

MASTER OF FLÉMALLE. Nativity. Dijon Museum (*34 x 27½*)

Plate 52

MASTER OF FLÉMALLE. The Annun

P

Collection, Westerloo, Belgium (*24 x 25½ – 10⅛*)

MASTER OF FLÉMALLE. Madonna and Child. Staedel Institute, Frankfort (56⅛ x 20½)

Plate 54

Roger van der Weyden

and

THE MASTER OF FLÉMALLE

THE MYSTERY that surrounds the brothers van Eyck is simple compared to that which envelops the figure of Roger van der Weyden, or Rogier de la Pasture, and the painter who, for want of accurate knowledge of his true name, is usually called the Master of Flémalle. The history of painting is full of gaps where interesting chapters are missing. Unfortunately, those gaps have incited many writers on art history to suppositions and inferences which occasionally lead far from the truth.

Sometime during the year 1859 a scholar named Alexandre Pinchart, who was delving in the records of the city of Tournai, discovered an entry which, when he announced it, sounded like a thunderclap in the ears of the art world. To understand the consternation of the learned gentlemen, who were then authorities on Flemish painting, it must be told that for many years a number of pictures, obviously of the Flemish school and including the famous *Nativity* in the Museum at Dijon, had been attributed to the great Roger van der Weyden, town painter of Brussels.

This master, who is known to have been a native of Tournai where the language spoken then, as now, was French and not Flemish, was generally known to the art world by the French form of his name, Rogier de la Pasture. In English, we would call him simply Roger Fields.

The entry which M. Alexandre Pinchart found in the archives of Tournai read as follows:

Rogelet de la Pasture, natif de Tournay commencha son appresure le cinquiesme jour de Mars l'an mil CCCC vingt-six (1426), et fu son maistre Robert Campin, paintre, le quel Rogelet a perfaict son appresure denement avec soudict maistre.

This tells us that a certain Rogelet de la Pasture began his apprenticeship in Tournai under the painter Robert Campin in 1426. Another document in the archives states that this Rogelet attained the rank of master painter in 1432.

M. Pinchart, confusing Rogelet with Roger de la Pasture—van der Weyden—proposed to ascribe to this painter's master, Campin, some pictures of earlier style which had long been attributed to van der Weyden.

But another entry in the same archives records that on November 17, 1426, some months after Rogelet was apprenticed, the city of Tournai gave a banquet, with eight lots of wine, to "maistre Rogier" —a greater honor than it ever accorded to Jan van Eyck.

Clearly the "maistre Rogier" who was feted in 1426 could not have been the same Rogelet who began his apprenticeship under Robert Campin in March of that year.

All that remains of the school of painting of Tournai created by Pinchart and his followers is a somewhat obscure Rogelet de la Pasture and his just as obscure master Robert Campin. Of the latter we know little more than that in 1432 he was expelled from the painters' guild of Tournai for his dissolute ways.

Many students of art grouped together the Dijon *Nativity*, the *Annunciation* triptych of the Mérode family in Belgium, and three panels in the Museum of Frankfort, creating on the basis of the similar style of all these a painter whom they called the Master of Flémalle. The panels in Frankfort which are said to have come from the Abbey of Flémalle are undoubtedly by the artist who produced the Mérode triptych.

Lately, however, some critics have been inclined to disregard the Master of Flémalle and to ascribe most of his pictures to Roger van der Weyden.

In spite of this judgment it seems that several of

the paintings attributed to the Master of Flémalle do not fit into the work of Roger van der Weyden. We must, therefore, accept the mysterious painter —this Master of Flémalle—who seems to have lived somewhere in Flanders during the first half of the fifteenth century, and was probably the master of van der Weyden, or at least influenced him very deeply.

Of the life of this mysterious master we know less than we know of Hubert van Eyck. But of his work it is possible to speak with greater assurance. Whatever his name was, and wherever he lived, there is no denying the fact that he painted several excellent pictures, and, after all, it is the pictures which live and have meaning for us today.

THE DIJON *NATIVITY*

This altarpiece, which would seem to have been painted at about the same time that Jan van Eyck was busy upon his *Adoration of the Lamb*, is amazing in its ingenuousness (PLATE 52). The scene is one which was popular in the Mystery Plays and is based on a story in the *Golden Legend* which derives from an ancient manuscript, the *Book of the Infancy of the Saviour*. In this apocryphal gospel it is told that Joseph summoned a midwife to attend the Virgin Mary. This woman, who was called Zelomi, exclaimed over the miracle in which the words of the Prophet, "Behold a virgin shall conceive and give birth," were fulfilled. The midwife went out from the cave, where she met another woman of the country, Salome by name:

And the midwife said to her, "Salome, Salome, I will tell you a most surprising thing which I saw, a virgin hath brought forth, which is a thing contrary to nature."

To which Salome replied, "As the Lord my God liveth, unless I receive particular proof of this matter, I will not believe that a virgin hath brought forth."

Then Salome went in and the midwife said, "Mary, show thyself, for a great controversy is risen concerning thee."

And Salome received satisfaction. But her hand was withered, and she groaned bitterly.

When Salome entreated the Lord for forgiveness for her lack of faith, an angel appeared in the cave and bade her, "Reach forth thy hand to the Child, and carry Him, and by that means thou shalt be restored." Which, when she had done, instantly healed her.[1]

In the *Nativity* by the Master of Flémalle, Salome,

[1]*The Apocryphal Books of the New Testament*, translated from the original tongues. David McKay, publisher, Philadelphia.

in a wide-winged white headdress, exhibits her restored hand. Behind her unfurls a banderole with the words, "I have proof." Zelomi raises her hands, marveling at the miracle which attests the virgin birth. The devout old Joseph sits beside the women and holds a candle in his hand. If this seems strange when the setting of the picture is in the full light of day, it is because the artist was following the traditions of the Mystery Plays, which, no doubt, he had seen staged before the magnificent cathedral of some Flemish town. In the plays it was conventional to have St. Joseph carry a candle or a lantern to symbolize the fact that the Nativity took place in the dark of night. As has been said, the medieval man always felt the idea of the thing to be more real than the thing itself. By means of the graphic symbolism at his command he conveyed his ideas quickly and clearly.

There is great realism in the painting of the stable with its thatched roof and the cow which can be seen through a hole in the stable wall. The artist was careful to paint a whole cow, one calculated to satisfy the eyes of the Flemish and Burgundian farmers, who might be expected to kneel in prayer before his picture. Angels, far less graceful but not less enchanting than those painted by Hugo van der Goes, fly overhead, carrying banderoles inscribed with praises. Their draperies billow in brilliant disorder. At an open door at the rear of the stable appear shepherds with bagpipes, but they are awed by what they behold and stand there mute and wide-eyed. The Virgin is magnificent and humble before the infant Christ. Far away behind the stable stretches a wide and open landscape through which winds a great highway down which, one knows, the kings of the East will presently come, bearing their gifts of gold, frankincense, and myrrh. In the far distance rise the towers and spires of a very Flemish Bethlehem. It is a landscape worthy of van Eyck, rich in story and symbolic suggestions and very different from anything ever painted by the more abstract and mystical Roger van der Weyden.

In his use of banderoles the artist shows how close he stands to the illuminators of manuscripts. He feels that he must use words as well as figures in his picture to tell the story he would convey. This use of the banderole, which was soon to be discarded, seems to indicate that the Dijon *Nativity* was painted early in the fifteenth century. Van Eyck used no banderoles in his *Adoration of the Lamb*, but he inscribed many words in the gold lunettes behind the central figures, in order to leave us in no doubt of his meaning. The amazingly rapid progress of the Flemish painter's art away from

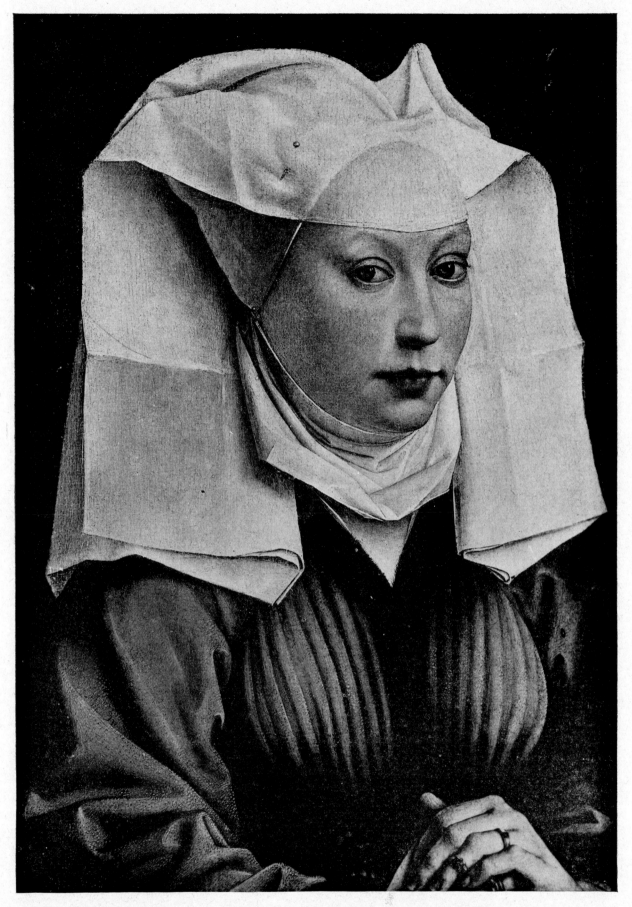

ROGER VAN DER WEYDEN. Portrait of a Woman. Kaiser Friedrich Museum, Berlin (*18¼ x 12½*)

Plate 55

ROGER VAN DER WEYDEN. Descent from the C

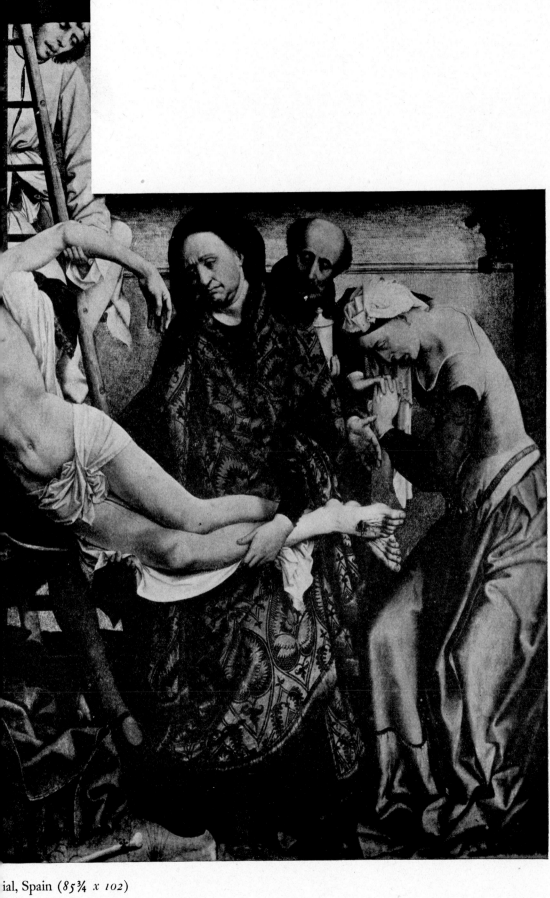

ial, Spain (*85¾ x 102*)

ROGER VAN DER WEYDEN.
ALTAR OF THE SEVEN SACRAMENTS.
Antwerp Museum (76¾ x 37¾)

PLATE 57

ROGER VAN DER WEYDEN. Wings of Altar of the Seven Sacraments.
Antwerp Museum (*48½ x 24⅜*)

Plate 58

ROGER VAN DER WEYDEN. Mary and John. Johnson Collection,
Philadelphia. Courtesy Johnson Art Collection (68⅛ x 35⅜)

Plate 59

ROGER VAN DER WEYDEN. Detail from picture of MARY AND JOHN
on opposite page. Courtesy Johnson Art Collection, Philadelphia

PLATE 60

ROGER VAN DER WEYDEN. Crucifixion. Kunsthistorisches Museum, Vienna (42¾ x 16¾)

PLATE 61

that of the illuminator of manuscripts is shown by the swift disappearance of the banderole and all inscriptions as the painter's skill in making the figures in the painting tell the story without the addition of text.

THE MÉRODE ALTAR

This altarpiece (PLATE 53) in the private chapel of the Countess de Mérode at Westerloo-Tongerloo in Belgium is said by Max Friedländer to date from about the year 1428. This places it somewhat earlier than van Eyck's *Adoration of the Lamb*.

It is a hearty, healthy picture, in keeping with the Flemish spirit. The forms are round and solid and rest heavily in their places. The folds of their draperies are broad and a bit angular; the figures have rather fat faces with very little expression. The perspective is clumsy, and the light is not all-pervading as in van Eyck's pictures. All in all, this is a very primitive picture, but it is certainly a milestone in the story of Flemish painting.

The identity of the donors of the altarpiece, whose coat of arms appears in the picture, is uncertain. But there is no doubt of the humility of this husband and wife who kneel on the outer doorstep of the chamber of the Annunciation. Within the room, which is furnished in accordance with Flemish custom with household utensils, candles, a pot hanging in a Gothic niche, and a long, snowy towel folded neatly on its rack, Mary reclines rather awkwardly on the floor, against a low bench. Every good medieval craftsman knew that the Annunciation occurred on March twenty-fifth when the weather in Flanders was still chilly and far from springlike, but this old master has shown the fireplace well blacked and the windows opened. Although it was usual in painting scenes of the Annunciation to show the Holy Ghost descending upon the Virgin in the form of a dove, the Master of Flémalle has given us a different and quite ingenuous interpretation of the Incarnation. The tiny Christ Child, bearing His Cross over his shoulder, slides down the golden rays from Heaven toward Mary. As He does so, He turns His head to smile out upon the world.

Meanwhile, Joseph works calmly in his shop, surrounded by all the tools of his craft. The shop shutters are open, showing that he is ready for more mousetrap orders from the good burghers walking the streets of this comfortable Flemish town.

Like the *Nativity* at Dijon (PLATE 52), this *Annunciation* is eloquent of the simple, childlike faith in the heart of the artist who painted it for men and women as realistic and direct in their approach to God as he was himself.

THE FRANKFORT *MADONNA*

Of the three panels painted by this anonymous "Master of the Mousetrap," as he was once called, said to have come from an abbey of Flémalle, the finest is the full-length *Madonna and Child* (PLATE 54). The drapery of the Virgin falls in heavy billows. She stands on a carpet of flowers, and behind her is a rich background showing repeated patterns of heraldic beasts. Behind the heads of the two figures are heavy halos which look as though they were made of gold plate. The painter of this picture is still under the sway of a distant Byzantine ideal, which governed the representation of the Madonna during the early centuries of the Middle Ages. There is no likeness in this figure to the Madonnas of van der Weyden, which, though abstract in sense, have much more character and drama. Van der Weyden and the Master of Flémalle both contrast vividly with van Eyck, whose figures were always surrounded by the full atmosphere of this earth.

ROGER VAN DER WEYDEN

Though van der Weyden was born in Tournai on the border of France, where doubtless he spoke French, nonetheless at the heart of his style he remains Flemish.

The first that is definitely known of Roger van der Weyden—aside from the rather doubtful clue discovered by M. Pinchart—is that he was made town painter of Brussels in 1435. It is amusing to note that in this position he was granted annually one third of a bolt of cloth. This was less than the town gave to judges and clerks, not because they were men of greater stature than the painter, but because they were learned and could speak Latin. He married Elisabeth Goffaerts, of Brussels, by whom he had three sons, two of whom followed in their father's craft.

Roger van der Weyden was a great traveler and is mentioned as having been in Louvain, Bruges, and Dijon. In 1450, the year of a papal jubilee, he was in Italy, visiting Rome and the court of Ferrara. He was praised there by Fazio in his *Book of Illustrious Men*.

As early as 1436 the town magistrates of Brussels decided that no one was to succeed van der Weyden in the office of town painter. In fact, the pictures he painted for the council chamber of the town hall were enormously admired. Dürer praised them in high terms and, according to van Mander, the great Lampsonius interrupted his political discourse in this hall to look up at the paintings and exclaim, "Oh, Roger, what a master you were!" which, after all, proved that Lampsonius was something of a diplomat and knew how to ingratiate himself with the people of Brussels.

That he was honored in his time, and beyond the boundaries of Flanders, is proved by a letter written December 26, 1460, by Francesco Sforza, Duke of Milan, to the Duke of Burgundy, in which he recommends the Italian painter Zanneto Bugatto in order that he may come to Brabant and study with the celebrated master, Roger van der Weyden. A second letter from the Duchess of Milan, written two years later, and addressed to Roger himself, thanks him for the generosity with which he had taught his art to the Milanese painter:

. . . And as much for the service rendered as for your modest way, and we put ourselves at your disposition in order to do anything we can do for you in your favor. . . .

Van der Weyden died in Brussels on June 18, 1464, and was buried in the Cathedral Church of St. Gudule. Later his wife was laid beside him. A notice in the archives reads, "Master Roger van der Weyden, eminent painter, and his wife rest in front of the altar of St. Catherine, under a blue stone on which is carved a skeleton." There are many other records which attest his good deeds and philanthropy. He had been a wealthy and a pious man.

When one approaches the work of van der Weyden, one is immediately aware that his art is the most idealized and the most abstract of all the Flemish masters. Many explanations have been offered as to what produced his distinctive style. Since he came from Tournai, which was the home of fine stonemasons, sculptors, and metalworkers, it might be assumed that he inherited to a degree their feeling for the essentially abstract quality of space. He gives the impression that he is accustomed to *feel* his way among things, and not merely to see them.

There is no doubt that Roger's way of seeing was not so direct and simple as that of many of his contemporary compatriots. As Friedländer puts it: "No lighting lends tone or atmosphere to the story. The images stand tangibly before us; overclear, close, in an airless space and in equal sharpness of outline. . . . Since he lacks that comprehensive way of looking at things, which is usual with a painter, and does not observe the play of light in the color sequence, the naturalness is less than one might expect."

There are two other points which must be grasped to understand the style of van der Weyden. The first is, as M. Focillon has pointed out:

The concentrated harmony which presses tightly the parts into composition, in a transparent and compact world, is a heritage of the miniature. Must one consider by contrast the knowing rhythms and the fine order of Roger van der Weyden as the result of the influence of the great decorative tapestries?

It is true that van der Weyden, more than any other painter of his time, saw the development of the Flemish tapestry industry. A wall hanging cannot be conceived like any other form of pictorial art because the expression is limited to what can be represented with woven threads. Large shapes must replace the exuberance of depth, if the eye of the observer is to be fascinated by the spectacle. It was this form of expression that Roger incorporated to a great extent into his art of painting. But he did this not because he was bound by the conventions of the tapestry designer, he did it as an expression of his own spiritual attitude toward the theme of his pictures.

The second point about van der Weyden's art which must be understood derives from his medievalism. His forms are graphic because of the contents. He intended them to be intensely symbolic of an idea. He was not a psychologist like Hugo van der Goes, and this explains the paucity of types in his repertory. In the best medieval sense he was a narrative symbolist. His power of expression is that of sculptured masses standing forth in a treeless and cloudless landscape. He seeks to impress by the finely drawn, clearly cut mass. He creates more from his head than from his heart, but the purpose of his art is to touch the soul.

Van der Weyden does all this like a true artist, making the relationship of form and content in his style result from the realistic demands of what he chooses to do. Naturally, in the range of his intentions he resembles van Eyck and van der Goes, but the means he employs are different. In fundamentals he remains true to the spirit of Flemish painting, but his personal genius sought and found a style of expression which epitomizes the last flowering of the Middle Ages. He is the great master of symbolic narrative.

THE *DESCENT FROM THE CROSS*

This picture, which was finished before 1443, now in the Escorial, is not only one of van der Weyden's greatest works, it is also one of the sublimest expressions of the religious faith which moved the people of old Flanders (PLATE 56).

The artist made it for the archers' guild of Louvain and it hung in their chapel in Our Lady Outside the Walls of that city until, during the sixteenth century, Queen Marie of Hungary acquired it by a clever exchange. She presented the chapel with a copy of the altarpiece made by Michael Coxie and an organ, taking in exchange van der Weyden's masterpiece. By this barter the picture found its way to Spain and the royal collection in the Escorial, only after a perilous voyage and rescue from shipwreck. Had the panel been lost at sea, the world would have been robbed of one of the most powerful works of religious symbolism. The *Descent from the Cross* marks a high point in the Flemish genius for the perfect union of the real and the super-real. It is narrative, but it is far more than that: it is symbolic. In no art save that of the ballet can be found such rhythmic cadences. No woman of this world could bend herself into the downward S-curve of grief assumed by the figure at the extreme right of the painting. The Magdalene is, in every sense, more than a human being: she is a posture and an attitude which crystallize a moment into an eternal expression. She is a dramatic symbol of anguish and remorse. On the opposite side of the picture St. John the Baptist balances the Magdalene. The faces of both are turned from the direct gaze of the spectator. By this means the painter conveys to us that they are essentially introspective—symbols of grief rather than individual portraits which express personal sorrow. The figure of the woman above St. John upsets the symmetry of the composition but adds a strong note of lamentation to the left side of the picture, which equals in power that of the Magdalene on the other side.

Like a pendulum, the right arm of the Virgin swings heavily down close to the hideous skull of Golgotha. The almost lifeless, weighty diagonal of her body echoes exactly that of the dead Christ. He is held up by a restrained old Nicodemus and a man who descends a ladder. The legs of Christ are held by the tearful Joseph of Arimathaea. He is the most striking in personality of all the figures, yet, like them, he, too, remains an actor in a symbolic role.

It is noticeable at once that the crossbar to which Christ had been nailed is much too short for the open spread of His arms. The reason for this is not that van der Weyden knew no better, but that, like a true son of the Middle Ages, he respected the architectural framework of his composition far more than the appearance of reality.

Unique and amazing is the fact that the entire group is placed in front of a gold background which adds much in giving the feeling of being beyond space and time. In other words, there is no specific place or moment in which this event is to be seen by the observer. It is universal and eternal. For van der Weyden, the Crucifixion was not simply a historical event, it was a constant tragedy in which every man plays a part.

THE ALTAR OF THE SEVEN SACRAMENTS

This triptych, which is in the Musée Royal des Beaux-arts in Antwerp, shows in three places the coat of arms of Jean Chevrot, Bishop of Tournai, and was probably made at the command of the bishop in 1445. It cannot be considered one of van der Weyden's finest pictures; the essential interest lies in the unique presentation of an unusual iconography (PLATES 57, 58).

The scene is a church. In the left aisle a priest baptizes an infant. Behind him two small boys receive the sacrament of confirmation while three others walk away unattended by their well-behaved little dog, who lies watchfully upon the tile pavement. The third sacrament, that of confession, is taking place openly in front of the choir screen.

The right aisle of van der Weyden's church is even busier. Here a priest receives ordination; a pair of young lovers exchange their marriage vows; and, amazingly enough, a dying man—deathbed and all —receives the sacrament of extreme unction before departing this life.

The large center panel shows the priest at the high altar, celebrating mass before one devout kneeling worshiper. This is the real world, and it is echoed from on high, from the realm of dogma, as Christ on the Cross while the lamenting Marys and St. John appear mystically in the foreground.

More than a century before Shakespeare immortalized the Seven Ages of Man, which became the theme of innumerable engravings and prints, persisting even down to the days of Currier and Ives, Roger van der Weyden painted his *Seven Ages of Man* in relation to the seven sacraments of the Church.

THE *CRUCIFIXION*

The museum in Vienna possesses a *Crucifixion* by van der Weyden which probably dates from about 1440 (PLATE 61). It reveals much of the master's method. The principle of scale organization is fundamental to the art of Roger van der Weyden, and produces a harmony of forms in the foreground rather than a harmony of spatial elements in a depthward progression.

In studying this picture, it becomes clear that van der Weyden's medievalism prevented him from becoming a great master of landscape painting. The little medieval city in the background, with its walls and parapets, its gabled roofs and towers, its church steeples and domes, is charming, but it and the landscape into which it is set remain undeniably flat and like a stage backdrop when compared with the extraordinary and exciting flow of space painted by van Eyck and by Dirk Bouts. This particular aspect of van der Weyden's style sets him off markedly from the other masters of the Flemish school. There is no confusing the painter of this picture with his so-called teacher, the Master of Flémalle, who painted the delightfully spacious and luminous landscape of the Dijon *Nativity*.

The figure of Mary, wrung with grief and collapsing at the foot of the Cross, in this picture is a conception typical of Roger van der Weyden. The interpretation of the Woman of Sorrows was destined to have a very powerful influence upon other painters who followed van der Weyden. This portrayal of the Mother of the Lord, as a symbol of lamentation and heart-rending pathos, is in keeping with the religious ecstasies of medieval mystics, like Mary of Ognies and Luitgard of Tongres. In his emotionalism, Roger van der Weyden shows himself to be the most southern of all the Flemish painters. Dirk Bouts, whose *Weeping Madonna* is an amazing interpretation of the Woman of Sorrows, may well be considered the most "northern" master of the Flemish school in the restraint he shows in handling this subject. It is extremely interesting to compare the mystical attitudes of Bouts and van der Weyden in relation to different conceptions of the Woman of Sorrows (PLATES 65, 68).

TWO PORTRAITS OF WOMEN

Roger van der Weyden painted many portraits, especially of men. However, not many of these that are extant have the extraordinary charm and character of the few portraits of women which are known to be his work. The two reproduced here are famous among all portraits of women of all schools.

The young matron in the violet-gray woolen gown and the starched white linen wimple (PLATE 55) is the picture of a deep contentment which borders on smugness. She is reserved, even a bit pensive; serious, but not, obviously, incapable of enjoying all the pleasures of this life. Her full face and large mouth seem to reveal a certain sensuality. The primness and erectness of the posture which to a large extent are due to the accepted style of the times as much as to van der Weyden's inability to unbend his figures, either physically or spiritually, are contradicted by her plump, ring-bedecked hands.

Friedländer believes that this portrait, which is in the Deutsches Museum in Berlin, was painted about the year 1435. It is interesting to compare it with van Eyck's portrait of his wife which was surely painted within the same decade. There is no doubt of the beauty of the design and workmanship, but compared with the penetration shown in Margaret van Eyck this picture reveals van der Weyden to have been removed from the full personality of the subject.

Here, too, the symbol takes precedence over personality. This plump, complacent wife of an unknown citizen of Brabant is representative of the prosperity which the province enjoyed during the reign of Philip the Good. One recalls Pirenne's phrase, *"ils regorgent de bienêtre."*

The second portrait is in the National Gallery in Washington, D.C. (COLOR PLATE 1).

This picture seems to have been painted some twenty years later than the portrait we have just considered. Although this woman does not look out to meet the eye of the observer, she has greater warmth and more humanity than the self-satisfied young wife. Perhaps she has learned of life a greater gentleness. It is also true that van der Weyden, in his later years, developed a deeper appreciation of human values.

The folded hands of this unknown lady are tense, revealing that she has great sensitivity. The arms and hands form a definite base for the portrait—a base which van der Weyden's strong sense of design would naturally feel necessary.

All that one observes in van der Weyden's art leads to the conclusion that he is a late, restless stirring of the spirit of the Middle Ages. He painted in great, triumphant symbols which, in turn, indicate the nature of a drama, pointing and elevating its meaning. His pictures seldom tell a whole story. As with his magnificent *Descent from the Cross*, all of van der Weyden's art had a timeless quality—the best and most necessary quality of an eternal symbol. Nothing that he paints is for the moment. He transcends time.

WEEPING MADONNA by DIRK BOUTS. Private Collection, New York, N. Y. (*Detail twice actual size*)

PLATE 62

Dirk Bouts

As INEVITABLY HAPPENS, when a country is enjoying prosperity and boom times, during the reign of Philip the Good the cities of his provinces in the Low Countries became a mecca for inventors of every sort of device, for scholars, skilled workmen, and clever young men who wanted to make a fortune or a name for themselves.

The city of Louvain, twelve miles from Brussels, had long been a clothmaking center. Its products commanded high prices. During the fourteenth century its population had grown to 150,000 or more, which made it one of the important industrial centers of western Europe.

Toward the close of the century the Louvain weavers began to protest against their working conditions and demand more rights for their guild. Three quarters of a century after the weavers and butchers of Bruges had asserted their power at the Battle of the Golden Spurs, the Louvain weavers staged a revolution in the course of which they broke into the town hall, seized thirteen of the magistrates, and hurled these unfortunate men out of the windows onto the spears of the angry mob gathered in the square below.

This labor unrest caused the Duke of Brabant to remove his court from Louvain to Brussels, which greatly increased the prestige and trade of the latter city. A few years later he came with an army and punished the rebellious men of Louvain, burning many buildings, and inflicting such heavy penalties on the citizens that thousands left Louvain to take up residence in other towns of old Belgium and in England, where inducements were offered to skilled clothworkers.

So it happened that for a period Louvain was threatened with industrial bankruptcy.

This was the state of affairs when Philip the Good, to whom the lordship of Brabant had come by inheritance, determined to bring back its former prosperity to this city of his. In 1426 he appealed to the Pope to aid him in founding a university there. This ultimately grew to be the largest, most renowned seat of learning in the Low Countries. The great Erasmus was one of its scholars. Only a hundred years after its founding the University of Louvain numbered forty-three colleges and had a student body of more than 4,000. It is to be recalled that its press published Sir Thomas More's *Utopia* when London publishers were afraid to sponsor so radical a book.

In carrying out his plans for the reconstruction of Louvain the duke ordered the rebuilding of several churches which had been damaged during the revolution, and in 1448 the town began to erect a new and magnificent town hall, resembling in style the halls of Bruges, Brussels, and Ghent. This striking example of the late Gothic style fortunately escaped destruction when the German armies burned Louvain in August 1914, at which time the historic university library went up in flames. As all the world knows, a new library building was erected by contributions from America according to plans made by Mr. Whitney Warren and his associates. Today this is in ruins, the victim of a second ruthless war.

Toward the middle of the fifteenth century, when the reconstruction of Louvain was going forward, it was natural that the news of these building projects should spread to every town in the Low Countries. Artists, architects, sculptors, woodcarvers, *ymagiers*, as well as carpenters and masons, packed the tools of their craft into little satchels, or wooden chests, and started for Louvain in search of employment.

Among those who came, about the year 1450, was a serious young Dutchman from the city of Haarlem, named Dirk Bouts. He was born sometime between 1415 and 1420, which would make him about thirty when he went to Louvain to open a workshop there. He already had a reputation as a painter. One old chronicler speaks of a painting by Bouts in Haarlem as "an exquisite picture, painted with infinite care." This comment might well stand for all of this master's work, for he was a conscientious workman with respect for his art.

He was a bachelor when he left Haarlem, but he did not stay so long. The first information we have of him in Louvain records his marriage with Catherine van der Bruggen. Her family had considerable standing and she brought her husband a substantial dowry. The entry in the town archives calls her "*mettengelde*," which means "with money." It would seem that Dirk was a provident Dutchman who found it just as easy to fall in love with a rich girl as with a poor one. The couple had two sons, who became painters like their father; and two daughters, who proved the family's piety by becoming nuns.

In 1464 Bouts set to work on an altarpiece, which occupied him for four years. It was ordered by the Confraternity of the Holy Sacrament for their chapel in the Church of St. Peter, one of the religious edifices then being reconstructed in Louvain. The confraternity asked for contributions to pay for making the altar. It is amusing to note that donations then were very much like donations for such purposes today. A citizen gave a *florin du Rhin;* a good woman, who declined to give her name, offered a half crown for the making of the altar; Bouts was paid on account. . . . The commission given to Bouts was signed by four masters of the confraternity and the actual receipt for payment for this great work, written in old Flemish and in Dirk Bouts's own hand, has been preserved:

"*Ic, Dieric Bouts, Kenne mi vernucht on wel betaelt als van den werc dat ic gemaect habbe den Heilichen Sacrement*

[I, Dirk Bouts, consider myself satisfied and well paid for the work that I have done for the Holy Sacrament]."

Shortly after Bouts started this altarpiece he was appointed painter to the town of Louvain. In his official capacity he was obliged each year to march in the Procession of the Holy Sacrament at the kermess. It is reported that he never missed one procession during his years in Louvain. As he marched down the cobblestoned streets, it is likely he carried himself with great dignity and moved with the angularity of many of his painted figures. Very likely, too, he held his candle carefully straight, so that no wax would drip on his beautiful robe, the cloth for which was allowed him each year by the town with an additional grant of ninety *pleken* for a lining. After the procession, like all the other officials, he received an allotment of Rhine wine. One feels sure that he did not drink this all at once, but conserved it thriftily, drinking a little each day, giving a small portion to his wife, and permitting his children to share it with him only when they were of a proper age to take wine.

After the death of his first wife, in 1473, Bouts married Elizabeth van Voshen, the widow of a butcher, who seems to have brought with her a portion not less substantial than that of Catherine van der Bruggen. Bouts lived only two years after this marriage, dying on May 6, 1475. At the time of his death he was engaged on a commission for the new town hall of Louvain—four panels commemorating the judgment of the Emperor Otto. Only two panels were partially completed. The work had not been paid for, and the burgomasters of Louvain summoned the painter Hugo van der Goes, dean of the painters' guild of Ghent, to appraise the value of Bouts's work on them. As a result of his judgment, the master's widow received the sum of 300 florins of the original price of 500 florins for the completed work.

Above all else, Bouts was a true burgher craftsman. He served the town of his adoption loyally and honestly, filling the commissions given him and living up to the responsibilities and requirements of his position. As one seeks to understand him through his pictures, it becomes apparent that he was a good family man, with very real piety and deep sentiment which his northern reserve could not altogether hide. Though Bouts's fame was great in his own day and during the sixteenth century, his pictures were passed over by art critics during the seventeenth and eighteenth centuries when the lavishness of Rubens and van Dyck was loudly acclaimed. People were slow to admit that this stolid and reserved old master was one of the great figures of the flowering of Flemish art.

Bouts's style of painting seems to have passed through three periods in its development. As a young man in Holland, he could have known the work of van Eyck, who was at The Hague between 1422 and 1424. After coming to Brabant, Bouts seems to have been touched by the style of van der Weyden, then regarded as the leading master of the Low Countries. But toward the last years of his life, Bouts seems to have moved out from the influences of other painters. He became more relaxed, as though he were developing a greater tolerance toward human nature. He seems to have

DIRK BOUTS. WEEPING MADONNA. Private collection, New York (14¼ x 11)

PLATE 63

LAST JUDGMENT. Rheims   LAST JUDGMENT by van Eyck

XV-CENTURY ILLUMINATION   LAST JUDGMENT by van der Weyden

ROGER VAN DER WEYDEN. The Braque Triptych. Louvre, Paris

Plate 64

WEEPING MADONNA by Bouts   SORROWING CHRIST by Bouts

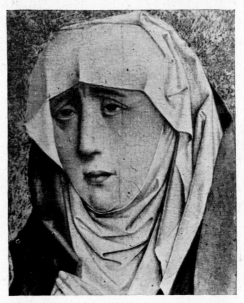

LAMENTATION by Bouts   FRENCH MASTER, XV CENTURY

DÜRER   EL GRECO

PLATE 65

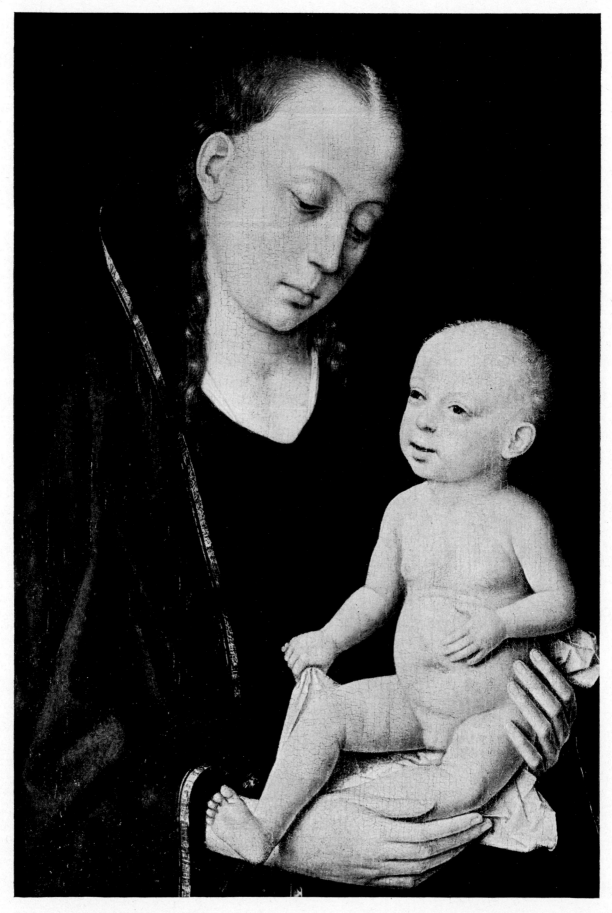

DIRK BOUTS. MADONNA AND CHILD. Private collection, New York (9⅞ x 6)

PLATE 66

felt life with greater tenderness. As life slowly begins to slip from the grasp of the great artist, he inevitably seizes upon its larger meanings. One may call this maturity; philosophers call it the wisdom of a full life. It is a noticeable quality in Bouts's *Last Supper* and in his *Adoration of the Magi* which he painted in his later years.

In PLATES 65, 68 comparisons have been made between the work of Bouts and van Eyck, Bouts and van der Weyden, and Bouts and van der Goes. The pictures represent only a small portion of what can be a lengthy and fascinating study. The work of Bouts shows by these comparisons a masterful restraint, calmness, and serenity. The true spiritual greatness of the Master of Louvain lies in the fact that his art seems, unquestionably, to be the supreme expression in painting of the faith of the last centuries of the Middle Ages.

Van Eyck was too rich, too conscious of the material world, too worldly to attain perfection of sentiment. Van der Weyden was too nervous and too exalted. His figures, especially in the drama of the Passion, approach the theatrical in their action. Van der Goes was wanting in qualities of peace and a balance of sentiment. Memling was too soft, too sweet; Bosch, too personal, gloomy, and pessimistic. Bouts was the one man in the Flemish school who translated with a kind of perfection the serenity of a soul bathed in the flooding words of the *Imitation*—the book which is the perfect blossoming of the most serene conception of Christianity that has been given to the world.

When one compares a *Madonna* by Bouts with one by van Eyck, it is at once apparent that the two masters approached this subject by opposing paths. The Madonnas painted by van Eyck are richly dressed and seated upon splendid thrones. The type is that of a well-fed, rather unspiritual, middle-class woman dressed in the robes of a princess. There is a lack of divinity in her character, and she, like the master who painted it, seems concerned with the beauties of this world. The Madonna type of Bouts, by contrast, is simple, calm, and radiant. Bouts seems to feel under no necessity to clothe the Mother of his Lord in rich and stately garments; for him it is enough that she is the Mother of God's Son.

THE BLUE MADONNA

In this picture, which is scarcely larger than the palm of a man's hand, Bouts attained the height of religious devotion and sentiment (PLATE 66). This is the simplest and most unpretentious of all the Flemish Madonnas; all that remains of the resplendence of the theme of the Queen of Heaven is a tiny gold edging on Mary's blue robe. She has no halo and no jewels. Her hair falls in simple plaits, brushed back from her high, sensitive forehead. She has the youthful bloom of a peasant girl who has spent her life walking beside the quiet canals and across the green fields of Flanders.

She holds the Child tenderly with quiet hands, protecting the soft little body from the wool of her mantle by a white cloth. There is peace in her downcast eyes, and docile obedience to the tremendous mission to which she has been called. There is also a kind of predestined strength and a radiance which is not of this earth.

The Christ Child, like all the infants painted by the Flemish masters, is ugly. One feels that He will grow into the suffering Christ. Nevertheless, He has a winning alertness which captivates the observer in spite of His angular posture.

This little devotional picture is pervaded with silence. In itself it is as much a prayer as a picture.

THE WOMAN OF SORROWS

It is revealing of the spirit of Bouts to compare an interpretation of lamentation by him with the same emotion described in paint by van der Weyden and by van der Goes (PLATE 68). The tragedy of Calvary provided the Middle Ages with a dirge, and the artists who composed upon this theme evoked many variations of the mood. The sadness of the event was yet filled with hope for devout Christians. In calling up a feeling of pity for Mary, the Woman of Sorrows, the theme had universal appeal.

In PLATE 68 a detail of the heads of Christ and Mary by van der Weyden has been reproduced beside a similar detail from a painting by Bouts. In the former representation Mary weeps with wild despair and an uncontrolled emotion that borders on the hysterical. This interpretation derives directly from the impassioned writings of St. Bridget, one of the great medieval mystics.

To Bouts this wild lamentation was an impossibility. For him the heartfelt beauty and pathos of the scene lay in a depth of spiritual grief, not in its outward demonstration. As he shows Mary holding across her lap the body of her dead Son he paints a woman wrapped in the overpowering silence of intense sorrow. She does not move, and she is possessed only of limited gestures.

In a picture of the entombment Bouts has filled his actors with the same kind of unutterable remorse and sense of loss. It is revelatory of Bouts's mind to contrast this scene with the mourners in a similar picture by van der Goes. Here one of the Marys throws her hands in the air; two others caress the nails of the Cross, and the man who thrusts the nails toward them seems to cry out in vengeful anguish.

To understand Dirk Bouts's approach to the sufferings of Mary it is interesting to compare his interpretation of this theme with that made by van der Weyden. In the latter's *Descent from the Cross* and in his *Crucifixion*, Mary gives way to wild grief and passion (PLATES 56, 61).

In his *Weeping Madonna* (COLOR PLATE 62) Bouts rises to a height of perfection and understanding that could come only with the simple piety and sentiment of a humble Christian craftsman.

This Madonna is the consummation of the religious sensibility at the end of the fifteenth century. Unlike van der Weyden's grief-stricken Virgins, she seems to have restrained her emotion, and for that reason she is more appealing and more deeply moving. She is timeless, like human suffering.

To the faithful of the fifteenth century, the Madonna was not only the Mother of Christ who died on the Cross, she was also the Mother of all suffering humanity. She was the one who understood and has ever endured throughout the ages.

This ideal was the one most beloved by the women of Flanders, who found in her the personification of all the tears that women's hearts can hold.

The origin of the theme of the Weeping Madonna goes back to the early representations of the Last Judgment of which we find so many examples in art; in the sculptures of the tympanum of the French cathedrals like that at Rheims (PLATE 64). Later this subject was selected by many painters, as by van Eyck in his *Last Judgment* in the Metropolitan Museum (PLATE 64).

The theme became very popular, always showing Christ judging men and Mary and John kneeling before Him and asking mercy for them.

In PLATE 64 we find an amusing example of the influence of the Mystery Plays on religious iconography. In the illumination of a fifteenth-century manuscript (PLATE 64) we see Mary seated beside Christ. The reason for this change is due to the fact that the Mystery Plays of the Last Judgment lasted several hours. The most beautiful young woman of the community was usually chosen to play the role of Mary. It was impossible to keep her kneeling for so many hours, and very politely the old playwriters decided to seat her on a chair beside Christ. The painters, seeing Mary seated beside Christ in the plays, pictured her as seated.

Roger van der Weyden in his *Last Judgment* remained faithful to the old composition (PLATE 64). Later on, in the Braque triptych of the Louvre, he

represented only the three principal personages—Christ, Mary, and John. There we find a striking likeness in the *Weeping Madonna* of Bouts to the *Interceding Madonna* of van der Weyden.

When you compare the *Weeping Madonna* of Bouts with his picture of Mary lamenting over the dead body of her Son (PLATE 65) in the Louvre, you realize that it is very likely that Bouts combined the idea of Mary at the Last Judgment interceding for sinners and the idea of Mary lamenting over the body of her Son. From this combination of ideas Bouts produced this theme of the Madonna praying for humanity and weeping, not over her Son, but for all the misery and sadness of the world.

This theme enchanted the dying Middle Ages and was indefinitely repeated later on in Flanders as in other countries. However, it never again reached the greatness of Bouts's composition and weakened itself by being repeated so often, as for instance in the *Madonna* of Dürer (PLATE 65) and of Joos van Cleve (COLOR PLATE 34).

The *Sorrowing Madonna* of El Greco, which completes this group of Madonnas, is still great, because El Greco succeeded in transmitting a portion of his mystic spirit into this painting.

THE VISITATION

There exists in the Prado at Madrid a polyptych which portrays the events of the Gospel from the Annunciation to the Adoration of the Magi. One panel which depicts the visit of Mary to Elizabeth (PLATE 70) is particularly interesting, especially as a contrast to the master's more mature creations.

In this early example of the style of Dirk Bouts one finds much of his characteristic serenity. He paints a glorious Dutch landscape, with the house of Zachariah high on a knoll in the hill country, raising its pointed Flemish gables above the misty horizon into a fair blue sky. Even in his earliest work, Bouts filled his panels with that human compassion that is the special merit of his art. As a painter of luminous atmosphere and ever-rolling landscapes he has perhaps no rival in the Flemish school. The figures in this early work have a solidity, even a peasant squatness, which Bouts was to give up as he grew older. It is interesting to compare these figures with those in the *Judgment of Otto* panels—a comparison which tells much concerning the development of Bouts as a painter.

THE *JUDGMENT OF OTTO*

To decorate the Hall of Justice in their new and magnificent town hall, the councilors of Louvain

DIRK BOUTS. The Judgment of the Emperor Otto. Brussels Museum (*127 x 71*)

Plate 67

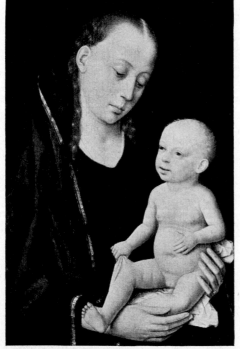

DIRK BOUTS. Madonna and Child   VAN EYCK. Madonna and Child

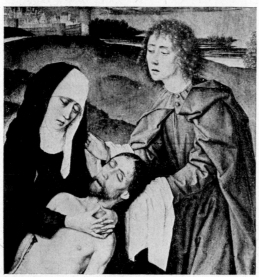

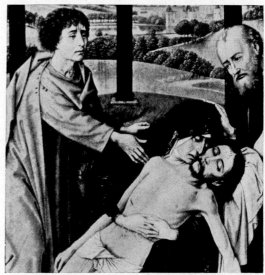

DIRK BOUTS. Louvre, Paris   VAN DER WEYDEN. Granada

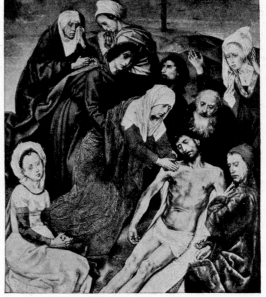

Entombment   Lamentation
DIRK BOUTS. National Gallery, London   VAN DER GOES. Vienna

Plate 68

DIRK BOUTS. Last Supper. St. Peter's Church, Louvain (70⅛ x 58⅞)

PLATE 69

DIRK BOUTS. The Visitation. Prado, Madrid (*31 x 21¾*)

Plate 70

commissioned their painter to make four panels based upon the legend concerning the judgment of the Emperor Otto (PLATE 67).

These panels are representative of Bouts's later style. The height of the figures is extraordinary, especially compared with the short, stocky forms the master painted earlier in his life.

There has been much speculation concerning the reason for Bouts's increasingly elongated figures. It could well be an effort toward greater spirituality and a more lofty, symbolic meaning. This solution is in keeping with the personality of the master as this is revealed in all his pictures. As Bouts grew older, he became more detached from the material world and more at home in a realm where all was dream and symbol. In Bouts one feels a serious and irresistible force, compelling him to express the religious soul of the expiring Gothic world.

It would seem that there is always a deep, secret instinct inspiring men to elongate the forms whenever they have sought to express something divine in the shape of man. The sculptures of Moissac, or of the Royal Portal, and the enigmatic angel with the sundial at Chartres demonstrate what men do when they want to let the enthusiasm of their souls sing in stone. The whole Gothic style, with its soaring spires and flying buttresses, bears the same witness.

Between the two extremes in the style of Dirk Bouts manifested in the Visitation and the Judgment panels there is a period of equilibrium.

THE *LAST SUPPER*

This picture, according to the contract made with the master, occupied all the creative energies of Bouts for four years. It has remained to this day in the chapel of the Confraternity in the Church of St. Peter in Louvain. Four wing panels made their way into German collections and were sold to the museums of Berlin and Munich. A special clause in the Treaty of Versailles enforced the complete restoration of the altarpiece.

Bouts's *Last Supper* (PLATE 69) is the finest expression composed upon this theme ever to have been painted in old Flanders. The quiet panel is in great contrast with Leonardo's emotional fresco at Milan. The two pictures are fundamentally unlike in theme. It would seem as though Bouts was determined to portray the scene with a realism that would be instantly recognized by all the simple good people in Louvain. The disciples gather around the homely table; their seating follows the ordinance laid down by the Mystery Plays, which invariably placed Judas opposite Christ, with his back to the

audience. The Savior is portrayed a little taller than the others. The moment which Bouts has chosen to commemorate is that in which Jesus, "having taken bread, He gave thanks and broke it, and gave it to them, saying, 'This is My body, which is given for you; do this in remembrance of Me.'" Leonardo chose for his moment the dramatic utterance of Jesus: "Behold the hand of him who betrayeth Me is with Me on the table." The two pictures, therefore, are quite different in significance and in feeling.

Special notice must be given to the flood of warm light which fills the room. The composition is most regular for a Flemish painting; notice how all the lines meet at a vanishing point directly above the head of the Savior. There is a tradition that the servants who appear in the picture are portraits of the masters of the confraternity, who ordered the painting. And the two small boys who stare curiously, as schoolboys do, at the solemn scene, are pointed out as portraits of the master's two sons.

Bouts has his place among the great masters, not only for his genius for color, for the harmony of his tones, for his new interpretation of landscape, which in his pictures lives a life of its own and tells its own story, but especially for having translated into painting the spirit of the Imitation of Christ. As one studies carefully his *Last Supper*, which at first glance appears cold, stiff, and dogmatic, a quality of peace comes from it to the observer. Soon one feels the enchantment of its subdued warmth and its artless sincerity. Even the woodenness of the gestures of Christ has the same hieratic quality that is found in all the work of men since the beginning of the world when they had endeavored to express divinity in a human form.

In a way, without knowing it, it seems as if the old Bouts were moving toward the crossroads where all religions meet and unite, because they represent man's earnest effort to know the reason for life, to find the explanation for sin and suffering, and to discover new reasons for wider justice and mercy. He speaks the same message as that given by the mysterious author of *The Imitation of Christ*.

By two things a man is lifted up from things earthly, namely, by Simplicity and Purity.

Simplicity ought to be in our intention; Purity in our affections. Simplicity doth tend towards God; Purity doth apprehend and taste Him. . . .

If thy heart were sincere and upright, then every creature would be with thee a living mirror and a book of holy doctrine.

There is no creature so small and abject that it representeth not the goodness of God.

Hugo van der Goes

ONE WONDERS what impression was made on the widow Elizabeth Bouts by the strange and moody painter who was summoned from Ghent to appraise the two panels left unfinished in her husband's workshop at his death. In this connection see PLATE 67.

At that time, which was in the year 1475, Hugo van der Goes held the office of dean in the painters' guild at Ghent. Little is known of his early life, though a record in the archives of Louvain gives Ghent as his birthplace. It is believed that his family was poor and his early life full of struggles and hardships. He was inscribed as a free artisan craftsman with the painters' guild of Ghent on May 5, 1467, and in the following year he was appointed an underdean of the guild. We know that he was employed on the decorations for the marriage of Charles the Bold in Bruges, in 1468. After that it would seem that he returned to his native town, as he held office in the guild there until Christmas 1475.

In the following year Hugo resigned his deanship and retired from the world to become a member of the religious community of the Red Cloister at Roodendaal, near Brussels, where his brother Nicholas was a lay monk. Of his life in the cloister we have more detailed information than we possess concerning his life in the world. From the diary of Brother Gaspard Ofhuys of Tournai comes the most direct account of Brother Hugo during the five or six years he spent at the Red Cloister:

I was a novice when van der Goes entered the convent. He was so famous a painter that men said that his like was not to be found on this side of the Alps. In his worldly days, he did not belong to the upper classes; nevertheless, after his reception into the convent and during his novitiate, the prior permitted him many relaxations more suggestive of worldly pleasure than of penance and humiliation, and thus awakened jealousy in many of our brethren, who said, "Novices ought not to be favored, but kept down." Often noble lords, and among others the Archduke Maximilian, came to visit him and admired his pictures. At their request, he received permission to remain and eat with them in the guest chamber. He was often cast down by attacks of melancholy, especially when he thought of the number of works he had to finish. His love of wine, however, was his greatest enemy; and of wine at the guest table there was no limit. In the fifth and sixth year after, he had such an attack of melancholy that he would have laid violent hands on himself had he not been forcibly restrained by his friends. They brought him under restraint to Brussels and so back to the convent. . . . When the prior saw that Hugo was struck with a mental sickness and that he did not cease to avow his eternal damnation, suspecting that Hugo was struck with the affliction that had tormented King Saul and recalling how he was appeased by David's playing on the harp, he allowed music to be made in the presence of Brother Hugo and to add other recreations of a nature that should dominate the mental trouble of the painter. In spite of it all, van der Goes did not get better and persisted to proclaim himself a child of perdition. . . .

People are rarely in accord upon the origin of the malady of our lay brother. In the opinion of some it was a kind of frenzy, in the belief of others he was thought to be possessed of the devil. He was preoccupied to excess with the question of how he was going to complete the works which he had to paint, and that, as it was said, he should scarcely be able to finish in less than nine years. As he was a man of the same nature as others, by the honors rendered to him and the homages that he received, his pride became swollen. God, not wishing to let him fall victim to it, put upon him this infirmity which really humbled him in an extreme manner. He himself, as soon as he felt better, understood this, and diminished his excesses; he aban-

HOLY FAMILY by Hugo van der Goes. Brussels Museum ($12\frac{3}{4}$ x $15\frac{3}{8}$)

PLATE 71

doned by his own free will our refectory and modestly took his meals with the lay brothers.

Brother Ofhuys has some anatomical opinions on the causes of Hugo's malady:

By an excess of imagination he was given to reveries and preoccupations, and he had been afflicted by that in a vein close to the brain. There is, in fact, as one says, in this region a small and delicate vein dominated by the creative power and reverie; when the dreams are too frequent this vein is tormented; if it is so troubled and wounded that it bursts, frenzy and dementia are produced.

In view of what is known of the general attitude toward mental illness during the Middle Ages, and medieval therapy for psychological disorders, it becomes clear that the prior of the Red Cloister was an extraordinary and wise man in his handling of poor Brother Hugo. He might have followed the custom of the time and sent his mentally ill charge to the shrine of St. Dymphna at Gheel, near Antwerp. St. Dymphna, an Irish princess who was beheaded by her heathen father in the year 600, was the patroness of the insane. Victims of all sorts of mental disorders used to be brought to Gheel and boarded out in the town, where it was hoped the influence of the martyr, whose bones reposed in the church in a magnificent reliquary, would effect a cure. It is still the custom to send those suffering from mental disorders to Gheel for a cure, where the Belgian Government maintains specialists in mental illnesses and hospitals for mental patients.

It is not without interest that the fifteenth-century prior should have experimented with the effect of musical harmony on a disordered mind—a form of therapy which is engaging the interest of present-day psychiatrists.

From the little that we know of van der Goes's youth, and from the testimony of Brother Ofhuys, it seems not unlikely that the painter suffered from dementia praecox, that malady which selects its victims among the brilliant and gifted, whose early manifestations are extreme conscientiousness and the tendency to overwork at the expense of physical strain. Van der Goes's record as a member of the painters' guild at Ghent proves how seriously he took his responsibilities and how conscientious he was in fulfilling them. His later anxiety about his work, the feeling he was unable to do all that he had undertaken to accomplish, his withdrawal from the society of others to seek seclusion, and perhaps the sense of security which he lacked within himself, in the cloister, as well as the alternating states of excitement and melancholy from which he sought escape

through alcohol, all point to the diagnosis of dementia praecox.

No one can doubt that he suffered intensely. The great works he has left are his monument; from them we know him and his powers. Whereas Bosch penetrated the universal spiritual miseries of his time, and van Eyck sought to penetrate the mystery of daily realities about him, van der Goes was concerned with a very personal spiritual examination of persons and events. The pathos of Calvary, the wonder of Bethlehem, the sorrow of the Dormition of the Virgin—these were his dramatic scenes which he interpreted psychologically. It is in the meaning of posture and physiognomy, not in shapeliness and grace, that his power lies. In revealing the psyche, he surpasses the vigorous but more formal van der Weyden, who was his only rival in the realm of drama. He had all the attributes of a true painter—a man of large and undivided vision, who suffered acutely and whose sufferings made him sensitive to all the emotions of humanity.

Many theories have been advanced to explain why van der Goes during the year 1476 decided to enter the monastery at Roodendaal. It is not known whether he ever married, and one theory advanced to explain his retirement is that of a disappointment in love. Another, no less fanciful, theory is that the young painter, studying van Eyck's *Adoration of the Lamb* in the Cathedral of St. Bavon, was overcome by the feeling that he could never equal the great Jan, and so, in disappointment, retired to a monastery. As one studies the pictures of van der Goes the latter theory seems most unlikely. Half a glance at his work proves that he in no way struggled to be Eyckian in his thinking, but constantly strove toward larger and more freely painted conceptions. He was far too competent a craftsman to fret himself about the successes of his predecessors or his contemporaries. He enjoyed high repute during his life in the world, was elected to the highest position in his guild, and, as we know from Brother Ofhuys, was sought out by "noble lords," who appreciated his genius. The man whom Tommaso Portinari selected to paint the altarpiece for his family chapel had no reason to feel himself a failure or to suffer qualms of inferiority.

No, neither of these theories adequately accounts for van der Goes's retirement from the world. One feels that in the cloister he sought peace for his sorely troubled spirit, relief from the loneliness that besets sufferers from his disease, and inspiration for the work to which his life was dedicated.

Of his last years we know no more than Brother Ofhuys has told us, but he was the most famed painter of his generation whose influence on the Florentine painters, through the Portinari altarpiece, was profound. The epitaph on his tomb reads:

*"Pictor Hugo van der Goes humatus hic quiescit
Dolet ars, cum similem sibi modo nescit*

[The painter, Hugo van der Goes, buried here,
rests in peace,
Art mourns, for she knows not his equal]."

MADONNA AND CHILD WITH ST. ANNE

According to the chroniclers, van der Goes painted a great number of pictures during his term as dean of the guild and before he entered the cloister. Of these only a very few have survived. Nor is the exact sequence in which he painted these pictures known. The little *Madonna and Child with St. Anne* (COLOR PLATE 71) may be a work of the master before he reached maturity. For lack of evidence to the contrary, and because this painting appears to be very much in van der Goes's style, it must be assumed that it is his.

In this little panel, which is in the Royal Museum at Brussels (PLATE 71), the charm is that of intimacy and family love. The theme of the Madonna and St. Anne was very popular during the fifteenth century, especially among women, who saw in it the exaltation of family life. Even the attitude of the monk, who was the donor of the picture, speaks of simple faith in purity and childlike innocence, not of awe of the Savior of the world.

St. Anne sits upon the wall of the enclosed garden, symbol of virginal purity. She looks upon the Child with a fondness suggestive of all doting grandmothers. Mary leans against her knees, supporting her Child upon the older woman's lap. As mother, she appears more critical, yet not less loving of the Child. The gestures of all the figures are filled with tenderness, and the hands—always the supreme glory of the art of van der Goes—are subtle, yet most demonstrative. These are Gothic gestures, full of the peace and wonder of the medieval soul. The hands of the friar are in the same posture and in the same mood as those drawn by Albrecht Dürer some twenty years later—perhaps the most famous hands in prayer in all art.

THE *ADORATION OF THE MAGI*

This magnificent picture (PLATE 76), which was probably painted by van der Goes before he retired from the world, was formerly one of the treasures of the Benedictine Monastery at Monforte de Lemos in the Asturias in northern Spain. In 1914 it was bought for the Kaiser Friedrich Museum in Berlin. The picture has a greater calm than is found in any of the master's other large works. In mood, it compares to the same subject in the Columba altar by Roger van der Weyden, but its difference from that work lies in its intense three-dimensional clarity. The king in the center of the picture sounds the keynote of calm and veneration, and his hands indicate the reverence that pervades the whole scene. From the foreground backward, through a rush of space, there is an intense feeling for distance. It does not halt or falter; it marches with a measured pace set so strikingly by van Eyck in his *Madonna of the Chancellor Rolin.*

In the master's interpretation of the so frequently painted scene Joseph drops upon his knees, awed, one feels, by the arrival of the three resplendent kings. He does not fully understand their presence at the manger, and his hands fumble self-consciously at his own poor garments. Mary is in full possession of herself; calmly and gracefully she presents to the Magi the solemn little Child upon her knees. Her left hand tenderly guides her Son's hand to make the sign of benediction. The Child alone gazes out to meet the eyes of all who look upon the picture.

The three kings are dignified yet reverent. One is about to take a chalice from his kneeling squire and to set it before Him who was to spill His blood into the Holy Grail. There is an old legend which said that the third king was a Moor, and in van der Goes's painting the youngest Magus appears to be a son of Africa. If so, this is one of the earliest appearances of the type in northern art. His lavish robe and pointed shoes recall the same figure in van der Weyden's Columba altar. Although not in appearance, the two works have much in common; yet there is a prouder reverence in this *Adoration* by van der Goes. The master has added grace notes to his magnificent work—the lilies behind the wall and, in the foreground, the delicate columbine springing from the rocks.

THE PORTINARI ALTAR

Tommaso Portinari was well established in his lucrative and influential position in Bruges when he saw fit to commission the master of Ghent to paint an altarpiece for the hospital of Santa Maria Nuova in Florence. One does not doubt that the shrewd Florentine considered carefully in making his choice, and that he selected Hugo van der Goes because he was well persuaded of this master's genius and of his ability to produce a picture worthy to hang in the city of Giotto, Botticelli, Fra Angelico, and Masaccio. Nor was he disappointed.

Hugo van der Goes, through this one picture (PLATE 73), would have attained greatness. Ranking

VAN DER GOES. Portinari Altar. Tommaso Portinari with His Two Sons
Antonio and Pigello, St. Thomas and St. Anthony Abbot.
Uffizi Gallery, Florence (97 x 53)

Plate 72

HUGO VAN DER GOES. Portinari Altar.

PLATE 73

THE NATIVITY. Uffizi Gallery, Florence (*37 x 118*)

HUGO VAN DER GOES. Portinari Altar. MARIA PORTINARI WITH HER DAUGH-
TER AND ST. MARGARET AND ST. MARY MAGDALENE. Uffizi Gallery, Florence (97x53)

PLATE 74

with the most sublime expression of all Christian art, the *Adoration of the Shepherds*, which is the central panel of the Portinari altarpiece, holds an unchallenged place in the realm of mystic realism.

Folly once led a small man, who wrote many books on art, to say that in order to be great an artist must produce many as well as good works. The reply to this is the reminder that *more* of anything is not equal to *much* of that same thing. In this altarpiece Hugo van der Goes has done much, and has done it superbly.

Before the most humble folk of the fields—shepherds and neatherds—breathed upon by the warm, fragrant breath of the beasts of the stall, in a manger, upon a bed of straw lies the Child who represents the great universal truths. They are the truths which, though often forgotten, are the foundation of moral conduct in the entire Western world. Later, these truths are to be witnessed and acknowledged by the great ones of the earth, symbolized by the three kings. They are to win the apostles, to challenge the power of Rome on Calvary, to endure with ever-increasing power through all the centuries to come. But here, in the stable at Bethlehem, they are revealed first to the poor and lowly, not by chance, but because this is a part of the divine plan for the redemption of the world.

It is an enchanted land that van der Goes envisions; the dramatization of a tale, told over and over again with elaboration of detail by the devout peasants of Flanders. The little angelic messengers have fluttered in from the starlit night. There is a dancing movement from the lower left and the lower right of the picture where the angels are gathered. Their draperies, heavy when at rest, in the air are weightless as gossamer. One of the loveliest little angels, with wing tips raised high, descends to join two of his fellows who adore at the end of the manger. They are of another world—the world in which little children feel at home, yet no one doubts their reality. They are as real as the faithful and simple St. Joseph, the good man into whose life this tremendous miracle has come. St. Joseph and the shepherds are the simple, hard-working plain folk of whom Mary sang in her *Magnificat:*

He hath put down the mighty from their seat, and hath
    exalted the humble and meek.
He hath filled the hungry with good things; and the
    rich he hath sent empty away.

And how eagerly, with what intense curiosity, the shepherds come running from the fields to peer in at the miraculously illumined manger, amazed, incredulous, awe-struck. Before their eyes the gates of Heaven are opened, the Word is made flesh. Here is that first Noël celebrated in innumerable carols which have come down to us from the singing fifteenth century in which van der Goes sang his "*in excelsis gloria.*"

Mary, the mother of God's Son, is serene and grave. She is not surprised by the angels though she, by her dress, belongs to the common people. She wears no crown, no jeweled robe, nor has she need of a halo to attest her sanctity, such as the saints on the wings of the altarpiece wear. Her motherhood makes her radiant.

The story of the Portinari patronage unfolds on the shutter wings of the altarpiece. To the left, the banker with his two little sons, Antonio and Pigallo, kneel reverently, under the surveillance of St. Thomas and St. Anthony, abbot. St. Thomas gazes afar off, as though doubting the virtue of the financier, who has invoked his intercession before the throne of God. After all, what rich man would not be slightly disconcerted to have the apostle, who questioned Christ's wounds, look into his record?

The irascible old abbot of Padua clasps his bell and leans heavily upon his crutch. His watch over the two small Portinari boys is like that of a severe schoolmaster (PLATES 72, 74).

On the opposite wing the donor's wife Maria, born Baroncelli, and her demure, well-behaved little daughter kneel under the direction of their two patronesses, St. Margaret and St. Magdalene. The Magdalene holds up her long, flowing draperies and lifts her jar of precious ointment. She, like St. Margaret, is beautiful and gravely remote. Their sanctity is revealed in their elongated figures, which remind us that van der Goes had just started work on this altarpiece when he was summoned to Louvain to see the two Otto panels of Dirk Bouts. Van der Goes's two saints, like the figures painted by Bouts, are far removed from the short, stocky Flemish types painted by other masters of the school.

Behind the donors and their saintly patrons the master has painted a landscape as real as anything of this earth and as ideal as anything in poetry. In the full light of open air and every day saints and mortals appear before the miracle of the Nativity. They gaze reverently upon the earthly arrival of Him who is their Lord. They seem to ask in the words of the French poet of their day:

Dost thou in a manger lie,
    Who hast all created,
Stretching infant hands on high,
    Savior, long awaited?
If a monarch, where thy state?
Where thy court on thee to wait?

Royal purple, where?
Here no regal pomp we see;
Naught but need and penury;
Why thus cradled here?

Van der Goes reminds the rich and worldly Portinaris that from those to whom much is given of this world's treasures more is expected than is expected of the poor shepherds. He reminds Tommaso Portinari that it is in the company of the humble and lowly men of the fields that he, the financier and the politician, must answer the sounding of the last trump (PLATE 75).

When one compares this conception of the Flemish master with the fresco which his contemporary, Benozzo Gozzoli, painted on the walls of the chapel of the Medici Palace in Florence, the contrast is almost overwhelming. Gozzoli used the procession of the three kings to do homage at the manger in Bethlehem, to exalt the prestige of the Medici. The Adoration of the Magi becomes an occasion for the display of the Medici's wealth, power, and magnificence. Van der Goes, the mystic, sees in the Nativity the birth of the idea of the brotherhood of man—that idea which had acted as a leaven on the thought and the way of life of the people of his native Flanders. It was these ideas, so powerfully presented by him, quite as much as the master's style, which brought the painters of Florence to study with unstinted admiration the altarpiece which Tommaso Portinari sent home from the Low Countries. Here in the city of Cimabue, Giotto, and the great masters of Tuscany the Flemish spirit spoke its vigorous message of democracy and humility. The message of St. Francis, which had traveled northward over the Alps to be received in the hearts of the Flemings, was sent back to Italy by van der Goes to inspire artists and laymen alike.

ADAM AND EVE

During his years in the city of Ghent, van der Goes must have gone many times into the Church of St. Bavon to study van Eyck's tremendous interpretation of the apocalypse. It is therefore interesting to compare van der Goes's painting of *Adam and Eve* (PLATE 38) with the figures of man's first parents portrayed by van Eyck. From these works it becomes apparent that Flemish painters of the fifteenth century studied the nude human body with no less and no more interest than any other phenomenon of nature. The masters treated the nude with the same direct and unembarrassed realism as they used in approaching other subjects.

Van der Goes's Adam and Eve, however, are not isolated symbols like the Adam and Eve of van Eyck. To van der Goes, the Temptation is an intimate family scene in which the first man and the first woman are brought together in a little paradise surrounded by the shrubs and trees that grow in the Low Countries. Here again we see the iris and the columbine, the flowers which it would seem van der Goes loved beyond all others. Eve has already taken and bitten into one apple. Finding its taste to her liking, she is about to pluck a second fruit for her spouse. She does not seem in the least concerned by her act of disobedience, whereas the more thoughtful Adam seems to hear the warning voice of his own guilty conscience. Neither Adam nor Eve appears disturbed by the lizard with a woman's head, who encourages them to the act of disobedience. This type of devil appeared frequently in the art of the fifteenth century, when it was not at all uncommon to give Satan female features, bearing out the teaching of certain theological writers that feminine charms were the root of all sin. These invidious tempters, half beast, half woman, appear in many of the Gothic carvings and tapestries, reminding the men of the north to beware of woman's wiles and her fascination.

The simplicity of the scene is in part deceptive, but this is quite intentional on the part of the master. With his own tragic sense of the inevitable, there is no doubt he saw in the fall of man the design of fate. The observer suddenly awakens before this picture and finds himself shaken by van der Goes's adamant and brooding certainty of man's dark destiny. His Adam and Eve are every man and every woman. They are of yesterday, today, and of tomorrow.

THE *LAMENTATION*

Van der Goes's *Adam and Eve* is one panel of a diptych, the other half of which is filled with a deeply moving *Lamentation* (PLATE 35). Taken together, as obviously the painter intended they should be viewed, the two pictures tell the story of the coming of sin into the world, its ultimate consequence, and the redemption of the world by the One who was without sin. Here is a tremendous subject, which has filled many hundreds of thick volumes, presented completely and dramatically in two very small wooden panels.

Just as much can be learned about each of the great Flemish masters by comparing their interpretations of the Madonna and of the Woman of Sorrows, so much is revealed by their individual approaches to the great subject of the Crucifixion.

The deep melancholy which enchained Hugo van der Goes's own spirit fills this picture. It is built

HUGO VAN DER GOES. Detail of the Portinari Altar. HEAD OF A SHEPHERD. Uffizi Gallery, Florence

PLATE 75

HUGO VAN DER GOES. Adoration of th

Pl

Friedrich Museum, Berlin (58 x 96¾)

HUGO VAN DER GOES. DORMITION OF THE VIRGIN. City Museum, Bruges ($48\frac{1}{2}$ x $46\frac{5}{8}$)

PLATE 77

upon a downward double diagonal of anguish which is suddenly broken horizontally by the stiff form of the dead Christ. The two corners of the grouping are weighted, as if by a prophet and a sibyl, with the calm and monumental figures of Joseph of Arimathaea and Mary Magdalene. Neither of them regards the scene, but, as though they have seen and understood enough, they now are a reflection of grief. As in all van der Goes's pictures, the hands of the figures are extremely expressive.

The man who thrusts the horrible nails toward the other mourners is filled with hatred for those who have crucified his Lord. Only a genius, such as Hugo van der Goes was, could have seized upon this mingling of human emotion—the love for the dead Christ and hatred for the instruments which caused his death—and made it live forever. The woman who flings her arms wildly in the air does not represent a profundity of grief, but—and this also must be put down to the credit of the painter—she is pitifully human. It is not given to all to lament as do the central figures in this monumental painting.

Over all fly the ominous black vultures, adding their note of horror to the scene on Golgotha.

DORMITION OF THE VIRGIN

This striking and dramatic picture (PLATE 77), which hangs in the museum of Bruges, is generally believed to be the last work of Hugo van der Goes. If so, it was painted at the Red Cloister and at a time when the master was undergoing great torment of spirit and disintegration of personality. One feels these things in the picture, as well as the penetrating, psychological analysis in the master's study of the twelve apostles. Compared with the childlike interpretation of the same subject by Petrus Christus, van der Goes's last work seems to belong to another era.

It was painted for the Abbey of Notre Dame of the Dunes. The subject itself is not common in Flemish painting, lending itself better to narrative drama than to the painter's art. This may be why van der Goes's *Dormition* is almost unique, being the second known example from the Flemish school,

and the most dramatic. The twelve apostles, who have been miraculously transported from the four corners of the world, are gripped by real anguish. Their grief is an electric charge, drawing their faces and gestures together into a unity of pathos. It is the same grief, but it has a variety from character to character which makes for an unending fascination as we study face after face.

The picture is not easy to read because the foreground is too low and the background too high. The bed lies almost crazily upstage. One feels the tormented spirit of the painter crying out because he has so much to say and so little time in which to say it. He is a long, long way from the master who created the Portinari altarpiece, with its eternal calm and its concern with unchanging values. He is a sick, lonely, self-distrustful man, striving desperately to express some of the anguish which fills his own soul as he feels the imminence of death.

The apostles painted by Petrus Christus seem serenely sure of the Assumption of the Virgin. Those of van der Goes reflect his own fear of the hereafter. Their lament comes directly from Brother Hugo's own heart. The Virgin alone is calm. She already sees the vision of Christ appearing to receive her soul. But the apostles, like poor Brother Hugo, are still in the dark valley of uncertainty. To them the Assumption is as yet an unrevealed secret. They sorrow as those do who cannot penetrate the unknown. Mary knows the joy of being welcomed in Paradise; they know only that she whom they loved and revered is dead. As a craftsman and as a mystic, Hugo van der Goes was essentially Flemish and essentially of the Middle Ages. The luminous and atmospheric spaces of his works are filled with tensions that are passionately religious, and which form themselves into logical and yet mystical drama. There is in his work the story of great suffering and of great exaltation of the spirit. The pictures he has left reveal a man who scaled the heights and plumbed the depths of life. To lament as he did is a catharsis of the soul. To adore as he did is an exaltation.

Hans Memling

According to the record of Memling's death, entered in the archives of the Cathedral of St. Donatian in Bruges, he was born at Mainz, or, probably, in the near-by village of Memelingen. For many years it was believed that he studied under Roger van der Weyden. Vasari and Guicciardini both say he was a pupil of the town painter of Brussels. Today, however, it is very seriously questioned whether Memling ever knew van der Weyden. There is no actual proof to substantiate the legend that the young German painter aided van der Weyden in the completion of his Columba altarpiece.

Aside from the record in the Church of St. Donatian, which links Memling with the Rhineland, the style of his paintings would seem to indicate that he was influenced to a certain extent by Stephen Lochner, the great master of the school of Cologne. That Memling knew Cologne seems certain from his accurate rendering of the partially completed choir of the cathedral, which he makes the background for the martyrdom of St. Ursula on the famous shrine.

Our knowledge of this master's life begins when he bought a house in Bruges around 1465. About that time he married Anna van Valkenaere of Bruges and became a citizen of the Flemish city.

Legend has it that Memling fought with the army of Charles the Bold at the Battle of Nancy in 1477. It is said that a certain "Jean Hemmellinck" returned from that disastrous engagement sorely wounded, and fainted on the doorstep of the Hospital of St. John in Bruges. The nuns nursed him back to health and, so the story goes, "when the spring had driven the leaden clouds of winter from the sky" the rehabilitated soldier took up his brush to paint an altarpiece and several other pictures for the chapel of the hospital. This legend, which seeks to account for the fact that Memling painted a number of pictures for the Hospital of St. John, including the marvelous reliquary to contain the bones of St. Ursula, is so romantic that one is tempted to accept it without inquiring further. As a matter of fact, the painter had been established in Bruges for almost fifteen years before the Battle of Nancy, and it is not at all likely that he was of the age or the temperament to meet the military requirements of the duke's army. It seems more probable that Memling, like other skilled craftsmen of his day, accepted commissions from the religious orders or from patrons who wished to make an appropriate offering to such a worthy institution as the Hospital of St. John.

Three years after the Battle of Nancy, Memling's name appears in a list of the two hundred and forty-seven richest burghers of Bruges, which would seem to indicate that he was well paid for his work. He had acquired three houses on the Vlamingdam, in a quiet quarter of the city where artists have chosen to live through all the centuries since Memling had his workshop there. Three sons—Hans, Cornelius, and Nicholas—were born to the painter and his wife. Anna Memling died in 1487. Her husband survived her until August 11, 1494, when he was buried in the cemetery of the Church of St. Giles.

One imagines him taking a quiet stroll along the Quai Vert, enjoying the view of the old buildings of the inner town; then down the narrow, twisting streets which have changed not at all since his day, loitering on one of the high-shouldered bridges across a canal, studying the reflections in the still water; walking more briskly along the Street of the Golden Hand and rounding the corner of the old Gothic Church of St. Giles where he would ulti-

HOC·OPVS·FIERI·FECIT·MARTINVS·D·NEWENHOVEN·ANNO·DM̃·1487

MADONNA OF MARTIN NIEUWENHOVEN by Hans Memling. St. John's Hospital,
Bruges, Belgium (17⅝ x 13⅛)

PLATE 78

mately be buried. No other painter is so closely and intimately identified with Bruges as this German who became so enamored of the Flemish town that, once he became a citizen there, he never left it, and who caught the spirit of Bruges so completely that for five hundred years his work has stood as a symbol of its serenity and charm.

Studying the art of Hans Memling, it becomes apparent that he was influenced to some degree by van der Weyden, whether he ever studied under that master or not. He lacked van der Weyden's sense of drama but he had—what van der Weyden lacked—a great feeling for nature. He was not so brilliant a colorist as van Eyck or Dirk Bouts and, though his technique was in the solid Flemish tradition, his sense of composed design was not so strong as that of the earlier and less decorative masters. He was drawing near to the time when conviction and purpose were to run thin in the Flemish school, due to the advancing tide of the Renaissance. However, he resists this better than does his follower, Gerard David.

One of Memling's claims to fame as a religious painter is his universal appeal to the little people. His art proves that Michelangelo's criticism of Flemish painting as a form of art which pleases women, nuns, friars, and devout persons is a compliment, and not a slur. Memling found a worthy and popular mode of expression within the milieu of his own time. He claims his place with those artists who find that simple realities of nature and faith are sufficient to fill a lifetime of creative work.

The criticism that Memling lacked imagination and had a rather mechanical way of working in his religious compositions is untrue of his landscapes, and especially untrue of his portraits, for it is as a portrait painter that he attains the height of his powers. Though not the intellectual and caustic penetrator of character van Eyck was, Memling is, in his own way, quite as great a portraitist.

His people do not live isolated lives; they seem to belong to groups and to represent whole sections of society. This ability to round off the sharp edges of a personality came in part from the fact that Memling painted toward the close of the fifteenth century, at a time when the individual was beginning to lose his sense of integral security within the great scheme of things. As the bounds of the then known world were extended, and as men also became increasingly aware of the history of mankind, the portraitist began to see in his sitters types of humanity. Memling, though belonging to the Middle Ages, feels the influence of this rising humanism. He tries, and succeeds, in giving his portraits a men-

tal alertness, deliberation, character, and thoughtfulness. They continue to live as individuals.

The Memling portrait is a superb example of saying the right thing about somebody. It is not over-specific to the point of being too curious or too sympathetic. Memling never bores his observers with petty details of cost, profession, or income. No critic, no matter how astute, could look at one of these panels and remark shrewdly: "Obviously this man was a lawyer whose name was Jan Smitte and he made an income of 5,000 guelders a year." It is the type of soul that characterizes the faces of Memling's portraits, and it is upon the inner life of these men and women that he based his interpretation of their personalities.

Typical of Memling's portraits is an imposing head in a narrow framework, clearly illumined in contrast to the heavier, darker chest area which forms a bustlike base. His subjects appear as though seen through a window of life. The margin of the frame cuts close and even crops off parts of hats and shoulders. This pressure of the frame gives a feeling of being pinched, a sharp contrast to the space which van Eyck put into even his smallest panels.

In many of his portraits of men the faces are framed in a growth of luxuriant curly hair which takes up a large part of the panel. The head is always seen in three-quarters view. Whereas the Italians made profiles, the northern Memling knew that the carved outline reveals less of spirit than does the modeled bust; and he knew that the bust should not be obtrusively frontal. The truly pleasing portrait never looks directly at the observer, nor does it look entirely away from the observer. The one form seems rude and presumptuous; the other, vague and unconcerned.

Memling usually paints at least one hand as if resting upon the ledge, or frame, of the lower margin. Thus he confirms the well-known fact that personality is revealed less through the configuration of the body than through the shapes of heads and hands. Memling's hands do more for his portraits than do the fingered designs of van der Weyden, the complacent hands of Bouts, or the demonstrative extremities of van Eyck. Memling inherits just the proper fraction of van der Goes's dramatic ability to make his hands expressive.

Memling's ability as a landscape painter has already been mentioned; in his portraits, this ability is a singular achievement. The opening up of a luminous horizon beyond the dark mass of the head not only provides the portrait with a pleasant vista, but tends to open out and expand the little milieu into a general and large one. Memling's men and women belong to the world, not to a narrow room.

There is a comfortableness about the open-air portrait. To place man before the open sky is a compliment to his destiny on earth; whereas to surround him with the appurtenances of his daily life is to lower him to the commonplace. Memling was never guilty of this fault. Even young Martin Nieuwenhoven, praying in his room, has behind him two open windows through which one looks one way across a bridge with people passing over it and the other way over treetops to a distant town.

In Memling's *Portrait of a Man with a Coin* (COLOR PLATE 83), the coin may be considered as a bit of storytelling detail on a par with the stained-glass panel showing St. Martin sharing his cloak with the beggar in Martin Nieuwenhoven's portrait. These things which seem like formulas and which make a pattern for portraiture are actually a system of composition.

The *Man with the Coin* (PLATE 83) was long thought to be the picture of Niccolo di Forzori Spinelli, the Florentine medalist who for some years was at the court of Charles the Bold. In recent years research has thrown some doubt on this, though the portrait is obviously that of an Italian gentleman.

The face harmonizes well with the delicate charm of the landscape background. The horseman, wearing a red cloak and riding the white horse which appears in so many of Memling's backgrounds, has drawn rein at the brink of the water to watch the swans. Far away, on a little hill, is a fairy-tale castle. Above this landscape is the luminous, cloud-filled sky of Flanders. One feels the touch of the breeze and the moisture which it brings from the sea.

The interesting *Portrait of Maria Portinari* (PLATE 5), in the Metropolitan Museum, New York, shows a woman of some importance and considerable pride. Memling has painted a more worldly aspect of the banker's wife than van der Goes saw, though the likeness is unmistakable. Her dress and necklace reveal her as a woman of fashion and authority in her world. Probably she was an exemplary housewife who managed her family and her household with great efficiency and success.

The companion portrait of Maria's husband shows him praying, as she is shown (PLATE 4). But though his hands are folded devoutly, Tommaso Portinari seems more intent on his rates of interest than on the state of his soul. This characterization of the head of the Medici "factory" in Bruges is all the more interesting in view of what we know of his business life; and what certainly Memling, like

every citizen of Bruges, knew. This story will be told in due course in connection with the altar of the *Last Judgment*, by Memling, in which he painted the naked and shivering soul of Tommaso Portinari being tried by the avenging angel.

Another portrait of an unknown man is intense in the quality of inner life (PLATE 82). Here, one feels, the master has found the perfect subject for his art. There are rare instances in Memling's work where an equilibrium is so finely balanced that the style seems inevitable. This picture has this quality of inevitability. The man portrayed is not good-looking, but he has a well-chiseled face. He is not yet middle-aged, and he seems not unacquainted with suffering, but he has found a peace in life which many older men might envy. Memling gives no clue as to who or what he is, any more than to say: "Behold a man!" A clear blue sky pales as it drops toward the horizon. Little orchards and meadows, between a castle and a village, stretch away to the calm sky. There is just enough of everything in the right place and with the right emphasis to make a beautiful composition. The master touch is the two fingers and the thumb of the man's right hand showing just above the lower margin. This hand does not pray or busy itself with papers, coins, or flowers; it simply echoes the intent expression of the face. In every sense the portrait is dynamic; one feels that this man could speak or act at any moment. This portrait of an unknown man is not a happy picture, but it is timeless, calm, and full of repose.

THE NIEUWENHOVEN *MADONNA*

This *Madonna with the Red Apple* (COLOR PLATE 78) expresses all the tenderness and dreamlike quality that one associates with Memling and with Bruges. It is rich and radiant. Mary is more a Princess of Heaven than a queen; she wears a pearl-studded fillet above her high, broad forehead, not a crown. Through one window one looks across a landscape where Memling's familiar red-cloaked rider on a white horse gallops across a green meadow. The stained-glass panel above this window shows St. George slaying his dragon. The other window has the Nieuwenhoven coat of arms, and below this, on one of the half-open shutters, hangs a little convex mirror in which one sees the reflection of Martin Nieuwenhoven venerating the Madonna in his own chamber.

The Christ Child is more appealingly childlike than many of those painted by earlier Flemish masters. Memling somewhat overcame the faults of the earlier masters in painting babies.

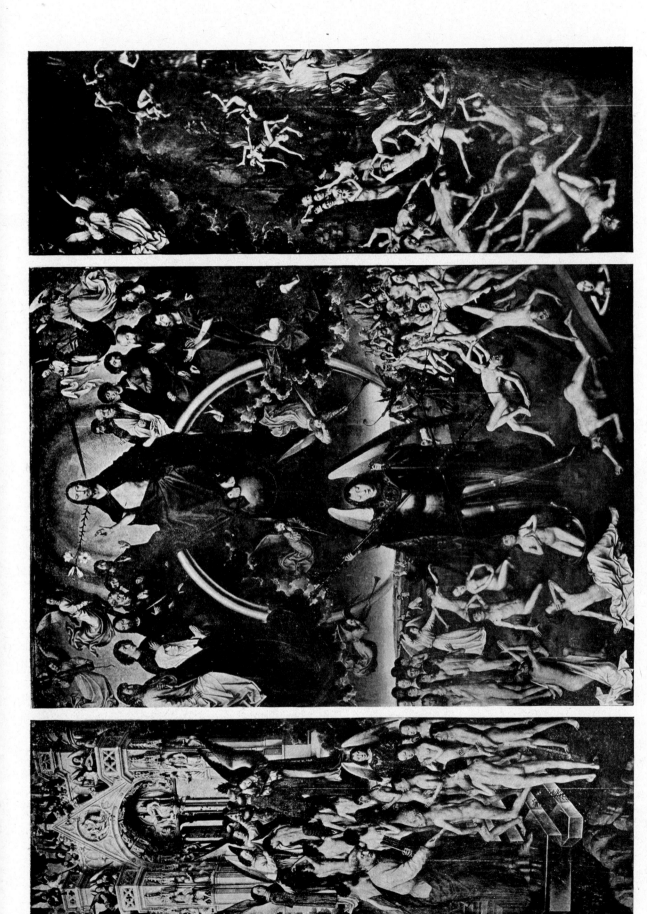

HANS MEMLING. Last Judgment. Marien Kirche, Danzig. Courtesy Frick Art Reference Library (87 x 62¾ – 31)

PLATE 79

HANS MEMLING. The Shrine of St. Ursula

Plate 80

Six Details of the Shrine of St. Ursula. St. John's Hospital, Bruges (33¾ x 12⅞ x 35⅜)

PLATE 81

HANS MEMLING. PORTRAIT OF A MAN. Private collection, New York (*12½ x 9*)

PLATE 82

THE *ANNUNCIATION*

This picture, now in the Lehman Collection in New York, formerly belonged to the Radziwill family in Russia (PLATE 23).

In his approach to this great religious theme, Memling shows the sweetness which was to be characteristic of his follower Gerard David and of other painters of the Renaissance. The picture falls short of the Nieuwenhoven *Madonna*, but it is splendidly made from a technical point of view.

There is a playfulness in the little angels who lift the long folds of the Virgin's robes, and even in the relationship of the two main figures as they bend and sway. One feels no awful solemnity about them, though the figures of the Virgin and of the archangel are elongated.

Memling holds true to the medieval tradition of painting a flower very prominently in the foreground of his *Annunciation*. According to M. Emile Mâle, "The doctors of the Middle Ages, as the chief of whom we shall quote St. Bernard, held that the Annunciation occurred in the spring *au temps de fleurs*. He (St. Bernard) believed he had proof of this in the name Nazareth, which means 'flower.' Accordingly, St. Bernard presumed to say: 'The Flower wished to be born of a Flower, in a flower, at the time of flowers.' "

This belief blossomed in a multitude of flowers of every sort in the stained-glass windows of many thirteenth-century churches throughout Europe. By the end of the thirteenth century it had become customary to indicate the time and place of the Annunciation by a single flower in a vase somewhere near the Virgin. It was the painter—not the Church—who selected a lily for this purpose. Thus the lily became not only the symbol of spring but of the purity of Mary—as we find it in the works of the fifteenth-century painters.

THE *ST. CHRISTOPHER ALTAR*

The triptych which Willem Moreel, head of the grocers' guild, commissioned Memling to paint is one of the master's most successful religious pictures (PLATE 36). The saintly giant, carrying the infant Christ on his back, is flanked by St. Maurus in his abbot's robe, reading a book, and by St. Giles, whose hand caresses the wounded doe, which, according to legend, came to him to be healed. In a cave in the rock behind St. Maurus appears a tiny figure of a hermit, leaning on a stick, with a lantern in his hand. The heads of the three saints are remarkably fine. In St. Christopher's eyes one reads bewilderment as he looks up at the Christ Child, as though asking why one so young and so small should weigh so heavily upon his shoulders. The rocky landscape behind the figures, with the reflection of the cliffs in the stream and the cloud-filled sky above them, reveals Memling at his best.

The wings of the altarpiece carry the portraits of Burgomaster Willem Moreel with his five sons, and his wife Barbara Vlaenderberghe with her eleven daughters (PLATE 37). The burgomaster is presented to the infant Christ and to St. Christopher by his own patron, St. William, who appears as a crusader with steel gauntlets and helmet, carrying a banner. The saint looks anxious, as though a trifle uncertain whether his namesake will be found acceptable; but the burgomaster apparently suffers no qualms of conscience. His mouth is firm and his eyes steady, fixed upon St. Christopher and the holy Child.

Of the five sons who kneel behind their father, only the eldest seems fully aware of the solemnity of the occasion. His junior is slightly less reverent, while the three much younger boys are frankly and humanly curious, even amused by their vision of the miracle. These five faces could have been painted only by a master who was deeply understanding of small boys and their characteristics. Indeed, after five hundred years the entire Moreel family still live dramatically in the wings of this altarpiece.

Behind Willem Moreel and his sons is an interesting group of buildings beside a canal which suggest the wharves and warehouses where the ships from the East, bringing spices and sugar, unloaded their aromatic cargoes. The head of the grocers' guild at Bruges drew his wealth and his prestige among his fellow citizens from the packets of precious peppercorns, nutmegs, and the baskets of cinnamon sticks brought from the Spice Islands to Bruges to be transshipped to England and to the ports of the northern Hanse.

Barbara Moreel is sponsored by her patroness, St. Barbara. Her eleven daughters are grave, well-behaved damsels, testimony to Barbara Moreel's maternal discipline. If she appears slightly more anxious than her husband, it is no more than must be expected of a mother with so many daughters to find husbands for. One daughter, presumably the eldest, is a Dominican nun and another, judging by her headdress, is already married. But there are nine little girls, with smooth, round, high foreheads and neatly combed hair, to be provided with dowries and trained in the housewifely arts after the Flemish tradition. One does not doubt that Barbara Moreel's prayers, like those of many another careful Flemish mother, are concerned with the welfare of her children.

THE *LAST JUDGMENT*

In Danzig there is a large picture of the Last Judgment, full of wonderful detail that has been attributed to Memling (PLATE 79). The history of this altarpiece is adventurous, to say the least.

It was ordered by Angelo di Jacopo Tani, who was the representative of the Medici at Bruges, and his wife, Catarina Tanagli, for their mortuary chapel in Florence.

In 1464—about the time Memling settled in Bruges—Jacopo Tani made his annual journey to Florence to render his financial report to his employers. During his absence, his junior partner, Tommaso Portinari, took occasion to discredit the senior partner with Cosimo de' Medici and to complain that Jacopo Tani showed too little confidence in his junior's business judgment. This was one of a number of steps Portinari took to oust his senior partner from the Bruges office. When Jacopo Tani was ordered to London two years later, to set in order the affairs of the Medici branch in that city which had become sadly tangled during the wars between the Lancastrians and the Yorkists, Portinari slyly pushed his campaign against his partner and succeeded in making a new contract with the Medici which gave him authority over their affairs in Flanders. Jacopo Tani came back to Bruges, after two years in London, to find himself ousted from his position. King Louis of France, learning that Jacopo Tani was planning to return to his native Florence, called him to Tours and offered him the post of Minister of Finance, which Jacopo Tani refused on the ground that he could neither read nor write French, and that he was too old to learn. He died a few years later, during an epidemic in Florence.

In view of these facts, it is amusing to discover that the tiny, naked, kneeling figure which Memling has placed in one half of the scales held by the angel of the Last Judgment undeniably represents the soul of Tommaso Portinari. The likeness of the face to Memling's later portrait of Tommaso Portinari and to the portrait of the same conniving businessman by Hugo van der Goes is extraordinary. Portinari is represented here being tried in the balance, and not found wanting. His soul weighs down one third of the scales while the writhing figure of a sinner in the opposite scale endeavors vainly to show as much solid worth. Clearly this representation of Tommaso Portinari was intended as a subtle compliment to the donor's junior partner, and it seems most unlikely that Jacopo Tani would have asked to have this compliment paid his associate had he then known of Portinari's machinations against him. Portinari may have taken an ironic delight in this portrayal of his soul, ordered and paid for by the man whose job he was scheming to secure. And it is a tribute to Jacopo Tani's character and appreciation of a work of art that he permitted the picture to stand as the master painted it, and did not record his new and bitter knowledge of Portinari's true character.

In 1473 the altarpiece was shipped in a galley that sailed from Bruges for Florence. The vessel was due to call at the port of London to take on more Medici cargo. In the English Channel the galley was seized by Paul Bennecke, a captain of the North German Hanse, and towed to Danzig, where it was turned over as a dividend to the pirates. There, in that great seaport of the north, the triptych intended for a chapel in faraway Florence has remained through five centuries.

Surely a more delightfully ingenuous conception of the sounding of the last trump has never come from a master's brush. From Christ, carefully balanced upon a floating sphere, emanates a sword of righteous wrath and a lily of peace. With one hand He blesses, with the other He condemns. He is surrounded by the twelve apostles, with Mary and John the Baptist. Angels, bearing the symbols of the Passion, and other angels blowing clarion calls on long trumpets, wing across the sky.

On earth, the archangel Michael, in a complete suit of Burgundian armor, tries the souls which rise from the graves, and on one side of the picture those found wanting are being driven by black vampire devils toward the open mouth of hell. The souls of the damned are shown tumbling into the bottomless pit of flames while an angel looks on, sounding a mournful note on his trumpet.

On the opposite side of the picture, the redeemed move in a delightful procession toward the steps which lead up to the Gothic portals of Heaven. The figure of St. Peter, clasping his key in one hand and with the other shaking hands with each newly arrived soul, is a gesture of naïve imagination, as are the angels on the upper steps of the staircase who form a sort of polite receiving line. In order that the souls of the saved shall not enter Heaven nude and ashamed, the angels at the door fit each entrant with appropriate garments.

One may imagine that the soul whom St. Peter greets so hospitably and who bends his knee respectfully before the apostle is that of Angelo di Jacopo

PORTRAIT OF A MAN by Hans Memling. Antwerp Museum, Belgium ($11\frac{5}{8}$ x $8\frac{1}{2}$)

PLATE 83

Tani himself. If so, he has advanced nearer the gate of Heaven than his junior partner.

In this picture, with its intense faith and its theology, one feels the impact of the Middle Ages. It is doctrinal, and it meets all the demands of a medieval altarpiece in that it is packed with instruction which stresses the advantages to be gained through living a godly life and the horrible consequences of sin.

THE SHRINE OF ST. URSULA

It seems inevitable that the legend of St. Ursula, one of the most charming and fairy-tale-like of all the legends of the little saints, should have engaged Memling's art. Of the Flemish masters of the fifteenth century, he was pre-eminently the one whose nature fitted him to immortalize the adventures of the young princess of Brittany who led her eleven thousand virgins to Rome and then home again as far as Cologne, where they all suffered martyrdom.

The reliquary is one of the treasures of the Hospital of St. John, and one of the most precious works of art in the city of Bruges. The sides of the shrine, which is a miniature Gothic chapel, contain six episodes in the story of the saint. On one end St. Ursula appears holding a palm, the emblem of martyrdom. Her great cloak shelters all her little virgin followers. At the other end of the shrine are paintings of two nuns, sisters of the Hospital of St. John.

In the six narrative panels along the long sides of the shrine the drama of the saint's life is unfolded, episode by episode. This series of pictures, which are so full of storytelling, might be considered a medieval conception of a motion picture; but here it is not the picture which moves before the observer's eyes, it is the observer who moves around the shrine, following the successive scenes of the drama. Such a form of presentation makes for suspense—that most necessary ingredient of successful storytelling. The effect is quite different from that produced by a panel picture in which the whole is seen at once (PLATES 80, 81).

No small amount of the popularity of this famous shrine results from its fairy-tale quality. The master is untroubled by any need for being realistic. Even the scene of the martyrdom is melodramatic, like a scene in a play which everyone knows will have a happy ending. The little virgins shriek and hide behind the gunwales of the boats in the Rhine. The arrows are let fly by the Huns who seem, however, to take no delight in the part they are playing. On the contrary, they appear very gentlemanly and a little sad that the storyteller has required them to massacre these innocent young maidens.

One delightful fairy-tale episode relates that when Ursula and her virgins arrived in Rome, she was met by the handsome young prince of England whom her father had selected for her and who had made the journey by another route. The prince and his followers—one worthy young man for each virgin—were baptized in Rome, converted by Ursula's piety. This event so moved the Pope (according to a tale which Memling has made the subject of one panel) that he resigned his high office to follow St. Ursula himself. His cardinals refused to sanction this pious elopement with eleven thousand maidens, and struck the name of the Pope from the records, thereby making it impossible to disprove the story which so charmed Memling.

Memling's paintings tell enchanting stories. The world of Martin Nieuwenhoven, of St. Ursula and St. Sebastian, and even of the Passion of Christ, is a wistful land where tragic events happen but where there is no malice. Evil to Memling was a bad dream, and not a reality to be painted. In this he is the opposite of Jerome Bosch. Memling expresses a completely different side of the late Gothic world than does the questioning and sad old painter of Brabant.

The last century of the Middle Ages begot two gentle sons: Memling and Fra Angelico. They rendered more eloquently than it has ever been done before or since the essential *tenderness* of Christianity. Two of the greatest shrines of Christendom contain their work—the venerable Hospital of St. John in Bruges, where the nuns move silently through the many courtyards and show visitors the panels in which Memling endeavored to lift men up to Heaven; and, at the opposite end of Europe, the peaceful cloisters and dim cells of San Marco, on whose walls Fra Angelico brought a tiny piece of Heaven down to earth.

For had they not both, the Fleming and the Florentine, obeyed our Lord's injunction, and become as little children? Had not both the northman and the Latin, each with his splendid talents and gifted hands, gone unto Him Who said, "Of such is the Kingdom of Heaven"? These are the two shrines of Christendom where this spirit still lives today. Among the mists that float softly over Flanders the music-making angels atop the gable of the shrine of St. Ursula seem to reply to the blue and pink heavenly minstrels who sound their golden trumpets from the walls of San Marco out into the sun-drenched hills of Tuscany.

These angels of Memling and of Fra Angelico are the Nordic and Latin voices that chant antiphonally the eternal song of the youthful heart and the child-like soul.

Gerard David

IN 1488, while Memling was working with characteristic quiet industry in his workshop on the Vlamingdam, Bruges underwent one of its fiercest political uprisings. The Brugeois, who were never known for their patience under oppression, rebelled against the stern military government of Maximilian, the widower of Mary of Burgundy. It was only eleven years since the defeat and death of Charles the Bold, and already the tide of splendor associated with the House of Burgundy had ebbed from Bruges. Mary's Austrian husband was resented by the Flemings as a foreigner who had neither sympathy for nor understanding of their way of life.

The indignant citizens moved quickly, as their forefathers had moved to defeat oppressors at the Battle of the Golden Spurs. They staged a revolt against the Austrian forces then in Flanders and captured Maximilian himself. They locked him up in the Cranenburg, the old fortress which fronts on the great square not far from the town hall. And there they held him for ten weeks, until he sulkily assented to their plan for a Council of Regency for Flanders.

The town officials of Bruges, for all that they were determined to defend their rights, had no wish to be disrespectful to royalty. Because his imprisoned majesty found the rusty bars across the windows of his prison annoying, the city council ordered these to be given a coat of cheerful red paint. In honor of their royal prisoner they did not give the house-painting job to an unrenowned painter; they commissioned a member of the Guild of St. Luke who already was regarded as a painter of promise. His name was Gerard David.

This is the first record of David's work. Like Dirk Bouts, Gerard David came from the northern provinces of the Low Countries. He was born at Oudewater, near the old cheese-making town of Gouda.

It is probable that he learned his craft in Haarlem in the workshop of Albert van Oudewater, along with Geertgen tot Sint Jans. It seems to have been a case of a successful man accepting as an apprentice a promising lad from his own home town.

According to van Mander who, strangely enough, leaves all mention of Gerard David out of his famous *Schilderboeck*, the first and best method of landscape painting was begun in Haarlem. Bouts, who had his early training in that city, showed great feeling and skill in painting landscapes; Gerard David's work in this field, while falling perhaps short of the high achievements of Bouts and Memling, is still full of tenderness, sweetness, and charm.

We do not know what brought David from Haarlem to settle in Bruges. At the time, the Flemish city was rapidly sinking into its long sleep. The trading ships which used to drop anchor off Damme and Sluys now went on to the new great wharves of Antwerp. With the passing of the high tide of Burgundian splendor, the demand in Bruges for fine works of art had practically ceased. There was no building going on there, no tournaments or royal weddings to demand the services of painters and craftsmen. Was it, one wonders, the presence of Hans Memling that lured the young Dutchman from Haarlem to quiet Bruges? Did he come as Memling himself had come twenty years before, following the star which first glowed in the sky over Flanders when Jan van Eyck was painting in Bruges, which had sparkled brilliantly in the work of van der Goes, and which now lighted the workshop on the Vlamingdam where Memling was at work on the *Madonna* ordered by young Martin Nieuwenhoven? There is no record that David was employed in Memling's workshop, but the younger painter's style underwent a marked change soon after he settled in Bruges. The *Christ* in the Dublin Gallery recalls a similar figure in van Oudewater's

FLIGHT INTO EGYPT by GERARD DAVID. National Gallery, Washington (*20 x 13⅝*)

PLATE 84

Raising of Lazarus—the picture which caused Hemskerck to exclaim: "What did these people eat?" meaning: "These painters must have had a colossal amount of energy to have accomplished such works of art."[1] The similarities to van Oudewater's painting now disappear; David's style begins to take on the characteristics of Memling.

David became a member of the Guild of St. Luke on January 14, 1483. Five years later, shortly after his embellishment of the bars of Maximilian's prison, he was made an officer of the guild. He was to rise to the position of dean soon after the death of Memling, and to be addressed respectfully as "Maître Gheraert." Bruges, which could be so bitter against foreigners who sought to curtail the hardly won privileges of its citizens, could be extraordinarily hospitable to foreign men of genius, in business and in the arts, who lent their powers to the town's enrichment and prestige. Memling, the German, found his spirit's true home there; and David, the Dutchman, seems to have been well content. Though he left Bruges for Antwerp in his later years, he never gave up his citizenship and official residence in the Flemish town. He came home to end his days there with his unmarried daughter, who alone of his family survived him.

Like his famous countryman, Bouts, David arrived in Flanders a bachelor. Again, like Bouts, he chose a wife with what seems to have been great prudence and discrimination. He took his time about it too. Thirteen years after he was admitted to the painters' guild, David married Cornelia Cnoop, the daughter of the dean of the Goldsmiths' Corporation of Bruges. The father-in-law was rich, and the marriage assured David of a high place in the patrician society of the town. But Cornelia Cnoop was much more than a rich goldsmith's daughter: she was also a skilled miniature painter, a Flemish woman who continued the tradition of "Margriete," sister of Jan van Eyck who, van Mander records, "was famous for her painting." "Margriete" remained unwed; perhaps eligible husbands were frightened away by her cleverness. Seventy-five years later, however, masculine views about a woman's right to express herself in the arts seem to have broadened. As far as we have record, Gerard David was the first and only one of the great Flemish masters of the Middle Ages to marry a career woman.

Toward the close of the century there was a marked increase in the religious confraternities which had been a powerful factor in medieval life.

One of these lay orders, the Confraternity of the Dead Tree, held services in a small Franciscan chapel on the dunes between Damme and Sluys. It took its name from a dead tree near the chapel. Petrus Christus made a Madonna for the "Dead Tree" chapel. Only the wealthy and socially esteemed were eligible for membership in the exclusive Confraternity of the Dead Tree. It is proof that David had risen to considerable prestige that he was made a member in 1508.

The political unrest, which was fermenting when David came to Flanders, continued throughout his life. During the minority of the Archduke Charles —later Charles V—the Low Countries were governed by that remarkable woman Margaret of Austria. Margaret held court in Mechlin, which brought wealth and importance to that staid little religious town which the widowed Margaret of York had chosen for her residence after the death of Charles the Bold. Mechlin is only twenty-five miles from Antwerp, which was then riding to the crest of its prosperity as the greatest commercial city of Europe. It was Antwerp's boast that sometimes 2,500 ships might be seen riding together at anchor on the Scheldt River. Antwerp was the copper and spice mart of Europe. Here were traded the laces of Mechlin and Valenciennes; tapestries made at Brussels; leatherwork, pewter, iron of Namur; *dinanderie:* Flemish sculpture produced for Spain or Greenland; Spanish cochineal and paints, books, and engravings; out of Antwerp "lives of saints by the mile" on tapestries.

In 1515, when the Archduke Charles was fifteen years old, he came to visit his aunt and governess in the Low Countries. Antwerp accorded him a *joyeuse entrée*, which was the most splendid commercial festival of Europe. Antwerp obviously intended to outdo in splendor the great festival at Bruges in honor of the wedding of young Charles' great-grandfather for whom he had been named. It was less than fifty years since that historic occasion, and the memory of it remained with many of the rich and powerful merchants who as lads had seen or taken part in the wedding procession.

The citizens of Antwerp spent £100,000 for their folk festival, representing the triumph of art, science, and industry, supported by trade. For three weeks competitions went on between the poets sent from fourteen cities to compete with each other, followed by two weeks of matches between the poets sent from all the Flemish villages. From Mechlin came bards, who called themselves "the peacocks," in a party of 300 riders, dressed in crimson cloaks with crowns of gold on their heads. Two

---

[1] *Dutch and Flemish Painters* by Carel van Mander; McFarlane, Warde, McFarlane, Inc., New York, 1936.

by two they rode into Antwerp, a pair carrying torches alternating with a pair carrying flowers. Brussels sent 1,000 men in antique helmets, white waistcoats, white gloves, and crimson robes, with eighty ornamental floats.

The preparations for this royal welcome provided work for artists and craftsmen from all parts of the Low Countries. Just as painters from other cities had been drawn to Bruges to design the decorations for the princely wedding years before, so now the new generation of artists and craftsmen was drawn to Antwerp. Among those who went was Gerard David.

David joined the painters' guild of Antwerp, then headed by Quentin Massys, and the two men became friends. Gerard David is the link between Bruges and Antwerp in the story of painting in the Low Countries. For the last eight years that he lived, he maintained a workshop in Antwerp, though he made periodic visits to Bruges. He died in the latter city in 1523.

Gerard David's drawing is more fluid than the dissecting draftsmanship of van Eyck. The lines of his draperies are easy, and move in such a way as to give quietness to his painting. He increased this effect of quietness by avoiding diagonals in his compositions and by emphasizing a harmonious symmetry of verticals and horizontals. The quality of his coloring and the fullness of his drawing are special merits of his work. He was very fond of subdued colors—two kinds of red, a soft blue in the landscape background, and a pleasant green in the grassy meadow. He used light with a fairly high degree of contrast, thus linking himself with the painters of the early sixteenth century. He composed in plastic masses, but his sculptural instinct was very largely offset by his studied light-dark effect and his luminous atmospheric space. Like van der Weyden, he had a tendency to compose his action in the foreground planes and not fuse his compositions into the background. The art of his landscapes derives directly from the tradition of Bouts and Memling. All his work is infused with a personal sense of calm; it is as though his own contentment with life—the life of a successful, prosperous, untroubled man who has risen from humble beginnings to comfortable and respected estate—directed his brush and led him to select subjects in tune with his own nature.

THE MARRIAGE AT CANA

Among the Italian merchants who were citizens of Bruges and important in the business affairs of Flanders was Giovanni da Sedano. In 1503 Sedano joined the Confraternity of the Holy Blood, the religious society dedicated to veneration of the relic which was brought from Jerusalem in the twelfth century. Da Sedano commissioned David to paint a picture of the Marriage at Cana, the scene of Christ's first miracle. In this da Sedano is shown as the donor, kneeling with his little son to the left of the picture (PLATE 87).

To commemorate the donor's membership in the Confraternity of the Holy Blood, the wedding feast at which Christ and His mother were guests is shown as taking place in the porch of St. Basil's Church in Bruges, where the confraternity had its chapel. Through the colonnade one sees the Palace of Justice and the Cathedral Church of St. Donatian, where stood van Eyck's altarpiece, commissioned by Canon van der Pael.

In this picture of Gerard David's the composition of the figures is crowded: platters of food, jugs of wine, showy flagons clutter the scene. The painter has not penetrated the hearts and minds of the wedding guests, who seem to evince little more than a mild, inattentive interest in the miracle which has changed the water in the jugs to the finest wine. This picture is an example of the kind of art that is highly desired by collectors for its technical perfection and the beauty of its workmanship. It is, however, little more than a conventional presentation and, therefore, disappointing to those who demand of a work of art that it have meaning and function.

THE BAPTISM OF CHRIST

The role of the donor in bringing about the production of many of the great works of fifteenth-century painting has been referred to many times. One of the most interesting altarpieces from the point of view of the donor is the Baptism of Christ by Gerard David, in the museum at Bruges (PLATE 88). The man who commissioned this fine picture was Jean des Trompes, a burgher of Bruges. He appears with his little son on the inside of the left-hand wing of the altar, presented by St. John the Evangelist (PLATE 32). The two small figures shown strolling in the romantic countryside which David painted as background were added by another painter some two hundred years later. Their costumes of the seventeenth century, suggestive of characters in a drama by Molière, betray them. On the inside of the opposite wing of the altar appears the portrait of the donor's first wife, Elizabeth van der Meersh, and their four daughters. The woman's patron is St. Elizabeth. The dedication of the central panel to Christ's baptism, with the introduction

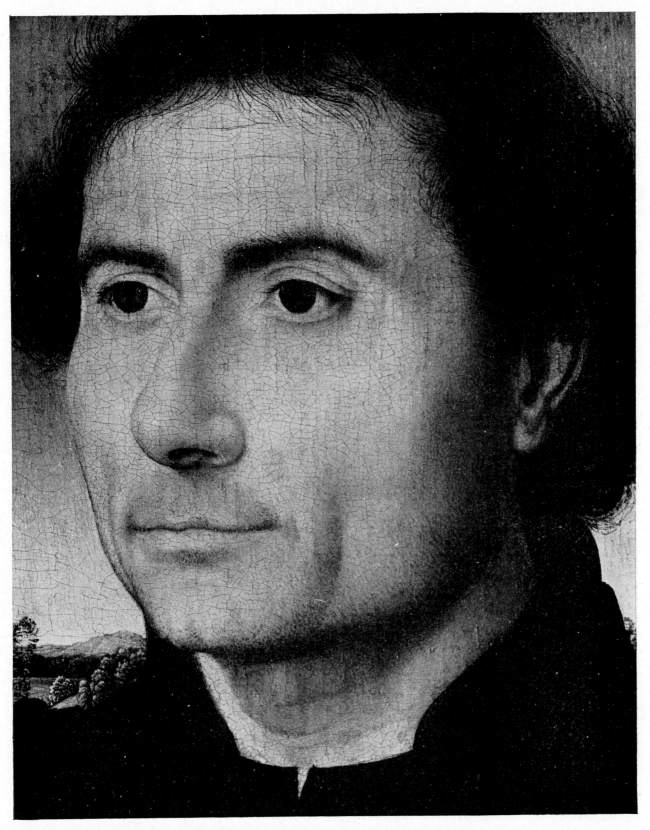

HANS MEMLING. PORTRAIT OF A MAN (*detail*). Twice original size

PLATE 85

GERARD DAVID. VIRGIN AND SAINTS. Rouen Museum (46¾ x 83½)

PLATE 86

GERARD DAVID. The Wedding at Cana, Louvre, Paris (37½ x 50)

PLATE 87

GERARD DAVID. The Baptism of Christ. City Museum, Bruges ($51\frac{3}{8}$ x $38\frac{1}{8}$)

PLATE 88

of the figure of John the Baptist, is suggested, logically, by Jean des Trompes's name.

Elizabeth des Trompes died in 1502. Her widower, with five little motherless children on his hands, soon began to think of taking to himself a second wife, and his choice fell on Magdalena Cordier. Perhaps he found himself very fond of Magdalena; at least he wished to give her and the daughter who was born to them a place in the memorial altarpiece. One wonders whether the solution of this problem was found by Jean des Trompes or by Gerard David, for it is decidedly clever. On the outside of the wing containing the portrait of Elizabeth van der Meersh, the master painted Magdalena and her daughter at prayer, with St. Mary Magdalene supervising their devotions. On the opposite wing appears a charming Madonna with the Christ Child on her knee. The representation is in the soft manner which suggests the Renaissance (PLATE 31). The Child holds a bunch of grapes, symbol of the Eucharist. David made use of the same symbolism in his *Madonna of the Flight into Egypt* (COLOR PLATE 84).

The records of Bruges reveal that Jean des Trompes was again left alone by the death of Magdalena in 1510. It is not known whether he married a third time. If he did, the third wife was, of necessity, excluded from the family altarpiece.

In the central panel, the Jordan River is no more than a tiny spring. Knee-deep in this stands a very Flemish Christ painted with the same bony angularity one sees in most of the fifteenth-century Flemish nudes. Yet His face is full of tenderness and sincerity. It reminds one of the faces painted by Dirk Bouts. This is certainly a pious figure filled with devotion continuing the medieval tradition. Of even greater religious conviction is the figure of the Baptist; in fact, one would have to search far for a more convincing action than is shown in the gentle movement of the cupped hand, poised momentarily over the head of the Savior. This co-ordinates with the motion of the left hand as it draws back the Baptist's robes from beneath the fall of the holy water. The angel who attends the scene is true to the tradition established by the Mystery Plays.

At the water's edge appear the little botanical miracles of the iris and the columbine which have become almost a tradition in Flemish art. Behind the figures stretches an endless greensward between two woods. It is flooded in the soft light of a Flemish summer afternoon which bathes and models the figures. Other distant figures move among the trees of the forest, and to the left the Baptist is shown preaching to a multitude of believers. The wonder and mystery of the enchanted forest, surrounding the source of the Jordan, touch the observer as the eye roves to the towers of a distant city. Above, on a far hill, rises a walled castle, but this reminder of worldly might is less significant than the dove which descends from God the Father. The Holy Spirit broods upon the face of nature.

It is impossible to deny the sanctity and even the sublimity of this painting made after the great period of Flemish art but still within the spirit of that art's highest tradition. One envies the joy of Jean des Trompes as he saw himself and his family so immortalized and included in David's rendering of the sacred event.

THE *MADONNA OF THE FLIGHT INTO EGYPT*

In the National Gallery at Washington is the *Madonna of the Flight into Egypt* (PLATE 84), by Gerard David, which is typical of his style. The Madonna wears a robe and mantle of blue, representing fidelity, over a rosy-red gown which appears below the hem of her mantle and at the sleeves, very much as van Eyck made the blue gown show beneath the crimson mantle worn by the Virgin in his tiny *Madonna* (PLATE 107). This change in the colors used in the Madonna's robes is due not only to the fact that at the close of the fifteenth century good blues were more easily obtainable than they had been in van Eyck's time, but also because of the development of feeling about the Madonna. As David and other painters of his time represented her, they chose to give prominence to the idea of fidelity, represented by the blue robe, rather than to the ardor of heart symbolized by the reds beloved by the earlier and more mystical masters.

In the *Madonna of the Flight into Egypt*, the Madonna is seated upon a rocky bank—all that remains of the medieval symbol of the enclosed garden—emblem of her virginity. Here, too, she offers the Child upon her lap a bunch of grapes. In the background St. Joseph, dressed like a Flemish countryman, is shown beating a tree for nuts. This idea is suggested by one of the tales in the *Golden Legend*, which tells that the Virgin, while traveling through the desert, saw a tree laden with fruit and besought St. Joseph to pick some for her to quench her thirst. He, manlike, was more conscious of the need to push on their way, to escape from King Herod's soldiers, than of Mary's comfort, and refused her request. Whereupon, according to legend, the Child commanded the tree to bow down and offer His mother its fruit, which the tree did. This tale was popular among all the European peoples during the later Middle Ages, and is found in many versions in paintings and carvings. There is a medieval Christmas carol, known as the "Cherry Tree Carol," which commemorates this little story. The carol was brought to America by the Scotch immigrants who settled in the southern Appalachians in the late eighteenth century, and is still sung by their descendants there. It has become one of the early American folk songs.

There is a prettiness in the faces of the Madonna and of the Child. Many persons have wondered why the Madonna, as painted by Bouts or van der Weyden, appears so exalted and of such spiritual beauty, when the Child in her arms is so unpleasing and frequently quite ugly. Many reasons have been suggested for the undeniable fact that the Flemish masters seemed unable or unwilling to paint babies. One reason that has been advanced is that it was the veneration of the Virgin which inspired these devotional pictures; therefore, it is the glory of the Madonna, who was to become man's intercessor at the Last Judgment, which was of the greatest significance. For this reason, she was made of finer proportions than the Child. Another explanation urges recognition of the fact that in those days very young babies were wrapped in swaddling clothes and bundled up against the damp cold of the Flemish houses. The painters were not familiar with the undressed bodies of little babies as painters in warmer countries were. This lack of knowledge of their bodies was equaled by the ignorance concerning child psychology. Most of the children of the donors of the famous altarpieces—notably the eleven daughters of Willem Moreel—seem replicas in miniature of their parents. There is very little that is childlike about them. Willem Moreel's three younger sons, by Memling, are a notable exception to this rule. When it came to painting the infant Christ, the early Flemish masters had to choose between painting a very stiff, unreal symbol of a child and one who would by its prematurely aged look and its marked unlikeness to the healthy babies of Flemish parents remind the observer that this Child was the true and only begotten Son of God. It is only when we come to Gerard David, painting at the close of the fifteenth century, that we find a realistic and charming Christ Child.

Toward the end of an epoch—and David lived at such a time—a culture tends to become more sensitive. In antiquity, it was the Hellenistic sculptor, not the classic Greek sculptor, who made beautiful babies of bronze. So, too, in Italy it was Verrocchio and not Donatello who created the dimpled little cherubs of Renaissance sculpture. In Flanders, Gerard David knew better how children sat, moved their legs and their hands, than did any of his predecessors.

These touches reduce the austerity of the true Flemish style in the hands of David, and give it an appeal which touches men of sentiment. Had he gone another step further, he would have become sentimental.

THE *ANNUNCIATION*

Probably done late in his life, the *Annunciation* by Gerard David, now in the Harkness Collection in New York, is a masterpiece of color, worked largely in cool tones against which the reds and golden lights make an impressive contrast (COLOR PLATE 25). A demure Virgin with obviously pious crossed hands kneels before a lectern. The pages of the Bible can be seen still turning within their tight binding. The rich reds of the bed hangings, usual in earlier paintings, have given way to bluish purples. The Holy Ghost descends in a radiant aura that is far more luminous than heretofore. The angel arrives in a swirl of drapery reminiscent of paintings by van der Weyden. There is a swing of movement in the figure that contrasts with the sweet calm of the Virgin. The whole scene has an elegance and luminosity that are born of a very conscious effort on the part of the master. There is a kind of planned beauty to these two joined panels that is not characteristic of the directness and simplicity of the school as a whole. This kind of arranged dramatics was known rarely before—except, perhaps, in the art of Roger van der Weyden. It is not necessarily a Renaissance quality, but it does come with the maturity of the Flemish style.

The actual condition of these two panels is excellent, and when they came to this country from the Hohenzollern-Sigmaringen Collection they commanded a terrifically high price. There is a possibility that they were not originally made to fit one against the other as can be seen by the unmatching patterns of the floor tiles. This is of little importance in considering their great technical and formal beauty, though from the point of view of content this treatment of the Annunciation is a bit overrich. It is slightly reminiscent of the style of the old Roger van der Weyden or of Memling. It lacks the robustness of van Eyck or the deep religious conviction of Dirk Bouts.

THE *VIRGIN AMONG THE VIRGINS*

In 1509, when David enjoyed the prestige accorded the leading master of Bruges, he painted an

[98]

altarpiece for the Carmelite Nuns of Sion in that city. The theme chosen was one very appropriate for a convent chapel—that of the Virgin surrounded by a number of the most popular virgin saints (PLATE 86). There is a touch of irony in the fact that David introduced his own self-portrait and the likenesses of his wife and daughter into the group around the Madonna.

Here again the holy Child, seated on the Virgin's lap, is shown holding a bunch of grapes. The saints are calm and remarkably self-possessed. They have something of the character of portraits. The placidity of the composition is remarkable, especially when compared with the contemporary work of Quentin Massys. The two music-making angels have a sweeping grace reminiscent of the sculptures of Rheims of a century and a half earlier. The larger forms of the Renaissance, combined with the dignity and reserve of these tender creatures, give the picture a classic harmony that is—even with all the sweetness and portraitlike gazes—truly impressive. It is one of the last honestly devout and religious pictures of the Flemish school.

This altarpiece, like so many of the old Flemish panel pictures, has had a somewhat adventurous history. It remained in the convent at Bruges until the end of the eighteenth century, when many of the religious orders were under pressure and their houses were closed. In 1785 the painting was sold at Brussels. It found its way into the Louvre, but in 1803 it was given to the city of Rouen and was placed in the Municipal Gallery there. At one time wings were added to David's panel and were decorated by another painter, but these have disappeared.

The course of the century has taken its way. By the time of Gerard David the fire of the Flemish style burns low. The robustness and intelligence of van Eyck, the humility and homeliness of Petrus Christus, the exaltation of van der Weyden, the anguish of van der Goes, and the serenity of Dirk Bouts have disappeared. Art is becoming decorative, yet against the pressure of man-made taste for beauty of the palette Gerard David makes a last stand. His green and blue vistas are still rich with God's inspiration. His light and figures still know the reality of mystery, and are impressed with being ineffable. Though coming short of the mark of the high calling of the masters who preceded him, Gerard David stands as a Christian artist of touching faith, tenderness, and humility. In this he declares his allegiance to the Middle Ages, though standing at the brink of the Renaissance.

Jerome Bosch

No PAINTER of the Flemish school has been so little understood and so variously interpreted as Jerome Bosch. "The droll one," he has been called, and proclaimed a satirist, painting with his tongue in his cheek as Jonathan Swift wrote. Others have protested that he is profoundly sad—a man moved by the tragic sense of life, whose deep melancholy prompted his choice of subjects and the manner of his painting. There have been those who declared him irreligious, a mocker and scorner of holy mysteries, with an unclean delight in the fantastic and macabre. And, retorting to these critics, others liken him to Savonarola, obsessed by the sense of man's sin and feeling under the necessity to remind men of the terrible consequences of their way of life.

Bosch, misunderstood, inveighed against, abhorred, laughed at, is the enigma of the Flemish school. Through five centuries he has presented the world with a mystery, at once fascinating and fearful, tempting and repelling.

Today, after the passing of more than four hundred years, the possibility of penetrating the mystery of his message seems less remote than at any other time since his paintings were completed.

As has been said, we of today are living in a period of transition between two eras, which bears a curious similarity to the period in which the medieval world came to its end and the modern world began. It was in this twilight between two worlds that Jerome Bosch lived. His oversensitive and fearful nature, which was prone to melancholy, introspection, and despair, apprehended the dissolution of the familiar world into which he was born about 1450. He foresaw the tremendous social upheavals, the abandonment of old ideals, and the setting up of new and frequently bizarre ones. He shuddered at the destruction of a world he had been taught to believe was eternal. And, like many a modern philosopher, he was filled with unrelieved pessimism concerning the human race.

The neurotic nature is satisfied to entertain its own pessimism without searching for its cause. Bosch was not neurotic. He was, in his way, an intellectual, like van Eyck. As van Eyck sought for realities in his world, Bosch hunted down the cause for the fears which filled his Gothic imagination with grotesque and horrible images. These he found in the decay of his time. Van Eyck had looked out upon his world and found it sound and good; Bosch peered from deep-set eyes upon a world which he saw full of evil. Nothing was good, honest, virtuous, or true. It was a *dies irae* which he saw and which he was under compulsion to portray. Out of this disillusionment and disgust he painted more than a score of pictures. In them, he blamed humanity for the catastrophe he foresaw. Like many modern philosophers, Bosch was afraid of what the future might bring. He had no trust in tomorrow, and he lashed out against his fellow men for their failure to safeguard for him the world into which he was born, which he believed he understood, and which he demanded should last at least to the end of his days. Bosch was a deeply religious painter, but his religion differed sharply from that of a master like Bouts—or even the melancholy van der Goes—in that Bosch missed the three spiritual graces praised by St. Paul in his Epistle to the Corinthians: " . . . and now abideth these three: faith, hope, love, but the greatest of these is love." Bosch had neither faith in mankind, hope for the human race, nor the love which throws its protection over a multitude of sins.

This lack which is in his own nature, not in his skill as a painter, makes him the saddest, and, at the same time, the most fascinating and the most baffling of all the Flemish masters who have attained fame.

HIERONYMUS BOSCH. The Prodigal Son.
Rotterdam Museum (*24½ x 24½*)

Plate 89

Fifteenth-century woodcuts of "Ars Moriendi"

HIERONYMUS BOSCH. Temptation of a Dying Man. Private collection, New York (36⅝ x 12⅛)

Plate 90

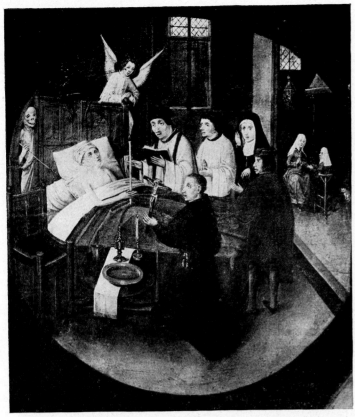

HIERONYMUS BOSCH. Death of a Man. Escorial, Spain   Fifteenth-century woodcut of "Ars Moriendi"

DETAIL of the Temptation of a Dying Man on opposite page

Plate 91

HIERONYMUS BOSCH. Triptych: The Temptation of St. Anthony. National Museum, Lisbon.
Courtesy Frick Art Reference Library (50⅜ x 45⅝ – 20)

PLATE 92

The little that we know of the life of Jerome Bosch can be put into a few lines. He was born about 1450 in Hertogenbosch (Bois-le-Duc), the old capital of North Brabant, some thirty miles from Utrecht. His grandfather was a painter and is believed to have done some wall paintings of a *Tree of Jesse* and a *Christ on the Cross* for the cathedral in the town. This magnificent late Gothic church of cut stone—one of the three most important medieval churches in Holland—was rebuilt in the first half of the fifteenth century after a fire. During the life of Jerome Bosch's father and grandfather the town had rung with the sound of the stone carvers' hammers. In the sculptures about the cathedral doors and the pillars of the lofty nave, in the carvings of the handsome choir with its chapels, the Gothic imagination found full and extravagant expression. Here, cut from stone and carved from oak, are thousands of creatures, half man and half beast, symbols of the fantastic elements in man's nature, which the Gothic imagination comprehended so amazingly and to which it gave expression, perhaps in the wholesome desire to free itself from the fears symbolized by these fantasies. It was inevitable that the youthful Jerome, the grandson of a member of the local painters' guild who had been employed in the decoration of this magnificent church, should have wandered frequently up and down the aisles. Inevitable, too, that his impressionable nature should have caught the message the older masons and *ymagiers* had left there to be read by such as he. These folk tales cut in stone were part of the childhood experience of the boy as they are of every child who is privileged to grow up in an old Gothic town.

It is not known where Bosch obtained his training as a painter. It seems probable that he never left his native Hertogenbosch. The individuality of his style and originality of his conceptions seem to prove that he was uninfluenced by the masters of painting of his time. The sources of his inspiration are found in the traditional thought of the late Middle Ages rather than in the influence of any master. At the same time, his expert technique gives rise to the belief that there may have been in Hertogenbosch at the time at least one highly skilled painter whose name is unknown, but whose fame rests in the fact that he instructed Bosch in the art of painting as this has been worked out and was practiced by the Flemish guildsmen of St. Luke.

He had so much to say that he packed his panels with figures and scenes, and his technique itself bears out the artistic fervor which inspired him. As Carel van Mander described the method of Bosch:

"On the white ground, Bosch quickly traced his whole composition with a pencil. Over the whole thing he passed a light-brown wash, and over this he painted his transparent colors." To see how dancing his touch was, it is only necessary to examine a detail of one of his pictures. Bosch's brushwork seems to make his paintings sparkle, but he did not use the same kind of deep, luminous glazes as van Eyck or Bouts. Bosch forecast the spontaneous vigor of the *alla prima* technique of the seventeenth and eighteenth centuries. In other words, in all his pictures there is an "all-at-once" effect, as though he could not hold back the flow of his ideas.

Bosch had no time to prepare careful monochrome underdrawings. If ever an artist was master of narrative detail, it was he. Even his largest works are scaled down to his astounding sense of detail. More than any of his contemporaries, Bosch sought to pull his compositions together by infinitely subtle color harmonies. Some of his works at first glance seem to be in *grisaille;* yet, actually, they are rich in color. But the range of their tones is limited to only a fraction of the complete palette of his day. His paint films vibrate with pearly iridescence—salmon and rose, light oranges, gray-greens, and enamel blues that might seem lost save in the harmony of the other tones.

We do know that between 1480 and 1516 he lived and worked in Hertogenbosch, where he was a member of the semi-monastic Confraternity of Our Lady. During the last half of the fifteenth century laymen were encouraged to join such brotherhoods, which undertook works of piety and charity and which had for their object not only doing good for the needy but the development of the religious life of the members. We know that Gerard David joined one of these confraternities in Bruges, membership in which did not prevent him from carrying on a normal life in the world. The Confraternity of Our Lady, which Bosch joined, seems to have been more strict and to have enforced on its members a more ascetic life while enjoining them to do works of charity in the world, which they were under solemn vows to reform. The members wore the tonsure, formed part of the choir in the Church, and were dedicated to work for the poor. As a member of the Confraternity of Our Lady, Bosch certainly staged and probably frequently acted in the many Mystery Plays which were given in the Church.

In a codex of portrait drawings preserved at Arras is one which is accepted as a portrait of Jerome Bosch, and which is undeniably evocative of the character of the man. The gaunt, aged face is full of vitality. The eyes under their shaggy brows seem to burn. The thin, straight lips remind one of portraits of Baudelaire. It is the mouth of a visionary and a cynic; and the full lower lip betrays the sensibility and the passion which moved Bosch and which made him a reformer.

The spirit of the reformer breathes in all his work. He is a man with a strong moral purpose, who intends his art as caustic criticism and a warning for his fellow men. His religious sense was profound, though he believed little in the goodness of man. In several of his pictures he shows God contemplating with sadness all the vices and crimes that distress the world—a world which He had created for the happiness and good of men. Many of these vices are painted with such intensity and power that they have drawn down on the painter's head the charge of delighting in evil for the sake of evil. Bosch's revelations of the blacknesses of the human soul so beguiled the morbid fancy of Philip II that he became an ardent collector of the works of Bosch. His great collection was placed in the Escorial. The walls of the King's cell there, in which he died, were covered with pictures by this extraordinary painter. A Spanish monk, Fray Joseph de Siguensa, who made the inventory of the King's pictures, wrote on the art of Bosch:

The difference which, according to me, exists between the paintings of this man and those of others, lies in the fact that the others aspired to paint man as he is externally; only he (Bosch) had the audacity to paint the inner man.[1]

Fray Joseph fell deeply under the spell of Bosch, and this led him to worry about the state of the painter's soul. He became his apologist against those who denounced Bosch as a heretic, advancing this rather naïve argument to prove the orthodoxy of Bosch's art:

I have such confidence in the piety and the soul of the King that I feel sure that if Bosch had been a heretic the King would not have had these pictures in his house, in his confidence, and in his chamber; on the contrary, all these places are filled with the work of this master.

THE *PRODIGAL SON*

The theme of the wayward soul which repents of its sin and turns to ask forgiveness of God and a chance for a new life is one which would, naturally, have interested Bosch as it has interested many other great painters. The comparison of Bosch's treatment of this theme with the famous portrayals by Dürer and Rembrandt reveals the unredeemed pessimism

[1]*Hieronymus Bosch* by Charles de Tolnay.

of Bosch's nature. Dürer selected for his famous engraving the moment of the Prodigal Son's repentance while he was in the field, feeding his master's swine " . . . and would fain have filled his belly with the husks that the swine did eat." Rembrandt chose to paint the moment when the father, seeing his son yet a long way off, ran to meet him and embrace him, manifesting his love even before the sinner could ask for forgiveness. Bosch sounds a note of despair even in the consoling parable of a sinner's forgiveness (PLATE 89).

Bosch's *Prodigal* carries with him a sense of guilt. His feet have been caught in the net, and the observer feels he will never be quite free again. Bosch has no faith in repentance or forgiveness. With a kind of puritanical righteousness, he feels that the Prodigal must be a marked man forever.

He shows him turning away from the ramshackle inn, which bears the sign the White Swan, whither his debaucheries have led him. His mistress in the doorway is already flirting with a new lover. In tattered garments, lean, bowed in spirit, the Prodigal is starting on his homeward way. Neither the other people about the inn nor the animals take notice of his going or seem impressed by his change of heart. One little dog lowers his head to growl at the Prodigal's heels. Bosch has elaborated his theme of failure and disillusionment with a number of little details— the unmated shoes on the Prodigal's feet, the pig's-foot good-luck charm, the cat's skin, symbol of bad luck,[2] and the wooden spoon hanging from his bundle. The spoon illustrates the old saying familiar throughout the Low Countries: "*die polopel hangt eem abt zide* [the wooden spoon hangs on his hip]," meaning "he is off on a debauch."

THE CARRYING OF THE CROSS

When Bosch approached the theme of the Crucifixion, he brought to it his own bitter judgment of humanity. The other great masters of Flemish painting—van der Weyden, Memling, Bouts—had seen in the Crucifixion the physical suffering of Christ and the anguish of His mother, the grief of the apostles, and, above all, the sublimity of the sacrifice made by the One without sin for the sins of the whole world.

When Jerome Bosch came to paint *Christ on the Road to Calvary* (PLATE 101), he seems to have felt acutely the wickedness of mankind which brought about the great tragedy. The menacing hate and evil which surround Christ in His last hours were so real to Bosch that he made them into a kind of nightmare. Christ, bowed under the weight of the

[2]A run of bad luck is still called a "cat's pelt" in the Flemish idiom.

HIERONYMUS BOSCH. Detail of central panel, TEMPTATION OF ST. ANTHONY. Courtesy Frick Art Reference Library

PLATE 93

HIERONYMUS BOSCH. Wings of triptych of GARDEN OF EARTHLY PLEASURES. Heaven. Hell.
Escorial, Spain. Courtesy Frick Art Reference Library (*Each 86¼ x 35*)

PLATE 94

HIERONYMUS BOSCH. Detail of Hell, Garden of Earthly Pleasures.
Courtesy Frick Art Reference Library

PLATE 95

HIERONYMUS BOSCH. Garden of Earthly Pleasures. Triptych.
Escorial, Spain. Courtesy Frick Art Reference Library (86¼ x 78½ x 35)

Plate 96

Cross, exhausted almost to the point of physical and spiritual collapse, is a man surrounded by his tormentors and unable to rise above them. His eyes are closed as though He were overwhelmed by what He has seen in the leering, taunting faces of the crowd. The executioners show a sadistic delight in the suffering of their victim. Veronica, holding her towel with the imprint of Christ's face upon it, has no kinship with van der Weyden's Magdalene bowed with anguish at the foot of the Cross; she appears to be a vain and foolish woman. The repentant thief is shown as a debauched man who remains stolid before the exhortations of his confessor. The latter is a grinning scoundrel who disgraces his monk's habit and brings to mind the Flemish saying, "He has the Devil for his confessor." At the lower right of the picture the unrepentant thief grimaces at two leering comrades. This little group of three is a conversation piece of imbecility, cruelty, and hate.

"See," Bosch seems to be telling us, "the world for which Christ suffered is full of evil, lust, and greed. These forces, active in the souls of men, crucified Him. These forces could look upon His suffering and remain unchanged to our day. This is the great tragedy. Not that Christ died, but that He died in vain."

THE *TEMPTATION OF ST. ANTHONY*

This picture (PLATES 92, 93), which is in the Museum of Lisbon, is one of the weirdest works of art which have come down to us from the Middle Ages. It is a portrayal, in extraordinary detail, of demonology; a veritable Witches' Sabbath.

The sources for the subject were available to medieval painters and engravers through the *Golden Legend*. There the story of St. Anthony being set upon by the devil and the legions of hell is told in graphic detail. When Bosch undertook to put this story into pictorial form, he elaborated upon the details given in the *Golden Legend*, emphasizing the temptations which beset the saint and creating a mad world in which inhuman creatures—half beast, half man—disport themselves like the figures in a delirium. St. Anthony, having turned from the devil, alone in this mad phantasmagoria faces squarely toward the observer. He does not see the half-hidden figure of Christ who, according to the legend, waits and watches to see how well His servant struggles against temptation. Directly across from the saint is one of Bosch's abortions—a man with head and legs but no body or arms. What this horrible creature symbolizes is not known exactly. Beside the saint is a female devil, the train of whose gown has transformed itself into a lizard's tail. A fool with a pig's snout carries the owl of wisdom on top of his head as though to make up for what his mind lacks. He carries a lute and leads a little dog, who wears the pointed cap of a jester.

There is a horrible fascination in this mad world which was opened before St. Anthony and which Bosch has interpreted with the insight of one who has himself been tormented by nightmares and the specters which rise from the unconscious. Each of these devils, like the figures in a dream, seems capable of transforming himself into something else in the twinkling of an eye. Shapes float in the air; villages burn; a troop of cavalrymen cross a dark river beside a ruined tower. A dog-snouted creature who is tonsured like a monk reads from a large book to two interested companions. Some critics consider this a performance of a black mass, but it seems more likely that Bosch has introduced here an evil creature called the Sea Monk, and described by Vincent de Beauvais.

In the central panel of the altarpiece of the *Temptation of St. Anthony* Bosch joins his fantastic world to the realistic. It is as though he reminded us that the world of madness and horror stands very close to the world of sanity; as though he reminded us that man carries within him at all times and even into holy places the grotesque shapes of his own imaginings and fears. One cannot study this extraordinary altarpiece, painted more than four centuries before the modern world accepted Freud's theories concerning the unconscious, without recognizing that Bosch, medieval mystic and painter, understood a great deal about the inner man and had drawn on this terrible knowledge in his painted sermons.

THE *TEMPTATION OF A DYING MAN*

Several pictures of Bosch dwell upon the theme of death. We know two of them were inspired by the woodcuts of a book called *Ars Moriendi* (The Art of Dying), which had an overwhelming success at the end of the fifteenth century and was meant to warn everyone to be prepared for the fateful hour which might be at hand.

In some of those pictures we see the devil urging the dying man to concern himself with what he was leaving behind—his family, his horses, his property. In another, on the contrary, we find the dying man's guardian angel struggling against the devil to interest the man in the state of his soul. The book ends by a consoling woodcut representing the forces of good vanquishing the forces of evil.

As a young man, Bosch painted such a picture in which the angels triumph over Satan (PLATE 91).

This hung in the death cell of Philip II at the Escorial, and comforted that tormented man in his last hours. Later in life, as his pessimism concerning the human race deepened, Bosch painted another, quite different version of the death of a sinner. This panel, which is only twelve inches wide and slightly over thirty-six inches long, tells the story of the death of a miser (PLATES 90, 91). This picture was inspired by illustrations in the first part of *Ars Moriendi*.

In the foreground the salmon-colored cloak, the helmet, spear, and gauntlet reveal the man's active youth. A little demon of vanity broods upon these mementoes. In the central portion of the panel the man himself, middle-aged and no longer a dashing warrior, bends over the chest in which he stores his hoarded gold. With one hand he drops more coins into the bowl held up by a demon of avarice, while his left hand fingers the rosary at his belt. "Verily," says Bosch, with a curl of his lip, "man is forever trying to serve God and mammon." Another writhing little imp holds up an unpaid note, revealing that the miser died without collecting all his outstanding loans—bitter blow to his last hours.

What can the death of such a man be like? In the background of the picture Bosch answers this inevitable question with his own penetrating insight into human character. The miser lies alone in a bare and narrow room. There is neither wife nor child to mourn his death; he has refused to let love into his life. All that is in that death chamber with him is his guardian angel, who urges him to fix his eyes on Christ on the Cross, who appears in the tiny, high window as Death steals softly in at the door and points his arrow at the man's heart. But the miser remains consistent to the end. One hand reaches instinctively for the moneybag which a frog-faced devil holds out to him. He seems to listen more intently to the imp which leans from the rafter over his head than to the pleadings of his guardian angel.

It is a tragic work, fascinating in the beauty of its unreal, soft colors—the reds that have become rose, the browns which have turned to gray indicate that we are no longer in the realm of the living. In it Bosch succeeds in making his composition of forms unusually telling. He displays the symbols of daily life in a shallow foreground plane; in the middle ground he paints the narrative of the miser's hypocritical life; then, when he seeks to depict the tragedy of death, he sets the scene deep into the background. The effect of mystery is heightened by the vault of the ceiling which extends darkly back over the struggle between God and Satan. In the handling of the perspective one feels the genius of Bosch as he seeks to lead the observer's eye from things temporal to things eternal and universal.

THE *GARDEN OF EARTHLY PLEASURES*

This triptych, which was also in Philip II's collection at the Escorial, is surely one of the strangest and most fascinating works of art of all times. As van Eyck painted Paradise and Heaven to inspire men to aspire to their joys, Bosch painted the seductive delights of this earth, and the hell which is the ultimate destination of those who embrace earthly pleasures.

It is easy to understand the relationship of the three panels. In the first the Fall of Man is forecast in the birth of Eve in Paradise. There can be little doubt that Bosch was a misogynist, and in this triptych he makes woman and her charms the central theme of the temptation to earthly pleasures. The central panel elaborates the theme suggested in the left wing, while the right wing shows that the fruits of license are reaped in a most horrible hell.

Bosch's *Garden of Eden* (PLATE 94) appears at first glance to be a happy, innocent paradise where beasts and plants live in harmony with God and man. But as one studies the panel, one discovers that already, as Eve is created and presented to her mate, evil and ugliness stalk through the garden. While beautiful and fantastic beasts come to drink of the fountain in the midst of the garden, an army of reptiles crawl from its waters up a rocky bank. The serpent coils about the palm tree, lying in wait for Eve. In the upper distance, several ungainly prehistoric monsters gambol, and a lion devours a deer—prophecy of the destruction toward which creation is moving.

Bosch's Eve, in contrast with van Eyck's and van der Goes's conception of the mother of all living, is a self-confident temptress whose coy downward glance reveals a weak but ardent nature. Adam seems naïve and pure, even startled by his first sight of woman; but Eve is already aware of her powers to seduce and ensnare.

The duality in nature, which seems to have obsessed Bosch all his life, is revealed in the symbols about the fountain of living waters where the owl, emblem of witchcraft and sorcery, and the cross of salvation appear in the decorations.

In the central panel of the triptych (PLATE 96) Bosch has created a pageant of wantonness and physical abandonment. The air seems damp and warm; it is as though this fantastic garden of the pleasures of the flesh were at the bottom of the sea. Animal and vegetable shapes are confused and intertwined, making a flamboyant Gothic tracery through which the figures move restlessly, like shapes in a dream. Of this extraordinary painting Charles de Tolnay says:

In the triptych of the *Garden of Earthly Pleasures* of the Escorial, where the symbol is king, Jerome Bosch does not content himself with borrowing from plastic and literary tradition, or with appealing to his own imagination; but, precursor of psychoanalysis, he makes use of all his penetration in order to draw out from his memory and from his experience the elements of these symbols of dreams whose import is as far-reaching as humankind. Moreover, this is neither a simple phenomenon of automatism nor a pure play of the mind. The artist is not dominated by his subject; on the contrary, he dominates it, and in his hands the symbols become instruments for the disposal of his will. The specific sense that he gives to them is intelligible only through a fundamental theme—the nightmare of humanity. Bosch is at the same time the one who dreams and the one who judges—the interpreter and the director.

There were several books known to the men of the fifteenth century which dealt with dream symbolism and its interpretation. In 1482 the *Dream of the Prophet Daniel* was published and circulated in northern Europe. There were also translations of an ancient writer, Artemidorus, who had written on astrology and dreams. As men sensed the coming end of an age they became increasingly curious about the future, and sought to read it in all manner of signs and portents. Bosch did not produce from the murky depths of his subconscious the fantastic beasts, birds, and fishes, the exotic flowers, or the procession of pleasure seekers, bearing various symbols of sensual gratification, who circle the pool where milk-white and ebony-black nymphs disport themselves. He was not intent on pouring out on his panels the tortured tale of his own frustrations and erotic imaginings. Bosch was a functional painter, as all the medieval masters were. He painted these extraordinary pictures on order and for use. He was commissioned by convents and by wealthy lay patrons, and he preached his terrific Jeremiad in a language which was understandable to the men of his time. They could read the warnings in the symbols he used.

He couched those warnings not only in allusions to the Scriptures, but in homely proverbs which were household expressions of the people of the Low Countries. In his *Garden of Earthly Pleasures* we find an amorous couple enclosed in a globe of glass—a reminder of the Flemish proverb: "Good fortune, like glass, is easily broken."

The incredible beasts which appear in this and in other paintings by Bosch have strayed from the pages of the innumerable bestiaries which formed part of the reading of the men of the Middle Ages. To the master's contemporaries unicorns, griffins, dragons, and other heraldic beasts were more familiar and easier to believe in than the elephant and the giraffe which Bosch carefully placed in his Eden.

The beasts which each age has created for its entertainment and enlightenment form an extraordinary Noah's Ark procession across the pages of history. This creative urge is not diminished in our day, which has produced Mickey Mouse, Donald Duck, and a score of other creatures which have national and political significance to millions of people in all parts of the globe. This twentieth-century bestiary reveals the thoughts, desires, fears, and aspirations of modern man no less than the fabulous monsters of the Gothic age gave expression to the medieval mind.

Typical of this fantastic menagerie is the porphyrion, described in detail by Isidore of Seville in his renowned *Etymologies*, which, written in the sixth century, was one of the most widely circulated books of the Middle Ages.

The porphyrion, according to the saintly Bishop of Seville, was a fowl with one foot like that of the partridge and the other webbed like the foot of a goose. It was by nature affectionate and exceedingly loyal to its master. It placed great value on all that belonged to him, especially his wife. If the wife was untrue, the little porphyrion crept into its master's bosom and died there of compassion and grief. Needless to say, the race of porphyrions is long since extinct.

It was from this picturesque, poetic, and frequently horrible treasury that Bosch drew, and this still lives in his pictures. He and many other men of his time still believed in these fabulous beasts, birds, and fishes as is evident from the work of many of the map makers of the fifteenth and early sixteenth centuries. Bosch explored the medieval spirit and recorded it with the fidelity of a scientist.

In the third panel of his *Garden of Earthly Pleasures*, completing this tremendous symphony of damnation, he paints the ultimate destiny of those who indulge in the pleasures of the senses. What a contrast there is between Memling's *Inferno* (PLATE 79) and the Hell conceived by Bosch (PLATE 95), which is as revealing of the master's psychology as his *Garden of Eden*. It seems clear that Bosch believed that music is one of the lures by which Satan wins souls away from God. Here, prominently displayed, are the ears through which man listens to the tempter's song; here, too, the musical instruments which Satan employs to do his evil will, and here are innumerable symbols of the erotic and soul-destructive thoughts which, Bosch seems to warn us, music engenders.

Bosch's Hell is a fetid, noisome, sulphurous pit, raucous with discords and the cries of miserable souls imprisoned within drums, impaled on flutes, and tortured by bestial demons. The plight of the damned has been the concern of artists and poets for many ages, but neither Dante nor Milton nor any other painter has given such an unforgettable representation of anguish as Bosch's conception of the man crucified upon a harp, whose fingers pluck desperately at its strings seeking an expression of his agony, and finding none. In this single figure is compressed all that is intensely dramatic in the philosophy of Jerome Bosch.

In the entire history of Western painting Bosch occupies a distinguished position. In his art he truly attained the gloomy purpose which he set out to achieve. He set his own problems and he solved them, not by relying on older methods, but by creating a completely new style of his own. For example, he was one of the first of the northern artists fully to appreciate movement in anatomy and composition, and his influence on the painters who came after him, particularly on Bruegel, is proof of his genius.

He and van Eyck must be considered the most imaginative and inventive masters of the Flemish school of the fifteenth century, though they are far apart; van Eyck the master of the objective realities of the world, and Bosch master of the subjective forces of the mind. Van Eyck penetrated daily life from the outside inward, and raised its common aspects to expressions of lofty ideals. Bosch explored life from the inside outward, disclosing ugly and evil motives behind many of man's occupations and aims. He must have shocked many of his contemporaries, though there seems to have been a demand for his pictures, and they were highly regarded in his own time.

He was a super-realist of the spiritual world in the years when the medieval world was dying. He bore no kinship to the modern surrealist, because he was a man with a fervent moral purpose. His art does not beguile for the sake of beguiling, nor is it intentionally bewildering.

All of the unhappy work of Bosch is situated at the crossroads of magic and faith, heresy and mysticism. Here we find a reflection of the pyre of Savonarola which had just lit up the great square at Florence. Certainly the demons which soon were going to haunt the cell of Luther at the Wartburg had the appearance of those which Bosch dreamed of and painted. One finds in the pictures of Bosch the premonition of all the drama of the Reformation where Luther tried to establish a new Christianity beyond traditional Catholicism. His work has no relation to the narrow sermons of the evangelist. A great tremor of mystic and visionary poetry runs through all of it. Perhaps it is the poetry of hopelessness; but Bosch is nonetheless one of the greatest poets that painting has given us. He reveals definite aspects of the soul of the fifteenth century which we would not know without him.

Bosch's art may be without hope, but he is not enchanted by the prospect of evil. He, who may be said to have produced the Fleurs du Mal of painting, is, above all others, the master painter of the want of God in the world.

HUNTERS IN THE SNOW by PETER BRUEGEL. Kunsthistorisches Museum, Vienna ($46\frac{3}{4}$ x $64\frac{3}{4}$)

PLATE 97

Peter Bruegel

IT IS part of the paradox of Jerome Bosch that some fifty years after his death he should have had a pupil. It is as though that ironic and punitive spirit were under some compulsion to project itself and its prophecies into the era which it had so deeply feared and inveighed against.

Bosch had enjoyed an enormous popularity during his lifetime and in the years following his death. His pictures were sought after, especially by Spanish and Italian patrons of art. Margaret of Austria counted at least one of Jerome Bosch's "dreams" in her collection, and we know that Philip the Handsome had commissioned the master to paint for him a *Last Judgment*, which was highly treasured; a fragment of it is in the Pinakothek at Munich. It remained, however, for Bosch's posthumous pupil, Peter Bruegel, to make the works of his fellow Brabançon known and admired throughout Europe. Through the engravings made after drawings by Bruegel in Bosch's style and published by Hieronymus Cock of Antwerp, the last and in some respects the greatest of the medieval Flemish masters influenced artists down to the eighteenth century.

Like Bosch, Bruegel was a native of North Brabant. He was born about 1530—fourteen years after Bosch's death—and probably in the village of Brueghel, which is between Hertogenbosch and Helmond. There is a tradition that he had his early schooling in Hertogenbosch, but this story may have been fabricated to account in part for his interest in and admiration for the great master of that city of northern Brabant.

The known facts concerning Bruegel's life begin when he was about fifteen years of age and came to Antwerp to be apprenticed to Pieter Coeck van Aelst, then an important figure in the art worlds of Antwerp and Brussels.

Bruegel's coming to Antwerp from a village in North Brabant may be likened to the coming to New York of a lad from a farm in some Midwestern state. One imagines him standing wide-eyed and agape at first sight of the ships riding the wind-ruffled waters of the Scheldt. At a time when Amsterdam boasted that 500 vessels with cargoes of grain and herring could be counted in her harbor, Antwerp replied that almost as many frequently came in on a single tide.

From the opening of the sixteenth century the business of Antwerp had prospered and increased to proportions hitherto unknown in Europe. As Miriam Beard in her *History of the Business Man* has said:

Perhaps never again will so great a proportion of the universal trade pass through a single harbor, or such an immense part of the world's credit-operations be transacted on a single exchange. Certainly, since Alexandrian times there had not been seen in the Old World so many products assembled from so many ports, dealt with in such amounts by companies so powerful and by men of such international orientation.

In the course of every week more than 1,000 freight wagons loaded with goods from Germany, France, and all the cities of the Low Countries creaked through the city gates to fill the shops of the merchants and to make Antwerp's daily market the busiest and richest in Europe. Whereas during the fifteenth century the city had had two great fairs a year, one at Pentecost, one on St. Bavon's Day, now the fair was continuous and perpetual. Here were traded the fine laces of Mechlin and Valenciennes, tapestries made in Brussels and in many places of Flanders; leather, ironwork from Namur, munitions—always a profitable industry—

copper, and spices brought in the Portuguese galleons. The city was like a great glowing hearth whose fire warmed and illumined all who gathered around it.

Above all, Antwerp was a city of the Renaissance. Pirenne points out that in contrast to Bruges, which clung to its medievalism and refused to readjust itself to the new, rapidly changing conditions, Antwerp welcomed and throve on them. Bruges had sought to revive its lost prosperity by curbing the activities of foreigners within its bounds, even to the point of passing an ordinance in 1477 which gave foreign traders the right to sell within the city only what they could carry through its gates on their backs. At the same time entry was forbidden goods purchased at the fairs of Antwerp and Berg-op-Zoom. The liberal views and vigorous democratic principles which had made the greatness of Bruges in the fourteenth and early fifteenth centuries were abandoned for a reactionary and self-protective economic policy.

Antwerp, with its eyes on the future, adopted those old Flemish ideas and expanded them.[1] The first article in the constitution was: "In this city all men are free and cannot be enslaved." Within his own house the citizen was safe from arrest. No restrictions were placed on foreigners; instead, over the gate of the Exchange this inscription was carved in 1531: "For the service of merchants of all nations and languages." The 5,000 men who gathered daily in that ornamental quadrangle bore testimony to the truth of the dedication. In all things Antwerp was determined to equal and excel Bruges in the older city's heyday. Bruges had had a school of art; Antwerp must have one. There had been a flourishing painters' guild in the city since 1450, but it was not until the end of the century that Antwerp produced a master who was able to aspire to the honors of Bruges' Memling, or—as the loyal citizens of Antwerp fondly hoped—to challenge van Eyck. This was Quentin Massys.

Though Massys had died some fifteen years before Bruegel came to Antwerp, his reputation as a painter was very high, and his influence on the Antwerp school was great. It was as inevitable that Bruegel should be subjected to this influence as that Memling should have felt the tradition of van Eyck when he came to Bruges. Some facts concerning Massys are therefore not out of place here. Though he followed the masters of the fifteenth century more closely than Bruegel in time, Massys had less kinship with them and their point of view than did

Bruegel, who arrived on the scene more than a century after the death of van Eyck.

Massys was born in Louvain a few years before the death of that city's great master, Dirk Bouts. He was twenty-five years of age when he joined the Antwerp Guild in 1491. There is a legend based on the inscription on his tombstone, "Once a blacksmith, afterward a famous painter," that Quentin forsook his forge and bellows to please the girl he loved and wished to marry. In a Latin poem placed under an engraved portrait of Antwerp's famous painter, Lampsonius puts these words into his mouth:

Quintijn Messijs, painter from Antwerp speaks:
A rough Cyclop blacksmith was I before,
But when my sweetheart was also courted by a painter,
She made me understand with some reproach,
That the thundering blows on the anvil were less
    pleasing to her
Than the silent play of the brushes,
The force of love made me a painter.
The truth of this is indicated by a little anvil,
Which I selected for a signature on my pictures.
As Cypris obtained from Vulcan the arms for her son,
O Great poet, You have turned a blacksmith into a
    clever painter.

Another less romantic, but no less touching, version of the story relates that the young blacksmith suffered a long illness which left him too weak to wield his hammer. At Shrovetide it was customary for the Lazarists who cared for the sick to have a procession through the city during which they distributed to the children in the crowd printed and colored pictures of saints. The Lazarist who had visited Quentin during his illness suggested that he color some of these pictures as a means of rehabilitation. This work stimulated the ex-blacksmith's latent gifts and led him to take up painting as a serious occupation.

There is no reason to doubt the possibility that Massys may have been a worker in metals, and a very artistic one, before he devoted himself exclusively to painting. He is not the first, nor the last, man to come into art by way of a craft. But it would seem as though these stories had grown up to explain the hardness and, perhaps, the metallic quality in Massys' able and clever work. He was, like all the masters who won acclaim in their time and have held their reputation through the centuries, an excellent craftsman. It has been suggested that he may have been taught to paint by Albert Bouts, and, if so, this explains much of his skill. His pictures are brilliant, the figures and details in them

[1]*Du Génie Flamand*, Jan-Albert Goris, Roseau-Peusant, New York, 1943.

expertly drawn. One readily understands why Antwerp greatly admired his work, which seems to express the materialism and the feeling of successful well-being which animated that city in the days of its prosperity.

Massys was the most important figure in the art world of Antwerp when Gerard David went to work in that city in 1515. He enjoyed the friendship of the great Erasmus and painted a portrait of him, and a much finer one of Erasmus' friend, Peter Gillis, as a gift to Sir Thomas More. The correspondence relating to these two historic portraits has been preserved. To honor Rotterdam's great scholar, Massys again became a metalworker and cast a bronze medal bearing the head of Erasmus.

When Dürer spent some time in Antwerp during the summer of 1520 and was feted by the painters' guild, he was taken to see Massys' fine house though its master was away from the city at the time. Six years later Holbein, on his way to England, visited Massys on an introduction from Peter Gillis. Holbein was then in his twenties and Massys sixty. There are critics who have found more than a trace of the older master's influence in the English portraits painted by Holbein.

Though one must admire the excellent craftsmanship of Massys, one is struck by a want of original and creative inspiration in his pictures. This lack extends even to his portraits, though these represent the best of his works.

Pieter Coeck van Aelst, to whom young Bruegel was apprenticed, had undoubtedly known Massys, who was the leading master of the guild when Coeck was admitted to membership. Coeck himself had been a pupil of Bernard van Orley, court painter to Margaret of Austria and the creator of a number of portraits which reveal how greatly van Orley was influenced by Massys. In his portrait of Dr. George van Zelle of the Hospital of St. John in Brussels (COLOR PLATE 106) van Orley follows the lead of Massys in introducing a great number of accessories intended to tell the observer certain facts about the physician. The clasped hands which form the decorative pattern of the embroidery behind the sitter indicate that the doctor and painter were friends.

Pieter Coeck was a son of the Renaissance. In his workshop and in his home to which Bruegel was admitted as a member of the family the young man was brought into close contact with Italian influences. Coeck had made a voyage to Italy and studied in Rome. He had translated for publication several books on architecture, including the writings of Sebastiano Serlio. Shortly before Bruegel became his pupil he had returned from a trip to Constantinople, where he had endeavored to secure a commission for tapestries from the Grand Turk. He brought with him a number of sketches which were published as woodcuts. These prints have furnished illustrators of *The Arabian Nights* with a careful record, as Coeck saw it, of the life lived on the Golden Horn early in the sixteenth century.

Coeck died in 1550, before Bruegel had completed his term of apprenticeship. He left a young wife and an infant daughter, Maria, whom the apprentice had often carried in his arms and played with, as he represents children playing in his great and symbolic painting, *Children's Games*. Years later, after he, too, had made his "Wanderjahr" to the south and had attained fame as a painter, he married Maria Coeck. They had two sons: Peter Bruegel the Younger (Hell-fire Bruegel) and Jan (Velvet Bruegel). Both became painters and were colleagues of Rubens and van Dyck.

By his marriage to his master's daughter, and through his sons, Bruegel continued the tradition of the medieval guilds which had encouraged the development of families of painters. And through his sons Bruegel became the important link between the medieval Flemish masters and the painters of the baroque period. In point of fact, though he belongs in time to the Renaissance and did most of his work in Antwerp where the spirit of the Renaissance flourished, Bruegel is closer in feeling to the masters of the fifteenth century than he is to Massys, who painted in the period of transition, or to Rubens, who followed only a half century later. The one outstanding reason for this is the effect of the work of Jerome Bosch on Bruegel.

Just when or how he came under the spell of the last of the great Gothic painters remains somewhat obscure. Judging from his very early work it seems unlikely that he was influenced by Bosch before or at the time he studied under Pieter Coeck. After Coeck's death, it is believed Bruegel entered the workshop of Hieronymus Cock, of Antwerp. Cock was one of the most noted engravers and publishers of his time. His brother, Mattias Cock, was a landscape painter of some note. It was as a landscape draftsman that Bruegel made his debut, and it was probably in the Cocks's studio that he first seriously studied painting and set himself to copy the drawings of Bosch.

Hieronymus Cock was a traveled man. From him, as from Pieter Coeck, Bruegel heard talk of Italy and what a painter could learn there. Soon after his admission to the painters' guild as a master in 1551, Bruegel set forth on a lengthy journey through France and Italy to Rome. There he visited, and, it is said, collaborated upon a picture with Giulio Clovio, the celebrated miniaturist who twenty years later was to befriend El Greco.

While in Italy, Bruegel traveled to Naples and Sicily and visited many learned men and persons of high position. Everywhere he went he made sketches. As van Mander so quaintly described them: "So that it was said of him that while he visited the Alps, he had swallowed all the mountains and cliffs, and upon coming home, he had spit them forth upon his canvas and panels."

It would seem that the greatest influence upon Bruegel by his experiences in Italy was in the conception of landscape. He introduces a new feeling for nature into the Flemish school which had long been famous for its handling of landscape. This feeling is Bruegel's own and a part of his philosophy. But it is akin to the feeling in some of Leonardo's drawings of clouds and mountains which recall the animism of the fifteenth-century philosopher Nicolas Cusanus: "The world, if I may say so, is a great animal; the rocks of it are the bones, the rivers of it are the veins, the trees, the hair."

Perhaps in Italy Bruegel became infected with this kind of respect for hidden gods in nature. In this he differs markedly from his Flemish predecessors, Bouts and van der Goes, who saw man made by God dwelling in a natural world. To Bruegel it is nature which dominates man, which reduces him in stature and significance, and which continues its ordered way regardless of his joys and griefs, his dreams of glory and beneficence.

This is the feeling he put into his *Fall of Icarus*, painted soon after his return from Italy to Antwerp (COLOR PLATE 12).

THE *FALL OF ICARUS*

In this interpretation of the myth of the son of Daedalus who dared to fly Bruegel drew on Ovid's telling of the old story. Intoxicated by success, Icarus forgot his father's warning, ventured so near the sun that it melted his waxen wings and caused him to fall to death in the sea. Ovid mentions three witnesses of Icarus' fall—a plowman, a fisherman, and a shepherd. All three are here in Bruegel's picture. Here, too, is the partridge which Ovid says beat her wings to jeer at the imprudent youth. But the partridge remains silent, and the three bystanders take no notice of the unhappy end of Icarus.

Moreover, Bruegel, again like the medieval masters, is not content with mere storytelling; he must needs teach a lesson. The lesson he finds in the myth is that kernel of wisdom contained in the old Flemish proverb: "No plow comes to rest because a man dies."

Here is the philosophy of the Flemish peasantry, the stoical endurance of a people who have suffered hardships and oppressions with profound patience and tenacity. And here, likewise, is the painter's own philosophy. He makes the plowman the center of the picture, and the unfortunate Icarus only a small spot in the composition. The event becomes merely an incident; the moment, a moment in eternity. The moving plow is a symbol of one phase of the endless cycle of the seasons. Bruegel's view of man and nature in harmony brought him to treat even human folly and vanity as unworthy of notice in the presence of eternal truths.

This one picture is sufficient to prove that however deeply Bruegel was impressed by the Italian feeling for landscape, the influence of the Italian Renaissance never swept him off his feet. These remained planted on the good black earth of the Low Countries. Although the grand manner of the Renaissance occasionally left its imprint on his art, he never fell victim to the mannerisms which his contemporaries and many of his immediate predecessors in Antwerp had adopted. Faithful to the older Flemish tradition, he took things as they came in daily life—the pots and jugs, the carts and animals, even the stolid Flemings in their ill-fitting, heavy clothes. Grave, single-minded Dirk Bouts knew a peasant when he saw one, though he frequently dressed him up in burgher's finery. And certainly Hugo van der Goes, with all his delicacy of feeling, had never been led astray from the paths of Flemish realism to make his types handsomely ideal. It is above all else this quality of careful observation and faithful record which keeps Bruegel within the tradition which goes back to van Eyck.

The second quality which makes him one with the Flemish painters of the fifteenth century is his craftsmanship. Like them, he was an oil painter *par excellence*, and the direct inheritor of a long line of highly skilled and disciplined craftsmen. There is no bravado in Bruegel's painting. There is sincerity, great seriousness—for all that he is sometimes called "Droll Peter"—and genuine humility. In his ability to draw and to mix colors he forms an important link between the artists who first perfected painting in oils and van Dyck and Rubens.

Yet in technique, as in his whole style of painting, he brought something new into the school. He

QUENTIN MASSYS. The Descent from the Cross. Antwerp Museum.
Courtesy Frick Art Reference Library (96½ x 98)

PLATE 98

HIERONYMUS BOSCH. The Way of the Cross   PETER BRUEGEL. The Way of the Cross

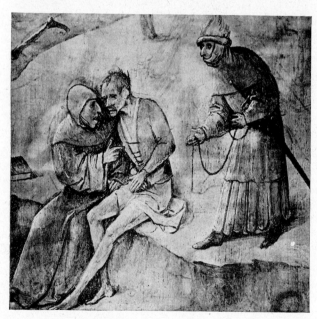

DETAIL OF ABOVE   DETAIL OF ABOVE

PLATE 99

HIERONYMUS BOSCH. The Prodigal Son

PETER BRUEGEL. The Robber of Birds' Nests

HIERONYMUS BOSCH. The Wedding at Cana

PETER BRUEGEL. The Peasant Wedding

BOSCH. The Blind Leading the Blind

PETER BRUEGEL. The Blind Leading the Blind

PLATE 100

HIERONYMUS BOSCH. The Way to Calvary. Museum of Ghent (28¾ x 31½)

Plate 101

may be said to have effected a harmony between certain forces of the Renaissance and some of the spirit of the Middle Ages, for Bruegel was not only taught by Italy and the so-called "New Learning," he was also a disciple of Jerome Bosch.

BOSCH AND BRUEGEL

Hieronymus Cock published the drawings which Bruegel made on the basis of his travel sketches as well as a skating scene on the canals just outside St. George's gates in Antwerp. This engraving had a ready market because the citizens were extremely proud of their new gate, which had been built by an Italian architect, according to the taste of the day. This engraving and several sketches made during the next year or two show Bruegel studying the village life of Brabant which in later years he was to make immortal in his paintings. Some time between the years 1556 and 1558 Hieronymus Cock engaged Bruegel to redraw for engraving a number of compositions by Jerome Bosch. In that experience it would seem as though Bruegel became obsessed by the spirit of the old Gothic master.

That obsession was never to leave him entirely. In Antwerp, where the spirit of the Renaissance and the Reformation was rapidly changing the texture of life, the medieval spirit, which had expressed itself through Bosch, was renewed through the work of Peter Bruegel. Far stronger than the influence of the Italian painters, whose works he had studied, or of the masters of the Antwerp school—Massys, van Orley, van Cleeve—then in high repute, was the impression which Bosch made upon Bruegel. Bruegel was like Saul of Tarsus on the road to Damascus, who suddenly saw a great light and heard a voice he was never to forget. Through Bosch, the medieval spirit laid hold on Bruegel, who might have said of himself in the words of St. Paul: "As one born out of due time."

There is great fascination in tracing the echoes of Bosch in Bruegel's own drawings and paintings. In PLATES 99 and 100 details from pictures by Bosch are compared with details from pictures by Bruegel. They make clear that Bruegel derived from Bosch occasionally not only the crowding and spattering of the picture surface with a multitude of little figures in a medieval, patternlike way which does not allow any corner to remain unfilled and meaningless to the narrative, he adopted also his type of human figures with elongated spidery limbs and with angular or expressively curving outlines.

It is also plainly seen that the younger man drew generously on the great treasury of fantasy he found in Bosch. It must be remembered that it was thought no dishonor to do this sort of borrowing. Any number of painters had taken for their own use ideas and even figures out of the works of van Eyck and van der Weyden. Massys was extremely impressionable in this respect. It is no sign of Bruegel's inadequacy that he made deliberate and excellent use of many of Bosch's ideas, compositions, and figures. Did not Shakespeare go to Holinshed for themes, characters, and plots?

At times Bruegel took over single motives from Bosch as may be seen in the *Way to Calvary*, which is in some features reminiscent of Bosch's picture based on the same theme (PLATE 100). In the middle ground of Bruegel's work is a cart in which the penitent thief rides. He is being confessed by a friar, as we see him also in the picture by Bosch. This is an essentially medieval touch which blandly ignores the fact that there were no monastic orders at the time of the Crucifixion.

On other occasions Bruegel seems to have drawn not only from the pattern of composition the type of figures or single motives but also from the whole idea of content. Bruegel's drawing in the Albertina "Big fishes eat little ones" was actually engraved and published by Cock as a work of Bosch, apparently an indication that it was based on an idea of Bosch. Another case is that of the *Blind Leading the Blind*, Bruegel's painting in the museum of Naples. It is one of his latest and most monumental creations, deeply tragic and stirring, and obviously was inspired by a similar composition of Bosch which has been preserved in an engraving published by H. Cock (PLATE 100).

These are cases of quite obvious influence of the Gothic master on the Renaissance master. There are others, where it would be difficult to prove a direct historical dependency, but the two artists nevertheless approach each other so closely that their affinity of mind becomes obvious. Such a case is that of the *Prodigal Son* by Bosch and of the *Proverb of the Bird's Nest* by Bruegel (PLATE 100). Bruegel expanded the dewy, sparkling spell of a Flemish farm on a summer morning. Man is set lonely and isolated in the framework of his native scenery, in which he nevertheless is rooted with a thousand fibers. The shy and reserved Prodigal Son of Bosch in his stiff demeanor is as well characterized as the broad, communicative, and exuberant peasant of Bruegel in his rolling way of carrying himself and addressing the spectator. Side figures in both paintings play a most secondary role, as much as is necessary for the explanation of the story. True, Bosch's work recounts a parable of the Gospel, that of

Bruegel, a popular proverb. The Prodigal Son looks back on the place of his former debauchery and misery. The peasant illustrates that only the one who seizes the bird's nest has it in reality and not the one who knows that it is on the tree and talks about it.

But the way in which a parable of the Gospel and a parable of everyday life are recounted is, in spite of the distance of time, so similar that at one time it was debated seriously as to whether Bosch's picture might not also be merely a general genre representation vested in a Netherlandish proverb. There is an inner affinity of mind which goes beyond the similarity. The many common details do not prove that Bruegel knew Bosch's picture when he painted his. There prevails a deeper affinity in both, which is independent of superficial contact. It may have been subconscious, though it does not exclude the possibility that Bruegel indeed knew the *Prodigal Son* by Bosch.

Even in creating a landscape background for the *Way to Calvary*, Bruegel drew on Bosch. As in Bosch's *Carrying of the Cross*, from the St. Anthony altar, a great crag rises from the plain. In a similar way a tree—larger in Bruegel's picture—grows to the right of the rock. Bruegel has added to this crag a windmill, as though he wished to stress the idea that though Christ is crucified for man, man is still dependent on the earth and its yield. It is the windmill, not the Cross, which dominates the scene. The windmill—homely, utilitarian, symbolic of the harvest fields, whose grain it turns to flour for the use of man—emphasizes the same idea expressed by the plowman in the *Fall of Icarus*.

MAD MEG

It seems probable that the inspiration for this picture of Hell (PLATE 103), with its host of fantastic inhabitants, including Megaera, one of the Furies, was found in not one but several works of Bosch. It is a nightmare realm under a flaming sky filled with the clash and clamor of war. Van Mander saw this picture in the collection of the Emperor Rudolph II and spoke of it as "an insane Margaret in the act of recruiting from the profits of hell." The figure seems to be a personification of the uselessness of war, and this is borne out by her unprofitable gleanings—two baskets, an apron full of odds and ends, including food, dishes, a silver pitcher, and a skillet. Under her arm is a little casket that may contain money. This lean Amazon wears an ill-fitting breastplate and a helmet that resembles a kitchen pot. From her waist dangles a

butcher knife, and in her right hand is a long, two-edged sword.

It is interesting, in view of the name which has become associated with this picture, *Dulle Griet*, to find that an old cannon, dating from the time of Philip the Good, which has stood for centuries in the market place of Ghent, is also so called, and there are records of Scottish and Irish cannon known to artillerymen as "Mad Meg" and "Roaring Meg."

In this picture Bruegel seems to say "War is hell." It is wasteful, brutal, and desolating. It is as far removed from the great realities of life as these fantastic and unreal creatures—part beast, part man—who play their games, dance, attack and devour one another, make love, and disport themselves on the battlements of Hell. Many of them have been taken straight out of Bosch's works—the lovers in the glass globe, the rotten egg in a walnut shell (symbol of gluttony), the harp with the spider stretched across its silent strings (surely a reminder of the harp with the unfortunate soul crucified upon it in Bosch's *Musicians' Hell*), the little beetles dancing merrily under their umbrella, the fishes, lizards, and nameless beasts, who swarm out of the waters.

The picture is full of noise, confusion, and incident, but it is a mark of the genius of Bruegel that the composition is controlled and has great expressive power. It is his invective against war for conquest, uttered at a time when the armies of the King of Spain were marching across the Low Countries and when rulers dreamed dreams of creating tremendous empires. Bruegel preaches against war for conquest in a subtle and unmistakable manner. In a period when he would have paid with his life for putting such words on paper, or speaking them in public, he paints this picture using symbols understandable to all, many of them recalling to mind familiar Flemish proverbs. No one could take exception to a picture of Hell; but those who had eyes to see and ears to hear could learn much from it.

Bruegel was essentially a man of his time. In Antwerp he lived at the crossroads of Europe. He had traveled, talked with famous and thoughtful men; he was an artist with a strong social sense. The procession of painters who emerged from the monasteries at the opening of the fifteenth century culminated in Bruegel. As the masters before him had used their powers to teach eternal truths concerning man and God, Bruegel, faithful to his medieval tradition, used his gifts to teach man for his good.

In our day we see how powerful an instrument for purposes of propaganda the cartoonist can be.

PETER BRUEGEL. The Harvest. Metropolitan Museum, New York. Courtesy Metropolitan Museum of Art

PLATE 102

PETER BRUEGEL. The Mad Meg. Van den Bergh Museum, Antwerp. Courtesy Frick Art Reference Library (44¾ x 62¾)

PETER BRUEGEL. The Wedding Feast. Kunsthistorisches Museum, Vienna (44⅜ x 63½)

PLATE 104

PETER BRUEGEL. The Magpie on the Gibbet. Darmstadt Museum (17⅞ x 19½)

Plate 105

Bruegel, as Goya was to do two and a half centuries later, gave inspiration and symbols for the use of political cartoonists down to our times.

Bruegel's attitude toward religion is difficult to define. He treats few traditional Christian themes in his paintings, and in handling these there is a feeling of agnosticism. There may be some truth in the supposition that Bruegel left Antwerp for Brussels for religious reasons and that a fear of religious persecution made him ask his wife to burn a number of his pictures after his death. In Antwerp at the time there were many groups of Protestants and certain sects which differed with the traditional church. Bruegel numbered among his friends some followers of Henri Nicholas, who, though remaining faithful to most of the precepts of the Roman Church, held that salvation was possible only through universal love. This teaching seems to be the keynote of many of Bruegel's pictures. In his art he seems always sympathetic to the lot of his fellow men.

HUNTERS IN THE SNOW

Throughout the Middle Ages, and even long before the Christian era, artists had often shown an interest in astrology and in the procession of the seasons. Floor tiles and ceiling frescoes were frequently ornamented with the signs of the zodiac. Calendars and prayer books, such as the famous *Book of Hours* of the Duke de Barry, were illustrated with the labors characteristic of the months. Bruegel inherited this tradition to which he was by nature extremely sympathetic. When he set to work upon his series of labors of the months he planned a cycle of seasonal landscapes into which the laborers were introduced as little more than accessories. Had they been completed, the twelve paintings would have formed a complete story of the earth of his beloved Brabant throughout the year.

Only five pictures remain to suggest the idea of this great plan, but they are indicative of what the master had in mind and of his sensitivity to nature and his attitude toward man. One painting shows men cutting fagots in the woods; the leaden sky and damp, chilly air indicate early spring in the Low Countries. The *Hay Harvest* is the subject of another picture which seems to represent the month of June—men and women are at work in the fields, cutting and raking hay, carrying baskets of vegetables and cherries to the waiting carts. The *Wheat Harvest* is the title of a third picture of the series, which is now in the Metropolitan Museum in New York. The wheat is bright gold under the blazing July sun, and the harvesters relax in the shade of a tree. The *Return of the Herd* through leafless woods may well be characteristic of November in a fourth picture.

Perhaps the most famous of Bruegel's five "Seasons" is the so-called *Hunters in the Snow* (COLOR PLATE 97). Like all the others it is sheer pastoral poetry in paint. The bleak, chill earth, covered with snow, rolls back to meet the gray-green sky beyond the horizon. Four black tree trunks mark off the slope of the hill in the foreground. The tired hunters with their shivering dogs make their slippery way toward the houses and the frozen millstream where the villagers are skating. Three little boys have joined hands; one hears the squeak of their wooden skates on the ice. Some old people and a little girl are working around a bonfire. Two ravens perch in the leafless treetops and a third glides across the snowy valley.

The village and the other hamlet which is seen in the distance are living through another winter's spell of frost and cold. The hunters have returned from the chase with perhaps a partridge and a few rabbits for the pot that hangs on the hearth. The hunt has been a hard run; dogs and men drag their feet in the snow, passing the inn where the sign, broken by the wind, hangs crazily.

THE *WEDDING FEAST*

This picture (PLATE 104) has gained Bruegel much fame. He seems to confirm the stories of how the painter and his friend Franckert dressed up in peasants' clothes in order to attend kermesses, harvest festivals, and weddings.

According to an edict of the government of the Emperor Charles V, who knew well the zeal of the Flemings for independence, no more than twenty villagers could gather together at a single time. No more than this number are seated at the wedding table; others wait their turn at the door.

The main preoccupation of everyone is the dinner. There is little gaiety and none of the buffoonery usually associated with peasant weddings. The bride is seated beside her mother, but the groom is nowhere to be seen. There is an old Flemish proverb which declares: "It is a poor man who is not able to be at his own wedding." And that seems to be the case here.

The unshaven bagpiper beside the bench in the middle ground of the picture does not make music. He wears a short blouse and puffy breeches. Three little coins dangle from the brim of his hat. He is called upon by somebody outside the picture frame while playing. We do not see the caller, but the musician's expression seems strangely tragic. He stares into space, seemingly oblivious to what is going on. And why not? He has seen and heard it many times before, as he will see and hear it again.

THE *PEASANTS' WEDDING DANCE*

The countryfolk who ate so heartily at the wedding feast have not changed in character in coming out of doors to dance (COLOR PLATE 7). To the sound of pipes they continue to lose themselves in their simple emotions. They dance with zest, but also with a certain driving heaviness of body. They are not transported by any spirit of joy or release from their daily toil; they are the same stolid men and women who, yesterday, cut the corn harvest, carried in baskets of vegetables and fruit, and who, tomorrow, will follow their beasts and carts into the fields again.

In this, as in his other paintings of peasants, Bruegel individualizes the faces slightly but the bodies not at all. They are all of one blood and bone, of one mind and of one mood. The figures tend to be color tones, each having its particular place in the composition. There is something of the decorative allure of the art of tapestries in this picture, sending the eye up and down to the rhythm of the shapes.

THE *MAGPIE ON THE GIBBET*

As has been told, Bruegel ordered his wife to burn certain pictures after his death, but one picture he asked her to keep for herself. It was his truly wonderful painting of a landscape with a gallows rising against the sky where a magpie perches upon the topmost bar (PLATE 105).

There has always been considerable discussion as to the meaning. It cannot be merely a superb bit of landscape painting; it seems to teach a moral or a truth—one which the master deeply felt or else he would not have painted this small panel with such perfection. Critics, recalling how fond Bruegel was of illustrating familiar proverbs, have sought for Netherlandish sayings which might hold the clue to this picture. One of these is "The way to the gallows leads through pleasant meadows." The company mounts a hill toward the gibbet. It is a gay crowd and the countryside is lovely; herds graze in a broad, flat valley, and the mists of a humid summer day veil the distant hills. The undergrowth and the bent old trees grow not as artists would will them to grow, but with all the beauty and force of nature. What else but peace and health is there in this great landscape?

Still in the foreground there is the gallows, the horrible machine of man's justice, which can be so far removed from that of God. It stands, stark and gruesome, against the beauty of the earth. Yet even the gallows, a symbol of violent death, cannot dim the radiance of nature nor quench the spirit of the merrymakers who approach it with less interest in it than in the magpie. Bruegel seems to have said that there is man's cruelty and demonstration of justice. But in spite of all this, there are great beauty and plenty in the earth; and these good gifts are undiminished by what man does to man.

These few of Bruegel's works are sufficient to prove in what way he was a great humanist and how deeply he felt the traditions inherited from the earlier masters. Like theirs, his work was full of motive and symbol. He intended his paintings to do something for the observer which would be not simply for his entertainment but also for his edification.

His art has enjoyed great popularity, and rightly so, because he was a clear and brilliant colorist, an excellent draftsman, and a composer who could make confusion speak as eloquently as order. He chose to see eternities in the immediacies of daily life, and to base his art upon subjects which found their inspiration in the daily concerns of ordinary people. When he painted stories from the Bible, legends of the saints or myths, he made them take place right in the midst of sixteenth-century Brabant. No man who loved proverbs and the homely wisdom of his countrymen, as Bruegel did, could possibly succumb to the pomp and circumstance of the Renaissance. He is one of the truly great landscape painters of all times, and his philosophy seems to have been that the lot of man was to be inextricably bound to nature and that man cannot avoid its forces or its destiny.

Bruegel's life was comparatively short. After removing to Brussels he lived only six years. During that time he painted his finest works, all of which pour forth his philosophy and show him growing in depth and artistic power of expression.

Out of his struggle for a synthesis between man and nature arose his sadness and his irony. He saw that the forces of nature are stronger than human reason and human will. His people move with the tides and seasons; they react to primitive emotions; in all their vitality they fulfill the laws of nature. The irony of human life, to Bruegel in his moral and satirical pictures, was that man is a part of nature, controlled by its laws and subject to its forces, yet he does not choose to understand his place in the great scheme of things, nor does he choose to elevate himself by his reason or become godlike in either the Christian or pagan sense. Hence, his "queerness" and his acting beyond that which is natural and reasonable.

Bruegel, therefore, in some respects was sad, as most philosophers have been sad. With all his positiveness and humor, he had something of the stern, resigned, and melancholy attitude of his stoic friends. Yet he devoted all his energies and his magnificent gifts to telling the story of these people who refused to see and to hear, and whom he loved so much.

The love which permeates the little panels of the early Flemish masters—love of God, of the Blessed Virgin, of Christ, and of the saints with whom they felt on such sweet and intimate terms—becomes in Bruegel a love of man. It is this love which unites him to the painters of an earlier century.

PART III

The Flemish Style

PORTRAIT OF DR. ZELLE by Bernard van Orley. Brussels Museum, Belgium (*15¾ x 12⅝*)

Plate 106

The Flemish Style

E HAVE considered the pageantry, the history, institutions, and social life of the people of medieval Flanders. We have looked briefly into their dreams and their religious mysticism. Out of these, inspired and fostered by these forces, came the great school of painting which established for all time what may be called "the Flemish style." It was the outward and visible expression of the prosperous culture of a civilization based upon ideals of individual liberty, self-respect, security, and well-being.

The characteristics which determine the style of a painting must be defined in terms of *form* and *content*. The two are not the same; but content dictates form and infuses it. Above all other things, the Flemish painter was concerned with the content of his work, which was to translate the beliefs of Christian piety into pictorial form. Had anyone asked him his opinion on the elements of form and content in his art, he would very likely have returned a blank stare and then made the simple reply: "I paint as best I can, and for the glory of God. That is all." The masters who created the rich heritage of the Flemish style were humble men—simple yet profound. They felt that an ideal of perfection was a goal to struggle toward but one seldom attained. They were moved by the same spirit which inspired van Eyck to sign many of his works "*Als ich kan* [As I can]."

As you study these pictures, you may often be amused by the stiffness and angularity of some of the figures; yet it is impossible to deny the competence of the men who painted them. They knew very well what they were about. They were not primitive painters employing the technique and materials of their art without meditation or inexpertly.

This mirror of life in medieval Flanders presents to view a thoroughly domestic world. It extols gentleness, reverence, and Christian piety. Its approach to the great truths of all time is made with humility and singleness of heart. It does not shrink from the commonplace. Indeed, in the hands of van Eyck and van der Weyden the commonplace becomes monumental and assumes an awesome dignity. It is the peculiar power of all the old Flemish masters to bring those things which are most profound and spiritual down to earth and within the grasp of the untutored but earnest men and women. The Flemish artist made the Christ Child a Flemish child; the Virgin, a Flemish maiden; and St. Joseph, a Flemish carpenter—perhaps fashioning Flemish mousetraps with Flemish tools. You are startled to find that what you took at first for a naturalistic portrait is really the visualization of a saint, or an angel, or a divine personage. For these old painters there was no definite boundary between dream and reality. The door between Heaven and earth stood always ajar. God, the saints, and the angels filled the vaults of their cathedrals and were thought of as far less remote than their overlord, the Great Duke of the West, with his courtiers and attendants.

This feeling of intimacy with the world of faith remains with the Flemings today and is characteristic of their religious life. Their old men have not lost entirely their ability to dream dreams nor their young men and women to see visions. These powers, of which many persons of other nations speak with diffidence, if at all, are an accepted part of daily life in modern Flanders. A servant, entering a new place, sometimes stipulates that she must have one free day each month on which to make a religious pilgrimage. Many men and women—hard working, thrifty, and intensely realistic—are on familiar but reverent terms with their patron saints and guardian angels. They speak of them affectionately and intimately, as they might speak of dearly loved, highly regarded great-uncles and cousins. They have preserved through five centuries the way of thought which moved the masters of painting to place the Madonna in a garden, which might have been in Bruges, and to depict the Passion of Our Lord as taking place in the fields of Flanders.

Look at most of the Flemish Annunciations. The symbolic event takes place in a bedroom such as might be found in any well-to-do home in medieval Flanders. Often outside the window is a charming little medieval garden. The painter's way of saying that he believes in this mystery and wants you to believe it is to make the scene as real as he can.

After looking at many versions of the Flemish Madonna, with her high, broad forehead, her downcast eyes, and her ageless and fleshless beauty, you come to feel that this type represents an ideal venerated by the painters and by the people for whom the image was made. This ideal was enshrined in the hearts of the people of medieval Flanders; it was not merely invented by the painters. They only used their skill to portray for their own time and for the generations to come the type of holy Motherhood in the way that they and their countrymen worshiped it.

The display of elegance in many of these pictures may be considered one of the characteristics of the Flemish style. This is not vulgar ostentation, nor—as the style came to be later, frequently during the sixteenth and seventeenth centuries—the exaltation of material values and physical beauty. It is, rather, the adorned embodiment of an ideal. Looking at many of these richly colored and richly ornamented scenes, you are reminded of the expression, "*en-dimanché*"; in every sense they are dressed up in Sunday clothes. And why not? These little pictures were meant to be seen by God and by man; consequently they wear their best attire. The brocade behind the throne of van Eyck's tiny *Madonna* (PLATE 107) is the finest to be found anywhere in all the Great Duke's counties. The room in which St. Barbara reads, warming her back at the blazing fire, is handsomely appointed (PLATE 21). The *Madonna*, venerated by young Martin Nieuwenhoven, is seated in a noble Gothic chamber, and she wears magnificent jewel-studded robes; though the only pride she shows is for her Son. In Petrus Christus' *Dormition of the Virgin*, the bed curtains are of heavy, lustrous scarlet (the *escarlate* for which Flemish weavers were famous the world over). They are carefully looped up exactly as the bed curtains are fastened in the Arnolfini nuptial portrait (COLOR PLATE 2).

THE REAL AND THE IDEAL

The Flemish masters are unique in the history of Western painting because they were so simple and so honest that their approach to their problems never allowed them to overload their art with earthly realism or heavenly mysticism. They were sane men because they were neither completely objective nor completely subjective in what they thought about the world. They could work as scientists yet still love the mystery of their glistening and gemlike enamels. They could work as mystics yet still respect the realism of their ineffable and Gospel-like visions.

If the subject matter of Flemish painting is essentially religious, that is only natural, because religion was uppermost in the minds of all the people. What seems strange to the modern man is that this deep concern with religious ideas, combined with a strong sense of objective reality, produced idealism in a realistic art.

The arrival of Hugo van der Goes's Portinari *Nativity* in Florence, shortly after 1475, caused a sensation among Italian artists. What impressed the Italians most forcibly was the "realism" of the shepherds. The astonished bewilderment and awe in the rough, unshaven face of the chief shepherd (PLATE 75) are clearly inspired by the thought that God has sent His only Son to man. This shepherd is just beginning to understand that his Savior is lying on the little pile of straw before him. He comes upon the scene breathless. The other two shepherds are in a quieter attitude of acceptance and belief. A fourth approaches in excitement, while two more are shown, about to leave their flocks on the distant hillside. The timing is done with perfection. A full gamut of emotion runs from the gesticulating arms of the man on the hill down to the calm love in the folded hands of the nearest old herdsman. It is all intensely, vividly real. But the realism conveys an ideal. In the face of the awestruck shepherd can be read the amazed, slowly mounting faith of humanity before the great truth of the Incarnation.

A further test will show to what extent the Flemish painter was at one and the same time idealist and realist. If the right side of the *Madonna of the Chancellor Rolin* (PLATE 44) is covered with a sheet of paper, what remains visible is the portrait of a pious and very real man. He is unmistakably a man of wealth and position; a shrewd, capable diplomat. Knowing, from his devout posture, that there is a

Madonna opposite him, it is interesting to ask: What should this Madonna look like, considering the half of the picture that is uncovered?

As soon as the right side of the picture is uncovered you find that van Eyck has not been disappointing. It is amazing, and yet infinitely satisfying, to see that the Madonna and Child are every bit as real as the Burgundian chancellor. An angel descends from Heaven with a filigree crown. The celestial goldsmith's work is no less wonderful than the work of the famous Flemish metalsmith, Hugo d'Oignies. It is as healthy as the flesh of the little Savior. Van Eyck does not make man in the image of God; he makes Christ the perfect image of man. He has determined in his mind what the healthiest Flemish mother and the healthiest Flemish child actually look like, and he paints the Virgin and her Son in their likeness. So he produces an ideal.

This Virgin, set before an infinite landscape, decked in the richest robes, enthroned in a magnificent loggia, handsome in the bloom of youth and motherhood, humble like a good burgess, yet grand like a strong queen, is a reality worthy of the veneration of chancellor and simple Flemish craftsman alike. This is what Mary and the Christ Child had to be like to be believable as a reality and adored as an ideal. By the time of Memling and David, this conception was somewhat modified in the direction of tenderness and softness.

With his strong sense of balance between the inner and the outer life, the real and the ideal, the Flemish artist found it necessary to harmonize time and place in his art. Medieval art was contemporary in every sense of the word. It was made for, by, and of the people of its time. Romantic plunges into the past were unthinkable to these craftsmen, who made objects of daily use and daily necessity. In order to render visible the undeniable immediateness and proximity of religious concerns, the artist chose a completely familiar language of forms—the personal idiom of his own times and country: like Shakespeare, who made his Italians, Greeks, Romans, and Danes speak Elizabethan English. This is why the saints and even historical and Biblical characters all wear Flemish clothes.

NARRATIVE AND DETAIL

The feeling for narrative fills all Flemish painting. This is just as true for a single head as for a whole sequence of events in a story. Dirk Bouts's *Weeping Madonna* (PLATE 63), with her reddened eyes and heavy tears, is powerful because of its sentiment. It is not in any way sentimental. The sentiment is expressed little by little; Mary's sorrow is told in storybook fashion. It is deep-set, but its depth cannot be felt all at once.

A symbol tells very little of a story. Realists, such as were the Flemings who lived at the very end of the Middle Ages, demand more elaboration and more information than a symbol can convey. Their painters satisfied this demand with a balance between symbol and narrative.

To examine detail after detail is a time-consuming process and its impact on the imagination is slow. By contrast, there are paintings by El Greco in which he makes a single brush stroke suffice to describe a high light running from the side of a head down the arm of a figure. It is a brief, shorthand notation of an idea, and it has suggestive (i.e., symbolic) power to connote the entire pictorial idea. It is like the notation of a melody: the observer must orchestrate the score for himself. The Flemish master, on the contrary, never left the visual instrumentation of his themes to the observer. He had a horror of leaving anything unsaid. He goes on and on in his careful, word-by-word description, telling his story by means of many carefully thought-out details.

Only in the hands of a great creative artist does the symbolic theme and its elaborated meaning remain clear when narrative is added. The Flemish painter had the ability to take a multiplicity of details and weave them around a central idea, still keeping the essential simplicity of the idea.

This use of detail in telling a story is said to have drawn from Michelangelo the following rebuke directed toward Flemish painting:

The painting of Flanders will generally satisfy any devout person more than the painting of Italy, which will never cause him to shed tears; this is not owing to the vigor and goodness of the painting, but to the goodness of such devout women who like it, especially very old or very young ones. It will please likewise friars and nuns and also some noble persons who have no true ear for harmony.

They paint in Flanders only to deceive the external eye, things that gladden you and of which you cannot speak ill, and saints and prophets. Their painting is of stuff—bricks and mortar, the grass of the fields, shadows of trees, and bridges and rivers which they call landscape, and little figures here and there; and all this, though it may appear good to some eyes, is in truth done without reasonableness or art, without symmetry or proportion, without care in selecting and rejecting, and finally without any substance or verve. And in spite of all this, painting in some places is worse than in Flanders. Neither do I speak so badly of Flemish painting because I think it all bad, but because it tries to do so many things at once (each one of which alone would suffice for a great work), so that it does not do any-thing really well. . . .

Michelangelo was speaking from the point of view of the humanist. What he attacks as senti-mental is in reality the reflection of the soul of the whole fifteenth century in northern Europe. What he attacks as "stuff"—the bricks and mortar, grass and trees—is the northern sense of realism. When he speaks of the endless enumeration of detail, "each one of which alone would suffice," he speaks as Michelangelo, the architect of the colossal. It is in fact the same kind of criticism which the Renais-sance leveled at the whole Gothic spirit, which it was trying to forget in favor of a new order and the "classic" harmonies. Where Michelangelo soars with Olympian power the Flemish painter touches hu-man life at every turn of its day-by-day existence. Michelangelo was an artist of apocalyptic moments; but the Fleming found no moment unworthy of notice as he wove his fabric of art out of nature, man, and God.

The Canon van der Paele as he kneels is holding a book and a pair of spectacles (PLATE 46). The lenses magnify the print and cast lights and shadows on the open pages of the book. Van Eyck recounts the minutest facts about the canon's wrinkled old face. No mark is missing in order to distinguish this particular man in this particular posture and act of devotion. The reporting of each single element be-comes poetry as the observer's eyes move here and there over the whole picture.

Or turn once again for a moment to the Nieu-wenhoven *Madonna* by Memling (PLATE 78). Each hair and strand of gold thread is treated as if it were a portrait in itself. In this painting Memling does not tire of telling something new; he is excited about what he has proudly painted and seems to say: "Look at this . . . and look at that!" To the Flem-ish painter the world around him presented an infinite awe and mystery; he felt that he had to probe into it and capture it if he could. He seemed to see things always for the first time, as if they were a completely new experience and adventure. His honesty did not allow him to suppress evidence if it contributed to the understanding of the case at hand, and that evidence was never unimportant.

If this seems building too strong a case for the Flemish love of detail, then look again at the Nieu-wenhoven *Madonna*, which is certainly one of the most elaborate of Flemish pictures, and see how harmonious and suitable to the whole each little part of the picture is. Each thing has its story to tell. The little round mirror above the Virgin's right shoulder

shows the young man in the act of prayer. His coat of arms appears in the leaded window.

INDIVIDUAL AND TYPE

Had the Flemish artist not had such a nice sense of the place of detail within the larger scheme of what he painted, he could not have painted his portraits.

He did not approach a sitter with a preconceived idea of what his portrait should be like. He formed his flowers from memories of real flowers; he had seen them growing in the fields, dipping their heads in the summer breezes. It is true that in comparison with the Italians, the Flemish painters lack apprecia-tion for the general principles of anatomical move-ment at work beneath the skins of things. This made for a stiffness and the rather unbending individual-ism in the Flemish figures. Memling was a typical portraitist and a great one in the van Eyck tradition. But, coming late in the century, Memling was more sensitive to the groupings of the little details that in the end make for the characterization of a type of person. Van Eyck saw only the individual.

With the classic examples of fifteenth-century Flemish portraiture, the inner and outer life of a man is harmonized in the individual. Yet the man still remains a man—a part of the great medieval synthesis which saw in men the likeness of God. The modern world has drifted away from such directness and loftiness; today a man is known and respected because he is a dentist, a politician, a preacher, a judge; a man's social position under such an emphasis of values depends entirely on what he does for a living and on how well he does it. He is not rated according to how good he is as a human being. In Flemish portraits you always find the feel-ing that the *man* comes first. Attributes of class, position, wealth, and other such minor details are decidedly secondary. This is particularly true in the work of Memling. This feeling changed markedly during the sixteenth century, and in later Flemish portraits dress, hangings, furniture, possessions, are made important. This was beginning to be the case in van Orley's *Portrait of Dr. Zelle* (COLOR PLATE 106).

THE THIRD DIMENSION

It is hard to realize that the third dimension was once an unexplored region, unknown to the artist as he made pictures. We are now so accustomed to photography that we forget there was a time when the illusion of distance on a flat surface was incon-ceivable to human imagination.

INCE HALL MADONNA by JAN VAN EYCK. National Gallery, Victoria, Melbourne, Australia (8¾ x 6)

PLATE 107

The illusion of the third dimension in painting reappeared for the first time since antiquity in two different places at about one hundred years' distance —with Giotto in Italy at the beginning of the fourteenth century, and then in Flanders with van Eyck. It was for Giotto to see in three-dimensional forms the opportunity to create sculptural and dramatically eloquent figures. His illusions are potent and intense, but they remain arbitrary. Felt and thought-out illusions of natural appearances became a reality for the modern world in the minds and upon the panels of the van Eycks. As an artistic means the principles were grasped and guarded by the whole Flemish school.

The Flemish painter had no precedent to follow. He had to teach himself how to master the serious problems involved in the rendering of three dimensions upon a two-dimensional surface. Moreover, these painters were never satisfied that space should wander gently off into the distance. To them space was so exciting that they created a very deep illusion of it.

Look once again at the *Madonna of the Chancellor Rolin* (PLATE 43). Two large figures and the Child dominate the foreground. The floor tiles recede like an elaborate checkerboard toward the arched openings at the back of the room. The space then dashes down to where two little men look over a parapet. Again, in a great hurry, the space rushes off into the distance where people, buildings, bridges, and wooded hills form a wonderland.

The Flemish painters could consciously deny space, as well as create it. Roger van der Weyden's impassioned *Descent from the Cross* (PLATE 56) is staged like a sculptured relief against a gold background. This represents a deliberate closing of the third dimension in the same way that the landscape represents its opening.

There are only two important ways in which a painter can create the illusion of depth upon the flat surface of his picture. One is by the use of diminishing forms and converging lines. The second method is to create the appearance of the actual existence of atmosphere. To this end the Fleming often used a warm brown foreground, a cool green middle ground, and a cold blue background. In creating airiness for his paintings he employed not only the effects of haze and mist, but he also cooled off his colors toward the horizon, massing his reds and yellows in the foreground.

Atmosphere has varying degrees of weight and density, depending upon climatic conditions. These factors very decidedly affect light radiation as it is reflected to the eye in traveling across certain distances. Atmosphere tends to break up and diffuse light waves, making things in the distance appear vaguer in outline and lighter in tone.

The opening up of the third dimension, with its powerful effects of far vistas, was as stupendous an artistic achievement as it was an intellectual one.

LIGHT

The Flemish artist, with his practical and common-sense attitude, never treated light as a thing of aesthetic pleasure in itself. In fact, by studying all the great early Flemish paintings, it is evident that the masters avoided strange effects of light, such as strong sunlight, spotlight, or moonlight. Van Eyck was the most forceful of them all in his use of lighting, but even he never actually painted *chiaroscuro* effects. The Flemish masters were so deeply concerned with painting a subject lucidly, that it never occurred to them to exalt the artistic means to the point whereby it became a subject matter itself—as is more or less the case with the French Impressionists of the nineteenth century.

Honest color, clear space, and emphatic shape were important to the clarity of the idea, and the Flemish masters did not compromise them. They never thought of color as being spectrally broken up light, nor as being of any special merit and interest in itself. They could not have been great colorists had they thought of light in terms of the science of illumination.

As everyone knows, the range of color possibilities in painting is far narrower than it is in nature. Considering the few pigments available to the Flemish craftsmen of the fifteenth century, they produced astounding results.

The secret of all color effects in art is a matter of distribution and tonal contrast, not a matter of the amount of color used. The Flemish painter ground his colors separately and set them in place in gem-like glazes. He never muddied a tone to lower it to shadow darkness. Always making his shadows luminous, he lowered the tonal value to create the impression of a shadow, at the same time keeping the identical hue. For the Flemish artist knew that to build a color was not to mix more color together in order to make it darker, but rather to keep the color transparent and clear and to add glazes, one on top of the other, until a deep shadow was slowly produced.

With the patience of silversmiths, the medieval Flemish painters ground and mixed their colors in oily media so that the effects have a jewel-like transparency. The paint is so well made that in the best untouched examples it retains all its original brilliance. There is no other school of painting which can boast such a high degree of technical achievement.

PLASTICITY

The term "plastic effect" refers to a painter's ability to portray a figure in lines and tones in such a way that it appears as though it could actually be touched with the fingers. This plastic quality is one of the characteristics of the Flemish style and is sometimes said to have come out of the long tradition among the Flemish masters of polychroming and gilding statues.

It is an interesting coincidence that the painters delighted in painting gray-and-white representations of stone figures, called *grisailles*, and used these to decorate the panels that come into view when the wings of the altarpieces are folded. Van Eyck, van der Weyden, and Memling all made some fine grisailles. Two of the most famous are on the covers of the *Adoration of the Lamb* altarpiece.

Another and perhaps more immediate cause for the creation of this plastic effect may be attributed to the practice of careful underpainting of the pictures. This was the preparation of black-and-white modeling over which the paint was finally laid in glazes. The unfinished *St. Barbara* by van Eyck (PLATE 29) is a fine example of a fifteenth-century panel in its stage of underpainting.

Roger van der Weyden was outstanding for his plastic effects. Bouts was too much a landscapist; but even so there is just a faint suggestion of carved and painted wood in all his figures. Memling was too suave, and his figures are painted in a more willowy fashion.

Van der Weyden went so far as to draw his figures with sharp edges; and on occasions he set those figures against a flat, wall-like background. His *Descent from the Cross* (PLATE 56) could almost be thought of as a sculptured frieze. It has the quality of a stony, symbolic lament for the dead carved upon a huge sarcophagus.

COMPOSITION

In studies of Flemish painting scant notice has been given to the greatness of the Flemish master as a composer. His point of view differed from that of the painters of any other country. Some have praised what is called the "naturalism of the groupings" in Flemish paintings. To praise a picture for such a form of composition seems to imply that the artist knew nothing more than the accidental placing of objects. On the contrary, the composition of the elements of form in Flemish painting is a highly

skilled and extremely subtle work of ingenuity. The composition of Flemish pictures is not premeditated; it is not worked out by compass and ruler. Yet, it is also not accidental. The harmony and balance of forms as they work themselves into position are achieved by a definite sense of stagecraft, which appears in the Flemish pictures as if it were known and felt, but never as if it were artificially arranged.

The mastery of scale required to make a whole large unit blend with its elements and yet, on closer and closer view, dissolve into other smaller wholes is a skill which reached its highest perfection at the hands of Jan van Eyck. Later masters have often confused photographic realism with a sense of scale; the two are not synonymous. True scale puts everything into a range of vision at one time.

The fact that the Melbourne *Madonna* (PLATE 107) appears so much larger than it is results from van Eyck's unusual sense of scale. His skill was to produce a monumental idea on a small panel. This is not simply a matter of measurement and proportion. The voluminous robe of the Virgin is enhanced by the presence of four or five objects of relatively small still life. It is interesting to compare them in scale with the great sweeping arc of the Madonna's flaming red robe.

In van der Weyden's *Christ on the Cross* (PLATE 61) the city in the background seems to push and pull for its position in the third dimension. But as a surface pattern of composition it is exactly the right size to catch the observer's interest and give an idea of the relative importance of all the elements in the design. Landscape is a factor of scale against which to judge the size of the foreground figures. Again, by comparison, Memling had a weaker sense of scale in his *Martyrdom of St. Ursula* (PLATES 80, 81). The figures are squeezed into the frame and seem on top of each other. This weakness gives the picture the appearance of smallness.

The concept of monumentality was often confused with a simple matter of geometric distributions. Triangles, pyramids, cubes, and rectangles in composition do not in themselves make for monumentality. Skillfully used by great artists, as they were by Raphael, Michelangelo, and other masters of the Renaissance, they strengthen the composition. Peter Paul Rubens was the greatest master of the ascending and descending spiral.

When one stands before the Melbourne *Madonna* it is immediately apparent that van Eyck created a great pyramidal composition in this minute panel, probably without being aware of having done so. The picture is scarcely larger than its colored reproduction in COLOR PLATE 107, yet it could be enlarged a hundred times and lose none of its power and dignity. Its monumentality is the result of a combination of factors: the sculptural modeling harmonizing with luminous light and atmosphere; the distribution of various yet counterbalanced areas of color; the geometric scale of the forms; and the single idea expressed with great clarity in orderly and rhythmic language of forms.

In these qualities this *Madonna* may be said to be one of the finest examples of the Flemish style of painting.

The *Last Supper* by Dirk Bouts (PLATE 69) has great charm and narrative appeal, but it is not a monumental picture because its organization is a bit too obvious. One of the greatest monument makers of all time was Roger van der Weyden. His *Descent from the Cross* (PLATE 56) is the work of a titan. It is conceived in a magnificently impressive way. The master saw no moment save the ageless, dramatic symbol. A bold critic might compare this picture with the *Pietàs* carved by Michelangelo. The comparison would not be unfavorable to the Flemish master.

STAGECRAFT

Monumentality in religious art demands that the thing created have the force of a theological demonstration. However, when dramatic quality is also required, there is need of stagecraft.

Everyone is acquainted with the little Christmas *crèche*, which usually consists of an open box and a dozen or so figures, representing angels, shepherds, the kings, the Virgin, St. Joseph, and the traditional ox and ass. The problem involved in arranging these to tell the story of the Nativity is one of stagecraft. When Hugo van der Goes set to work on his Portinari *Nativity* (PLATE 72), he was faced with exactly the same problem. The whole tableau as well as the individual figures had to have factual force. The business of one character in the drama could not detract from another. All the figures had to be clearly visible so that their expressions could be read, and the focus had to be upon the Christ Child. There is no need to dwell at length upon how tremendously successful Hugo van der Goes was in his Portinari *Nativity*. A single glance will immediately reveal the extraordinary degree of psychological as well as spacious clarity that this master infused into all his figures. In his *Dormition of the Virgin*, van der Goes gives us one of the greatest compositions of a psychological mood ever to have been rendered in paint.

On the other hand, Dirk Bouts in his quiet little pictures, that are so full of tender pathos, is perhaps less dramatically forceful; he does not smite the observers of his pictures with any astonishing effects. If his effects lack the excitement of those of van Eyck, it is because they are more melodious. He rarely composed on the geometric principle, except in the *Last Supper*, and relied on a serene harmony of extremely quiet and gentle action to draw his figures into unity. His great success as a composer lies in the fact that he effaced all effort at composition in an attempt to remain lyrical.

It must be remembered that all the swinging curves and counter curves, all the triangles and sweeping diagonals in the world, will not save the composition of a picture which neglects sound principles of stagecraft. The quality of stagecraft in Flemish painting was always to tell the story presented through vividly portrayed actors, distributed according to the importance of their stage business, and in designs that were psychologically as well as spatially composed.

THE PEOPLE AND THEIR ART

A work of art is misjudged unless it is seen on its own terms—not in the terms of other works of art. If it is misunderstood, the work of art must not be blamed for it; the mind of the observer only must be made responsible for such a mistake. Popular appeal is in direct ratio to popular comprehension. It is a measure of merit, if the level of popular comprehension is high; it is no measure at all, if popular comprehension does not exist.

It is a well-known fact that art lovers have spurned pictures of the theme of the "Nursing Madonna." Because of the lower sales value of these pictures, dealers have secretly wished to have them repainted. But the little Madonna within her gilded frame dreams on, loving and cherishing her Son as a true mother should, oblivious of all the criticism launched against her.

Some Flemish paintings were as simple as everyday words. One of them could have been shown to a cook in a medieval kitchen, and she would have understood it perfectly. Although often commissioned by men in high places—bishops, princes, or wealthy merchants—they were made for places where all men came to worship, equal in the eyes of God. In chapels and on private altars these paintings were the property of guildsmen, of businessmen, and artisans. They registered them in their inventories and wills as among their most priceless possessions. These pictures do not speak in hidden allegories nor of new cults or philosophies. Nor were they the playthings of amateurs. These are not "pretty pictures," nor do they talk down to the people as do many modern books and movies of "popular appeal." Popularity of a work of art in old Flanders meant wide spiritual meaning and an artistic purpose common to all men.

There is a striking similarity between the fifteenth century and our own times in that both ages have been extremely picture conscious—even if the pictures differ greatly. At a time when there were few books and when few persons could read at all, pictures were immensely important. Today, after the passing of five centuries, there is a marked swing away from the dependence on words which the Renaissance brought about. Once again we are strongly picture conscious as medieval man was. We take our information and our inspiration from motion pictures, tabloids, and illustrated magazines. We are thrilled by war posters on billboards and are inspired to buy articles by colored advertisements. All this should help us to understand the people of the Middle Ages, who also depended on pictures to learn things.

In looking back at the great masters of fifteenth-century Flanders, one must admit that there is a certain worldliness about van Eyck which will always keep him from being the most loved of the Flemish painters. Bouts and Memling hold the cherished places in the hearts of the Flemings. Van Eyck was universally praised, but less universally felt and understood. Though the parent of genius, he remains in his lavishness, his exacting realism, and by his courtly haughtiness, above the popular appeal of van der Weyden, van der Goes, and Bouts. It was through these three masters that the Flemish style made its greatest foreign conquests.

CONCLUSION

In the Middle Ages every man was a particular kind of artist. Art was a way of doing things. The average man, from the servant in the house to the artisan in the workshop and the farmer in the fields, was anxious to do the things he had to do as well as he could. Why not? If a thing is worth doing at all, it is no more expensive and it is much more satisfying to do that thing well. Good art inspires high demands; high standards of popular demand inspire good art. Art is democratic when it is understandable and easily conveys its meaning to all alike. The best art of all times has not only been democratic, but it has also been functional. This is as true of the work of our Flemish painters as it is of that of the Gothic builders and the best craftsmen of all times.

There is an indefinable instinct in the average man which tells him that anything, in order to be good, must serve a clear purpose. It has to work well. The average man in old Flanders would not have tolerated works of art in his churches which would not have answered his spiritual needs. This attitude prompted his ideas on portraiture; a portrait was good when its likeness reminded him of the man portrayed. The more it was like him, the better was the portrait.

Good works of art hold no unexplainable mysteries. Flemish painting was (and still is), good art because it had popular meaning. But that meaning arose out of mutual understanding. Popular comprehension of works made by the craftsmen was on as high a level as was the art itself. It is difficult for the modern man to understand how extremely sensitive the man of the Middle Ages was to a visual impression. He always looked through and behind what he saw for its meaning.

To the medieval man the whole world as it stretched out before him was a huge symbol. He agreed with Honorius of Autun who said: "All creation is the shadow of truth and life."

Reality existed, because the artist knew that no reflection could exist in the mirror of the mind if the mirror did not reflect the world. He knew, too, that without meditated reflection the world would remain only an ever-passing appearance. Thus he sought to raise reality to an ideal and to make the individual into a type; he also had a sufficient sense of balance to know that to be convincing he must retain qualities of solid reality and selective individuality. This he accomplished through a harmony of lines, tones, and shapes. Flemish painting had ideas to put across—ideas of monumental importance to the artists and to the people. The devout Fleming wanted, and received through the Flemish style, certain visual images of his belief. He knew what he believed and how to evaluate its representation; yet, on the other hand, he received instruction in his belief through the iconography of the Flemish style—truly a *Biblia Pauperum* (the Bible of the Poor). The popular quality of Flemish painting was high, because the general visual comprehension of the average man was high. And the opposite was also true—the Flemish style was lucid because of popular critical demand.

The Flemish style left its indelible mark upon the thinking of Western men. It brought realities into harmony with the sublime. It became unwittingly one of the cornerstones of inductive thinking in painted form.

The history of art is the story of mankind. A work of art is never a dead thing; it is the living reflection of actual men living on this earth, hoping, struggling, loving, dreaming, praying, dying, but always believing. Art is a universal inspiration to tolerance, for it reveals that all man's anguish and his highest hopes strive to find ultimate expression in beauty. It is the evidence that Truth bears many names and wears many faces, according to those who seek her.

In art all the gods in whom man has believed and all the saints he has loved and trusted join hands. The sublimity of Pallas Athene, the dream of the Buddhas of China, the mystery of the Indian Shivas, the calm of the old gods who brood over the Valley of the Nile guard the same secret as the smiling little saints of the *Golden Legend* painted by the medieval Flemish masters. All these, in many tongues but speaking the language of the heart, tell of man's eternal longing for more justice and loving-kindness.

Through the slow course of the centuries one European people after another has provided the hearth for the divine fire which has warmed and illumined our civilization. Greece exalted her splendid youth in the friezes of the Parthenon; Rome built grandly a framework for the Western world; later, in the mosaics at Ravenna and in the miracle of Hagia Sofia, Byzantium produced the first perfect expression of Christian art uniting memories of the beauty of Greece and the power of Rome with the splendor of the East and the vigor of the young Gothic tribes.

Then came the turn of France. A mighty *Te Deum* sounded through western Europe as the magnificent cathedrals rose stone on stone, with their soaring towers and their windows of flower and flame. It is to the everlasting glory of the Flemish masters of the fifteenth century that when the Hundred Years' War halted the building of the huge stone churches in France, they prolonged that sublime effort of love and exaltation on their frail panels of wood.

This era lives on in every one of us today, though we may frequently be unaware of it. As Henri Focillon says: *"L'image de l'homme conservera longtemps la chaleur et la passion qui lui viennent du moyen âge. . . . Ainsi les époques ne meurent pas d'un seul coup; elles se prolongent dans la vie de l'esprit* [Man's image will keep for a long time the warmth and the passion which came to him from the Middle Ages. . . . In this sense, epochs do not die suddenly; they are prolonged in the life of the spirit]."[1]

It was in Flanders that the Middle Ages came to die. There in the misty plains and in the quiet little towns beside the slow canals, the Middle Ages lingered for a while. The exaltation of spirit, the childlike mingling of realism and mysticism, the deep concern with values that are universal and eternal, which marked the medieval mind, are the sources of fifteenth-century Flemish painting which may truly be called the last flowering of the Middle Ages.

[1] *L'Art d'Occident* by Henri Focillon.

ACKNOWLEDGMENTS

Grateful acknowledgment is made to the following:

The Reference Collection of Photographs, Metropolitan Museum of Art; The Frick Art Reference Library; The Pierpont Morgan Library; The Detroit Institute of Arts, for photographs.

Art News, New York, for color plates 25, 34, 39, 71, 83, and 106; Knoedler Art Galleries, New York, for color plate 47; Simon & Schuster, New York, for color plates 1, 2, 7, 12, 78, 97, and 107; and National Gallery of Art, Washington, for color plate 84.

Francis G. Mayer, for photographs and comparative photographs.